A CONCISE HISTORY OF TEXAS

FROM THE TEXAS ALMANAC

BY MIKE KINGSTON
EDITOR, TEXAS ALMANAC

PUBLISHED BY

The Dallas Morning News

ISBN - 0-914511-08-4 *(paperback)*
Copyright 1988, A.H. Belo Corp., Communications Center, Dallas, TX 75265
P.O. Box 655237

Distributed by
Texas Monthly Press
P.O. Box 1569
Austin, TX 78767
1-800-288-3288

A Miscellany of Texas History

Acknowledgements

This short history of Texas from prehistoric times to the present was prepared especially for the Sesquicentennial by Mike Kingston, editor of the Texas Almanac. As in any project of this magnitude, Kingston had the help of many people. He particularly wants to thank Ruth Harris, Mary Crawford and Paula LaRocque of The Dallas Morning News for proofreading and editing the material.

Several professionals critiqued the manuscript, and their comments and suggestions were invaluable. Included among these were: L. Tuffly Ellis, former director, Texas State Historical Association; Dr. Alan Skinner, an independent professional archaeologist of Dallas; Bob Forrester, an amateur archaeologist of Fort Worth; Dr. David Weber, chairman of the Department of History, Southern Methodist University; Dr. Archie P. McDonald, professor of history, Stephen F. Austin University; Dr. Fane Downs, professor of history, McMurry College; Dr. Paul Lack, professor of history, McMurry College; Dr. Alwyn Barr, chairman of the Department of History, Texas Tech University; Dr. Adrian N. Anderson, chairman of the Department of History, Lamar University; and the late Dr. Ernest Wallace of Texas Tech University. Also, Dr. A. Ray Stephens' Texas history seminar at the University of North Texas, Denton, was an invaluable resource. Any errors, of course, are those of the author alone.

Prehistoric Texas 1

MANY factors make the once-simple picture of early humanity in Texas a much more complex and interesting problem. More than 30,000 archaeological sites have been registered with the state, and new ones are discovered regularly. Archaeologists, with the aid of scientists from other disciplines, are bringing more sophisticated techniques to bear on the studies of the clues that prehistoric Texans left. New discoveries and more detailed information open additional dimensions to our knowledge of early man in the state.

The picture of early humans in Texas will not be brought into final focus for decades. But indications are that these first human inhabitants of the state were probably more intelligent, more resourceful and more culturally developed than the often conveyed image of the "squatting savage."

One basic theory remains unchallenged — how these people got to the New World. Early Texans were descendants of those Asian groups that migrated across the Bering Strait during the Ice Ages of the past 50,000 years. At intermittent periods, enough water would accumulate in the massive glaciers worldwide to lower the sea level several hundred feet. During these periods, the Bering Strait would become a 1,300-mile-wide land bridge between North America and Asia. These early adventurers worked their way southward for thousands of years, eventually getting as far as Tierra del Fuego in Argentina 10,000 years ago. These migrations populated both North and South America in a relatively short time. It is generally accepted that these people walked to the New World, although some scientists suggest that groups may have come by sea.

By land or sea, they brought a paleolithic technology. Their primitive tool kit contained projectile points, scrapers and other simple stone tools. Atlatls, or spear-throwing sticks, were used to launch projectiles. Basically these people were big-game hunters and may have followed their prey across the land bridge.

Biologically they were completely modern homo sapiens sapiens. No evidence has been found to indicate that any evolutionary change occurred in the New World. Dressed in modern attire, scientists say, these early Texans would be indistinguishable from those of today.

Four basic periods reflecting cultural advancement of early inhabitants are used by archaeologists in classifying evidence. These periods are the Paleo-Indian (20,000 years ago to 7,000 years ago); Archaic (7,000 years ago to about the time of Christ); Woodland (time of Christ to 800-1,000 years ago), and Neo-American, or Late Prehistoric, (800-1,000 years ago until European contact). Not all early people advanced through all these stages in Texas. Much cultural change was made in adaptation to changes in climate. The Caddo Indians of East Texas, for example, reached the Neo-American stage before French and Spanish explorers made contact in the 16th and 17th centuries. Others, such as the Karankawas of the Gulf Coast, advanced no further than the Archaic at the same time. Still others advanced and then regressed in the face of a changing climate.

The earliest confirmed evidence indicates that these humans were in Texas between 10,000 and 13,000 years ago. "Midland Minnie," which was identified from only a few pieces of skull, was discovered in Midland County in 1953. Dated by chemical methods, these remains were determined to be 10,000 years old. In 1983, the discoveries of two burial sites dating to about the same period or earlier were announced. Archaeologists with the State Department of Highways and Public Transportation uncovered the complete skeleton of a woman in the excavation on a farm-to-market road project near Leander, north of Austin in Central Texas. Material found in the grave site was radiocarbon dated at 10,000 to 13,000 years old. The site also was a well-preserved ceremonial burial with artifacts such as a grinding stone and beads found with the skeleton. A rock, which could have been a primitive headstone, also was found in the grave.

Shortly after the Leander discovery was announced, amateur archaeologists working an excavation near Waco reported the discovery of a double burial of a man and a child. Material from this grave site was radiocarbon dated at 10,000 years, too. In addition, the two skeletons were covered with several large stones, which, along with other evidence, indicated a ceremonial burial. Artifacts — apparently from the High Plains and the Gulf Coast — were found in the grave, indicating the people participated in a wide trade territory.

Paleo-Indians have long been considered successful big-game hunters. Artifacts from this period are found across the state but not in great number, indicating they were a small, nomadic population. Some of the artifacts have been found in conjunction with kill sites of large animals. Texas' climate was cooler and much wetter during this period, providing lush grasslands to be grazed by large animals. Early Texans hunted prehistoric bison, which were seven feet tall at the shoulder, and small horses. Although the horse evolved to its modern state in the New World, it had become extinct and had to be returned to the New World in the 16th century by European explorers.

Prehistoric Texans used the same hunting tactics for thousands of years. In one area on the Rio Grande in Val Verde County, sites ranging in age from Paleo to Archaic to Pre-Historic indicate that bison were driven over the edge of a cliff to their deaths and then butchered. The ages of the sites vary from hundreds to thousands of years.

Archaeological studies came relatively late to Texas, and the delay probably cost the state a place in the terminology of science. In 1924, a man and a boy walking down the dry bed of Lone Wolf Creek near Colorado City in Mitchell County found the skeleton of an ancient bison eroding from the bank. Within the rib cage of the skeleton were found three projectile points that are described today as "Clovis" points. Large and with a characteristic design, Clovis points are now benchmarks for dating the earliest evidence of man in North America. The Texas discovery could not be dated to the satisfaction of scientists of the day. In 1936, similar points found at a kill site near

Clovis, N.M., could be scientifically dated. The New Mexico city is now honored as the namesake of the points. Folsom points, which are smaller and fluted, also are named for a New Mexico community near which the first of these points was found and dated in 1926.

Prior to the discoveries near Leander and Waco, only four or five complete skeletons of Paleo-Indians had been discovered in the New World. These people had long been considered to be nomads with an egalitarian society. With evidence of ceremonial burials and artifacts indicating broad trade territories, new dimensions will be added to the cultural assessment of these early Texans.

For example, the projectile points and other artifacts found in the Paleo sites of Texas differ significantly from those excavated in Northern Mexico sites, indicating two distinct cultural traditions within a narrow geographical range.

As Texas' climate changed at the end of the Ice Age about 7,000 years ago, inhabitants adapted. Apparently the state experienced an extended period of warming and drying and a population increase. Archaic Indians accommodated the change by broadening cyclical hunting and gathering patterns and by becoming less selective in game. They stalked smaller animals, as well as large beasts, as indicated by the reduced size of the projectile points found at these sites. Their tool kit was expanded to include stone drills, axes and knives used to work bone and wood. And these Texans began to harvest fruits and nuts when in season and exploited rivers for food, as indicated by the fresh-water mussel shells in ancient garbage heaps. Archaic Indians also had broad trade territories. Flint from the Alibates quarry in the Panhandle was transported throughout a territory thousands of square miles wide, and chert from the Edwards Plateau was used to make projectile points and other artifacts found in North and East Texas.

Several burial sites from this period also have been excavated. The bodies were buried with tools and sometimes dogs. A site near Houston contained dozens of burials, indicating that these early people had returned to the same area over hundreds of years to bury the dead. Dating between 5,000 and 6,000 years old, the site produced artifacts made of chert from near Little Rock, Ark., and sea shells possibly from Florida.

The people were involved in a much wider trade territory than previously thought. At about the time of Christ, the Woodland stage began to emerge in parts of Texas. This period is distinguished by the development of complex, settled societies. The people were less nomadic. While they still ranged widely in search of game, crops and local wild plants provided much of their diets. And the first evidence of social stratification is found. The bow and arrow came into use, and the first pottery is associated with this period. Between 750-800 A.D., Pre-Caddoan Indians in East Texas had formed primitive villages and were building distinctive mounds for burials and for rituals.

Some Indians reached this stage and then reverted when the climate changed, as it did in the Texas Panhandle and along the Rio Grande. In these areas, evidence has been found of agriculture-based communities that ceased to exist.

The Neo-American period, which is best exemplified by the highly civilized Caddos of East Texas, is dated between 800-1000 A.D. and the time of the European contact with New World natives. Early Texans that reached this stage had very complex cultures with well-defined social stratification. They were fully agricultural and participated in exotic trade over wide areas.

When the Europeans arrived, they found people in Texas living in cultures that ranged from the very primitive to the highly complex.

Archaeologists often are frustrated by the theories propounded by amateurs and speculators who propose that similarities between cultures in different areas indicate a contact. Other questions are raised that simply cannot be answered by the present stage of research and understanding. Some of those will be reviewed here.

One of the most enduring, but unresolved, theories is that Prehistoric Texas was on the route that colonists of the Olmec or Toltec civilizations in early Mexico followed to the Mississippi Valley and the Southeast United States. There are many similarities between the early Mexican civilizations and the Mississippi cultures. Both built large ceremonial mounds, had similar social organizations and shared other cultural traits. In Mexico, these early tendencies evolved into the massive pyramids also characterizing the Maya and Aztec civilizations that greeted early Spaniards. Although some amateurs have found tantalizing evidence of an overland migration between these New World cultures, acceptable scientific proof has not been established.

The earliest evidence of the presence of humans in Texas also has been clouded by enigmatic finds. In the 1950s, for example, amateur archaeologist R. King Harris and other members of the Dallas Archeological Society found a Clovis projectile point along the shoreline of Lake Lewisville in Denton County before the dam was completed. Radiocarbon dating of material found in the hearths associated with the point ran off the scale of the day. According to these tests, the points were associated with material that was almost 40,000 years old — much before early humans were in the New World, according to conventional wisdom. Subsequent investigations in the early 1980s found that the dated samples were contaminated with lignite, a hydrocarbon that would throw the dating far askew. The final evaluation of the hearths, which were restudied when a drought lowered the water level in the lake, was that they were about 10,000 years old. But the sites do represent the first use of a fuel other than wood for a fire in the New World.

Another question not so easily answered is the case of the Malakoff-Trinidad heads found in Henderson County in the 1920s and 1930s. These are three largest ones that have apparent hand-carved human features. They were found in the bottom of a gravel stratum over an eight-year period. And with the exception of the final stone, no scientific archaeological surveys were made of the discovery sites. If the heads were deposited in the bottom of the stratum in which they were found, they indicate that humanity was in Texas — and the New World — 40,000 to 50,000 years ago, again far earlier than thought by many of today's scientists. Because of the lack of a professional survey at the time of discovery, this question may never be answered.

Other mysteries also exist. On a West Central Texas hillside, a series of vertical and horizontal lines firmly engraved in sandstone have been deciphered as a form of ancient Celtic line writing in a Celtiberian language. Barry Fell, a marine biologist turned epigrapher, has been criticized by professional archaeologists for errors and misinterpretation of engravings in rock in other sections of the country. But he holds fast to the theory that these inscriptions were left by Celtic adventurers and traders, giving travel instructions to others. The inscriptions are examples, Fell contends, of a well-developed trade between Europe and the New World long before Columbus or even the Vikings and Irish monks ventured westward.

In another case, a plaque bearing what was interpreted as ancient Libyan writing was found in the Big Bend in the early 1960s. The plaque itself was lost, but pictures of it have been deciphered by Fell. These, too, verified his contention that even African peoples were trading in the New World long before the usually accepted discoverers of North and South America took to the sea.

This curiosity is compounded by an incident mentioned by Spanish colonizer Jose de Escandon in the middle 18th century when he came upon a tribe of black Indians near the mouth of the Rio Grande. These "Indians" told the explorer that their ancestors had come to the New World by boat from a homeland that must have been

Africa. They were identified as Negroids, and the blacks fought with spears and shields unlike those used by other Indians in the area. Escandon speculated that the blacks were survivors of the wreck of a slave boat or that they had escaped from a slave colony on an island in the Gulf of Mexico. No further mention is made of this tribe by later colonizers or explorers. But the blacks had intermarried with local Indian women, and chances are that they were absorbed by other bands in the area. Nevertheless, in recent years, there has been speculation, based on the Negroid features on some Olmec and Toltec statues, that blacks from Africa visited the New World — and possibly Texas — long before Columbus opened the New World for European colonization.

No definitive answers to these puzzles are expected or obtainable. They stand outside the usual realm of archaeological research. But they still present questions about the prehistory of Texas that should be borne in mind. Studies have found that legends often have a basis in fact. Other enigmas are based on enough evidence to put them a degree beyond rank speculation. But these ideas have yet to rest on the foundation of solid scientific evidence necessary to make them a part of the state's prehistory.

2 *The Spanish Period*

SPAIN'S conquest of the New World was one of the first acts of a vigorous, emerging nation. For 700 years, the Spanish fought to oust the Moorish invaders from the Iberian Peninsula. Regional and ethnic divisions hampered the effort, but the marriage of Isabella of Castile and Ferdinand of Aragon unified the country under a single monarchy.

Under Ferdinand's leadership in early 1492, the Spanish army conquered the province of Granada, completing the reconquista. Later in the year, Ferdinand and Isabella took a major stride toward shaping world history by commissioning Christopher Columbus to find a western route to the Far East.

Some historians characterize this voyage and subsequent subjugation of the New World as an extension of the Christian crusades against the Muslims. From the beginning, Columbus' exploration had religious, as well as economic, goals. In a papal bull in 1493, Pope Alexander VI gave Spain the right to develop any new lands that might be discovered west of the longitude 100 leagues west of the Azores and Cape Verde. But the assignment was conditioned on the Spanish making "God's known there." The ultimate goal of Columbus' voyage was to establish contact with the Great Khan, a mythical figure as it turned out, in the Far East. Initially trade was to be developed, and Christianity was to be taken to the pagans. Ultimately, however, the Spaniards hoped to form an alliance with the powers of the Far East to put the Muslims in pincers and to break their control of the rich overland trade routes through the Middle East and to secure Christian dominance of the Holy Land.

From Columbus' first contact with New World natives, missionaries were in the forefront of the exploration. Early in the conquest, the Spanish crown decreed that the pagans must submit to Christian authority and receive religious instruction. If the natives refused, a "just war" could be initiated against them with enslavement to follow. And the Spanish conquest of Mexico and Central America was accomplished with astonishing speed. Between 1519-21, Hernan Cortez conquered the Aztecs in the Valley of Mexico and partially transformed the sophisticated Indian culture into the image of Christian Spain. The Aztecs of Central Mexico and the Mayans of the Yucatan and Central America, however, were settled, civilized people, much accustomed to following hierarchical leadership and to paying tribute or taxes. Although they

12

stubbornly resisted the Spanish, the ultimate conquest was relatively simple.

Unlike Anglo-Americans, the Spanish had little racial prejudice in the modern sense. Throughout the long struggle with the Moors, the great gulf was between Christians and infidels, not between races. However, dark-skinned people were considered inferior, for most were thought to be infidels. From the initial contact, Spaniards intermixed with Indian women. The only social or religious limitation was the qualification that the women accept Christianity.

Spanish monarchs and religious leaders agonized over the treatment of New World natives. The conquest was bloody, as might be expected in a war. And afterward, other natives resisted conversion to Christianity. Spanish occupation policy also produced atrocities. Throughout the reconquest of the Iberian Peninsula, the Spanish required tribute from the conquered peoples. To reward the conquistadors for the perilous adventure in the New World, an encomienda system was established, in keeping with the practice used throughout the reconquista. The Spaniards were granted land and the use of natives. For this, the grantee was required to protect the Indians, to provide for their needs and to see that they were taught the faith. Too often the system was abused and degenerated into a form of slavery.

By 1540 the concern about treatment of the New World natives became so serious that Charles V suspended expeditions while a junta considered arguments about the proper policy toward treatment of the Indians. Pope Paul III in 1537 issued a papal bull asserting that the Indians were not "dumb brutes" and should not be enslaved. Bartolome de las Casas, a Dominican missionary with many years of experience in the New World, urged a humane policy. He suggested that priests be given strict parental control while the natives received religious instruction. The mission system that developed reflected some of Las Casas' suggestions. Others disagreed with this argument and harked back to Aristotle's theory of natural slavery. The argument held that some segments of mankind were born to serve a leisure class. The Spaniards, of course, were to be the leisure class.

Official policy of Spanish kings and popes was to treat the New World natives as reasoning human beings. They believed that all humans could be improved with patient instruction. In 1573, an ordinance was promulgated decreeing that "pacification," not "conquest," of the New World was Spain's goal. But policies and pronouncements often did not survive the trip across the Atlantic. The king's policy might always be obeyed, it was said, but it was not always enforced.

Humane treatment of the Indians had more practical sides, too. While England and France had excess populations to colonize the New World, Spain was a relatively sparsely settled nation. Therefore the crown's policy incorporated the Indians as an integral part of the colonization effort. They would be turned into good Spanish citizens. To this end, the mission system was developed with two basic goals: to convert the Indians to Christianity and to make them economically productive citizens. With the protection of the military, the aborigines in an untamed area who expressed a willingness to receive instruction would be congregated at a mission to be taught the faith and a trade as well. When the Indians' training was completed, the mission would be secularized as a church. The missionaries would move to another area. The system worked with varying degrees of success, although the zeal of the Franciscan, Dominican and Jesuit missionaries seldom waned.

"Pacification" of the New World became more difficult as the Spaniards moved north of the Valley of Mexico. The fierce Chichimecas resisted the Spanish yoke as vigorously as they had the Aztecs. These were nomadic Indians whose culture had little resemblance to that of the Aztecs or Mayans. In 1528, two expeditions launched by Cortez from the Rio Panuco crossed the Rio Grande but did not stay. No doubt other explorers briefly probed the region north of the Great River.

As early as 1519, Alonso Alvarez de Pineda, a captain in the service of Francisco Garay, governor of Jamaica, mapped the coast of Texas. Early historians credited Alvarez de Pineda with exploring the Rio Grande from its mouth to the Brownsville area and with referring to the river as the "Rio de las Palmas." But recent research questions this interpretation. The first recorded exploration of today's Texas was made in the 1530s by Alvar Nunez Cabeza de Vaca, two other Spaniards and a Moorish black slave named "Esteban." They were members of the expedition commanded by Panfilo de Narvaez that left Cuba in 1528 to explore Florida — which included most of the southeastern United States and all the land westward to the Rio Grande at the time. Ill-fated from the beginning, many members of the expedition lost their lives, and others, including Cabeza de Vaca, were shipwrecked on the Texas coast. Cabeza de Vaca and his companions, although separated at intervals, survived and lived with a series of Indian tribes that inhabited much of southwestern and far western Texas. Through a combination of good luck and skill, Cabeza de Vaca gained a reputation as a healer, and after a time he was held in great esteem by many Indian groups. At one point in his wanderings, the Spaniard performed the first recorded medical surgery in the state by removing an arrowhead from a man's chest. Wherever the little band of Spaniards went, however, stories circulated about the lands of great wealth to the north — the Seven (Golden) Cities of Cibola. When Cabeza de Vaca was reunited with his countrymen in Mexico in 1536, these tales excited the interest of authorities.

In 1540, Francisco Vazquez de Coronado, governor of New Galicia, was commissioned to lead an exploration of the American Southwest. The quest took him to the land of the Pueblo Indians in New Mexico. Here his interest in riches was further enhanced with tales of Gran Quivira, a land rumored to be even richer than Cibola. Native Americans learned it was best to keep the Europeans away from their homes, so they would suggest vast riches could be found in other areas. So Coronado pursued a fruitless search for the riches across the High Plains of Texas, Oklahoma and Kansas. Missionaries on the expedition found the number of potential souls to save overwhelming and stayed in the upper Rio Grande Valley.

While Coronado was investigating Texas' High Plains from the west, Luis Moscoso de Alvarado assumed leadership of Hernando de Soto's expedition when the commander died on the banks of the Mississippi River. In 1542, Moscoso's group ventured as far west as Central Texas before returning to the Mississippi. While sailing for Mexico, the group was shipwrecked for a time at the mouth of the Sabine River. Here they used oil from seeps to caulk their boats, ignoring the claims of local Indians that the petroleum had great medicinal properties. This was the first recorded use of the mineral in the state — the mineral that has become synonymous with Texas.

But an era was ending. Cortez had found great riches that could be easily reaped in the Aztec and Mayan kingdoms. Other conquistadors had been equally successful, and even lesser adventurers had profited within the encomienda system. These vigorous, ambitious men who had fought first to free Spain from the Moors and then to conquer the New World were aging. The Coronado expedition is considered by some historians as the last of the old regime. Certainly the makeup was different. More non-Spaniards participated, and the men were younger, without the battle experience of the older warrior-explorers. And the northern territories were unlike central Mexico in climate, culture and economic potential. Quick wealth was not to be found. A new generation of explorers and settlers would be required to venture into the harsh northern territories.

One of this new breed was Luis de Carvajal, a member of a Jewish family that converted to Christianity. He was given a huge land grant stretching from the Rio Panuco in Mexico to an area near present-day San Antonio. As part of the bargain, he agreed to introduce cattle into the region. Though it is not known if Carvajal ever visited Texas, cattle that he brought into Mexico are thought to have migrated north of the Rio Grande. Carvajal died while imprisoned during the Inquisition for failing to denounce his sister as a Jew.

Spain had no precedents from which to develop an administrative system for the New World colonies. What evolved was cumbersome procedure that stifled initiative and action. The Council of the Indes administered New Spain, as Mexico was called, and viceroys supervised regional affairs. Philip II completely centralized the system upon taking the throne in 1556, however. Several administrative councils became only consulting bodies. Philip made all final decisions on affairs of state, down to the most inconsequential details. Consequently, decisions had to filter through a bureaucracy that stretched across the Atlantic. The process could — and did in some cases — take years. Philip's successors delegated authority to ministers after his death in 1598, but the system remained cumbersome and troublesome.

Forty years passed after the Coronado and Moscoso expeditions before Fray Agustin Rodriguez, a Franciscan missionary, and Francisco Sanchez Chamuscado, a soldier, led an expedition into Texas and New Mexico. Following the Rio Conchos in Mexico to its confluence with the Rio Grande near present-day Presidio and then turning northwestward in the Great River's valley, the explorers passed through the El Paso area in 1581. Among the Pueblo Indians great material wealth was not found, but the missionary was satisfied with the spiritual potential of the pagans. Father Rodriguez died a martyr. The following year, Antonio de Espejo led a relief expedition up the Pecos River from the Rio Grande to the Pueblo Indian area only to learn of the missionary's fate.

Permanent colonization of the upper Rio Grande Valley was accomplished as the 16th century drew to a close. Juan de Onate was granted the right to develop the area in which the Pueblo Indians lived. In 1598, he blazed a trail across the desert from Santa Barbara, Chihuahua, to intersect the Rio Grande at the Pass of the North — today's El Paso. For the next 200 years, this was the supply route from the interior of Mexico that served the northern colonies. And the El Paso-Juarez area developed as a way station. The first permanent settlement in Texas was established in 1681 after the Pueblo Indians rebelled and drove the Spanish settlers southward. The colonists retreated to the El Paso area, where the missions of Ysleta del Sur and Socorro del Sur — each named for a community in New Mexico — were established. Ysleta pueblo originally was located on the south side of the Rio Grande, but as the river changed course, it ended up on the north bank. Now part of El Paso, the community is considered the oldest European settlement in Texas.

Texas was attractive to the Spanish in the 16th and 17th centuries. Small expeditions found trade possibilities, and missionaries had ventured into the territory to instruct the Indians. Frays Juan de Salas and Diego Lopez responded to a request by the Jumano Indians for religious instruction in 1629, and for a brief time the priests lived with the Indians near present-day San Angelo.

Missionary efforts also were made north of the Rio Grande. In 1675, Fernando del Bosque and Fray Juan Larios led an expedition to gain insight into the Coahuiltecan bands in the region. Capt. Juan Dominguez led an expedition that established a mission among the Jumano Indians at the La Junta — the confluence of the Rio Grande and the Rio Conchos. This mission was closed in 1688, and a priest blamed its problems on the military and others who enslaved many Indians to work in the north Mexico mines. But the Spanish crown was preoccupied with affairs in Europe. The colonial wealth also was diverted to these activities — and to extravagant living at court — rather than to investment in development of the New World. Ironically, it was affairs of state in Europe, rather than the resources and natural attractiveness of the territory, that first riveted Spain's attention on Texas. From 1681 to 1697, Spain and France were at war on the Continent, as they had been for much of the 17th century.

Spain's claim to the vast stretch of the New World from Florida to the Pacific Ocean rankled the French. In 1682, an ambitious and courageous Rene Robert Cavalier, Sieur de la Salle, explored the Mississippi to its mouth at the Gulf of Mexico. LaSalle claimed the vast territory for France, cutting the heart out of Spain's North American territories. Two years later, LaSalle returned to the New World with four ships and enough colonists to establish hs country's claim in this segment of Spanish America. Some historians think that LaSalle's expedition was blown past the mouth of the Mississippi by a Gulf storm and ended up on the Texas coast by mistake; others think Texas was his planned destination. Nevertheless, though short of supplies because of the loss of two ships, the French colonists established Fort Saint Louis at the head of Lavaca Bay. Hostile Indians, bad weather and disease took their toll on the small enclave, althugh LaSalle managed three expeditions into the surrounding countryside. Based on these explorations, the French made a weak claim that the Rio Grande was the western boundary of Louisiana Territory. In 1687, LaSalle and a group of soldiers began an overland trip to find French outposts on the Mississippi. Somewhere near present-day Navasota in Grimes County, the great explorer was murdered by one of his men. His grave has never been found.

When Spanish officials heard from Indians about the French colony, a frenzied search for LaSalle was launched. Five sea expeditions combed the Gulf Coast from the Rio Grande to today's Florida. And six land expeditions into Texas' interior provided Spanish officials with the first detailed information about the territory. Finally in 1689, Capt. Alonso de Leon, governor of Coahuila, re-entered Texas at a ford near present-day Eagle Pass and headed eastward. He found the charred remains of Fort Saint Louis at the head of Lavaca Bay. Indians had destroyed the settlement and killed many colonists. DeLeon continued tracking survivors of the ill-fated colony into East Texas.

On this journey, Father Damian Massanet accompanied the official. The priest was fascinated with tales about the "Tejas" Indians of the region. "Tejas" meant friendly, but at the time the term was considered a tribal name. Actually these Indians were members of the Caddo Confederacy that controlled parts of four present states — Texas, Louisiana, Arkansas and Oklahoma. They were the most culturally developed of all Texas Indians. They farmed, had a well-developed leadership structure and traded across a broad area. Unlike other Indians, they had judicial and diplomatic procedures to settle disputes between groups within the confederacy. The Caddo religion also acknowledged one supreme god, which the Spanish felt made them prime candidates for conversion to Christianity. For years, the Tejas had been brought to the attention of the Spanish by the Jumano Indians who traded with them and with the Pueblo Indians of New Mexico.

Usually the Caddos did not let strangers enter their territory. Trade usually was carried on at annual fairs that were held on the periphery of their settlements. But with the French trading with the Caddos' enemies, the East Texas Indians were anxious to develop contacts with Europeans to obtain trade goods, guns and horses. Hence the Spanish were quite welcome.

When a Tejas chief asked Father Massanet to stay and instruct his people in religion, the Spaniards quickly promised to return and establish a mission. The pledge was redeemed in 1690 when the mission San Francisco de los Tejas was founded near present-day Weches in Houston County. A few months later, a second mission, Santisimo Nombre de Maria, was established nearby, only to be washed away by a flood in a few months.

Twin disasters struck this missionary effort. Spanish officials soon lost interest in the French threat. And as was the case with many New World Indians who had no resistance to European diseases, the Tejas soon were felled by an epidemic that killed many. Some Indians blamed the illness on the holy water used for baptism by the priests. Soon the mission languished. It was difficult to supply, being so far from the other Spanish outposts in northern Mexico, and the Caddos remained committed to their native religion. Also the priests often insulted the Indians' leaders and medicine men, and the soldiers were troublesome.

In addition to being the first European settlements in East Texas, the missions also brought ranching to the region. The herds of cattle driven to the area by de Leon were the first organized movement of livestock in Texas.

In 1693, Spanish officials closed the missions, however, leaving the Tejas to the stealthful ministrations of French traders for two decades.

3 *Europeans and Indians*

ALTHOUGH Spain had not made a determined effort to settle Texas, great changes were coming to the territory. The French had opened trade with Indians along the Mississippi River and its tributaries and had made contact with Indians on the High Plains. French guns and horses were changing the nature of warfare among the Indians.

Spain introduced horses into Texas and the Southwest. No one is sure when or how the Comanches got mounts. But in the late 17th century they began moving onto the Plains from their Rocky Mountain homelands. On foot, the Comanches were not intimidating. They were short and stocky and somewhat awkward in appearance. They were among the best horsemen in the world, however, and were fierce warriors, spreading terror wherever they went.

The southward movement of the Comanches and their allies on the Great Plains played havoc with the established homelands of several groups of Indians. The Apaches were the first to be displaced. And the Apaches were the first of the fierce Plains Indians to worry the Spanish. In the 1720s, the Apaches moved onto the lower Texas Plains, taking the traditional hunting grounds of the Jumanos and others. The nomadic Coahuiltecan bands were particularly hard hit. Attempts by these Indians to gain Spanish support against the Apaches were fruitless until the late 1720s, and by that time, many of the Apaches' enemies, like the Jumanos, had joined the raiders. As early as 1707, the El Paso area was under siege by the Apaches.

Although the Spanish stayed out of the Indian wars in the beginning of their excursions into Texas, they were soon drawn into the fray. In 1699, the French established a colony on the Mississippi River in Louisiana and began trading with the Indians in East Texas. The Spanish had to respond to the challenge to protect their interests.

Spanish officials became committed to opening Texas for trade and colonization. In 1700, the mission San Juan Bautista was moved to a site on the south side of the Rio Grande near present-day Eagle Pass where two excellent fords provided access across the river. The mission became the gateway to colonial Texas from Mexico, and many figures who shaped the territory's future passed through this portal.

In Europe, Philip V, the grandson of the French king with aspirations to the

French throne, ascended to the Spanish throne in 1701, becoming the first of the Bourbon kings. He instituted reforms in the clumsy administrative system, but it remained an impediment to development of the New World frontier.

In 1709, Fray Antonio de San Buenaventura y Olivares made an initial request to establish a mission at San Pedro Springs (today's San Antonio) to minister to the Coahuiltecans, who were suffering at the hands of the Apaches. The request was denied. But the Spanish were xenophobic about the French, and quickly responded to any threat, real or perceived, by their European enemies.

Religious intrigue involving the French spurred the Spanish into action that led to the establishment of permanent missions and the colonization of Texas. Father Francisco Hidalgo had served at the Tejas missions in East Texas in the early 1690s and longed to return. When Spanish officials turned a deaf ear to his request, the priest secretly wrote the French governor of Louisiana in New Orleans seeking help in establishing a mission among the Tejas. Always anxious to open trade with the Spanish, the governor dispatched Louis Juchereau de Saint Denis, an adventurer and explorer, to find the priest and to enter into trade negotiations. While crossing Texas, Saint Denis was impressed with the number of wild cattle that roamed the region. These no doubt were the offspring of the cattle left at the East Texas missions, and the result of de Leon's practice of leaving a cow and a calf at each river crossing while traveling to East Texas in 1689. When Saint Denis arrived at San Juan Bautista, the Spanish were aghast at his temerity. Fears of new French incursions into Texas were fanned. Though Saint Denis vowed he wanted only to open trade — which was strictly forbidden by Spanish colonial policy — he was sent to Mexico City for questioning. Upon release by Spanish authorities, Saint Denis returned to San Juan Bautista, married the commandant's granddaughter and served as a guide for the expedition that established the second set of missions in East Texas.

Father Hidalgo's dream of returning to the Tejas was realized when he accompanied Capt. Diego Ramon on the expedition. The mission San Francisco de los Neches was established in 1716 near the site of the old San Francisco de los Tejas mission. Nuestra Senora de Guadalupe was located at the present-day site of Nacogdoches, and Nuestra Senora de los Dolores was placed near present-day San Augustine. Two other missions were located in the area, and another was built across the Sabine River in Louisiana. The East Texas missions did little better on the second try. Saint Denis, who was well-liked by the Indians, planned to stay in the area to set up a trading post. But the suspicious Spanish forced him to leave, to the distress of the Indians. Supplying the missions also was a problem, as it had been in the 1690s. The Indians were unhappy with the trade goods and the delays in receiving supplies. Soon it became apparent that a way station between northern Mexico and the East Texas missions was needed.

In 1718, Spanish officials consented to Fray Olivares' request to found a mission at San Pedro Springs. Because the Indians of the region often did not get along with each other, other missions soon were established to serve each group. And for a time these missions flourished and each became an early ranching center. But the missions' large herds of cattle and horses soon attracted trouble.

About 1720, the Apaches made their first appearance in the San Antonio area. One settler was killed and scalped and raids on the missions' herds began. Punitive retaliation by the Spanish only outraged the Apaches, and religious authorities opposed the military operations. Attempts to negotiate a peace with the Apaches failed, but the raids subsided between 1726 and 1731.

War broke out between the French and Spanish in Europe, and the East Texas missions were temporarily abandoned a second time in 1717 after a comic-opera incident in which the mission at Nacogdoches was engaged by French soldiers from Natchitoches in present-day Louisiana.

The expulsion from East Texas prompted the Spanish to return with the largest military operation of the period. The Marquis San Miguel de Aguayo, a nobleman of Coahuila, was ordered to launch a retaliatory offensive, but the orders were soon changed. Texas' defenses were to be strengthened. Because of the time lag in receiving orders, Aguayo's expedition did not get into the field until 1721. With 500 men, 4,000 horses and large herds of livestock, he reached San Antonio in April 1721, and after strengthening the presidio there he headed for East Texas.

Unknown to the Spanish in Texas, the French had suffered a financial disaster. John Law, a Scottish banker, had launched an investment scheme that involved the issuance of paper money in France to finance the development of colonies on the Mississippi River. The bubble broke in 1720, and the French government all but abandoned the colonization effort while retrenching to repair the damage to the nation's economy. In some cases, Indians in the Mississippi valley attacked French traders in rebellion against the diminished trade. But Saint Denis had been given command of French troops in Louisiana and tried to arrange a truce with Aguayo to prevent the remanning of Spanish missions and presidios in the region. The ploy did not work. Forts and missions were re-established, and a presidio was built at Los Adaes to keep an eye on the French at Natchitoches. This presidio, which was located near present-day Robeline, La., became the capital of the province of Texas for the next half century.

Aguayo was successful in strengthening the defenses in Texas. He re-established six missions, founded three more. Two new presidios were established, one re-established and a fourth strengthened. When Aguayo left Texas, 269 soldiers were on duty in a territory that previously was defended by only 60 to 70. He also separated the province of Texas from Coahuila for the first time, drawing the boundary along the San Antonio and Medina rivers.

While Texas' eastern frontier was threatened by the French in the 18th century, the greatest problem for the Spanish existed in the thinly populated areas of western Texas. The Comanches began their southward movement from the Northern Plains at the beginning of the century, relentlessly pushing the Apaches and others before them. The Apaches moved westward and southward. Attempts by the Jumano Indians to have missions established in the Big Bend near the junction of the Rio Grande and the Rio Conchos — the Junta de los Rios — were thwarted by hostiles in 1717-18. A mission built near present-day Del Rio suffered a similar fate. And San Juan Bautista, built unfortunately close to one prong of the Comanche trail crossing the Rio Grande, was under constant threat. Only the most adventuresome Spaniard or Mexican braved the hazards of this frontier to attempt colonization, and often the price paid for a display of courage was the settler's life. By the middle 1730s, the Apaches were raiding mercilessly south of the Rio Grande. Monclova and Saltillo were endangered, and the province of Sonora was on the brink of destruction. The Spanish concentrated their defensive efforts south of the river to protect the silver mines and ranches in northern Mexico. The province of Texas was actually "behind enemy lines" for much of the time.

The San Antonio missions felt the Apache wrath. The mission system, which attempted to convert the Indians to Christianity and to "civilize" them, was partially successful in subduing minor tribes. But the Spanish realized that more stable colonization efforts must be made. Mexican Indians, such as the Tlascalans who fought with Cortez against the Aztecs, were brought into Texas to serve as examples of "good" Indians for the wayward natives. In 1731, descendants of the colonists of the Canary Islands were brought to Texas and founded the Villa of San Fernando de Bexar, the first civil jurisdiction in the province and today's San Antonio. But the province remained thinly populated, much to the despair of Spanish officials.

As desperate as was the plight of Texas, the Spanish were more concerned about another area. One of Spain's most successful colonization efforts in the New World came in the Lower Rio Grande Valley. But the history of the effort underscores the lengthy process of decision-making in Spanish Texas. In the late 1730s, officials became concerned over the vulnerability of Seno Mexico — the large area between the Sierra Madre Oriental and the Gulf Coast in Northern Mexico. The area was unsettled, a haven for runaway Indian slaves and marauders, and it was a wide-open pathway for the English or French from the Gulf to the rich silver mines in Durango.

For seven years the search for the right colonizer went on before Jose de Escandon was selected in 1746. A professional military man and successful administrator, Escandon earned a high reputation by subduing Indians in Central Mexico. On receiving the assignment, he launched a broad land survey of the area running from the mountains to the Gulf and from the Rio Panuco in Tamaulipas, Mexico, to the Nueces River in Texas. In 1747, he began placing colonists in settlements throughout the area. Tomas Sanchez received a land grant on the Rio Grande in 1755 from which Laredo developed. And other small Texas communities along the river sprang up as a result of Escandon's well-executed plan. Many old Mexican families in Texas hold title to their land based on grants in this period.

Escandon's colony became the state of Nuevo Santander, named for the founder's home province in Spain. The boundaries extended to the Nueces River, placing the Lower Rio Grande Valley outside of Texas.

Escandon also contributed to the early development of ranching in South Texas. In 1753 he granted Capt. Jose Vasquiz Borrego 433,800 acres of land to develop a ranch. The headquarters was located near the present-day town of San Ygnacio in Zapata County. Other large land grants also helped establish large-scale ranching in the area, although Texas never developed the hacienda concept that was used in Mexico. Ranching helped the economy, but the livestock also attracted Indians.

As devastating as the Apaches were to Spanish settlements, they were getting the worst of their fight with the Comanches and their allies. By 1747, the Apaches around San Antonio were ready to make peace and said they were ready to enter missions. Attempts to gather them in existing missions failed because other Indians feared and hated them after many years of bloody warfare. In 1757, officials established the mission of San Saba de la Santa Cruz in present-day Menard County. One year later, the Spanish encountered the Comanches in Texas for the first time. The Comanches, with their allies from the Plains, devastated the mission, killing several priests and Indians. Spanish officials were irate. After much debate they launched a punitive expedition to punish the raiders. Col. Diego Ortiz Parrilla led a mixed army of Mexican Indians, Lipan Apaches and Spanish soldiers. The force engaged a mixed group of Plains Indians at Spanish Fort on a bend of the Red River in present-day Montague County. Entrenched in a stockade with a crude moat, the Indians fought with French weapons and used disciplined tactics in the field. Abandoned by their allies, the Spanish suffered a humiliating loss, the worst inflicted on them by Texas Indians during the colonial period.

The battle of Spanish Fort was a turning point in Indian warfare. The Plains Indians proved they could adapt to European field tactics. And for a time, they had set aside tribal animosities to present a united front against the colonizers. The Spanish had easily defeated sedentary Indians in Mexico, but the Plains Indians were a different breed, as the defeat of the Spanish proved. Obviously, new tactics were needed if the Spanish were to stay in Texas.

4 *The Demise of Spain*

SPAIN'S final 60 years of control of the province of Texas were marked with a few successes and a multitude of failures, all of which could be attributed to a breakdown in the administrative system. Charles III, the fourth of the Bourbon line of kings and generally recognized as an enlightened despot, took the throne in 1759. Soon he launched a series of reforms in the New World. The king's choice of administrators was excellent. In 1765, Jose de Galvez was dispatched to New Spain (an area that then included all of modern Mexico and much of today's American West) with instructions to improve both the economy and the defense.

Galvez initially toured parts of the vast region, gaining first-hand insight into the practical problems of the colony. And there were many that could be traced to Spain's basic concepts of colonial government. Texas, in particular, suffered from the mercantilist economic system that attempted to funnel all colonial trade through ports in Mexico.

In a typical trip, trade goods bound for Texas would enter New Spain at the port of Veracruz. From there they would be shipped to Mexico City and then Saltillo before reaching Texas. At each stop, charges would be added. By the time the goods reached Texas, they would be prohibitively expensive. Texas' economy was limited. Ranching was its foundation, and there were few markets for Texas cattle and horses. The mines in northern Mexico were serviced by haciendas in that region. Texas' market was limited to the army, the missions and the few colonists who lived in the province.

Also, because of the mercantilist approach, trade with the French in Louisiana Territory was strictly forbidden. But Spanish Texans were practical people. When a demand for Texas cattle and horses developed in Louisiana, a healthy smuggling trade arose. Texas' livestock became a medium of exchange for low-cost trade goods provided by French traders. And government officials in Texas often were bribed to look the other way.

Problems with the Comanches, Apaches and "Nortenos," as the Spanish called some tribes, continued to plague the province, too. The Marquis de Rubi was commissioned to inspect the defenses of the entire northern New Spain frontier from California to Louisiana. Rubi reached Texas in 1767 and was appalled by the deplorable condition of the province's defenses. At San Saba mission, there were not enough horses for each soldier, although each should have had four or five mounts to be properly equipped. Soldiers at Los Adaes had only two guns and two shields for the entire 60-man contingent. Morale was low throughout the province. In some cases, officers were selling equipment and uniforms to soldiers at greatly inflated prices. Rubi recommended sweeping reforms in the defense system. But some changes were based on faulty assumptions.

In 1762, France ceded the Louisiana Territory to Spain in compensation for Spain's help in the losing effort in the Seven Years War in Europe. The politics of the day convinced the French that it was better that this huge — and largely undefined — area be in the hands of the Spanish than the British. For the Spanish in Texas, the cession was a mixed blessing, however. True, the French were no longer an immediate threat on the province's eastern boundary. But the fact lulled Rubi into a false sense of security.

With the need to defend East Texas from the French diminished, Rubi moved to construct Texas' defenses around the needs of the mining and ranching areas in northern Mexico. This meant closing the East Texas missions and presidios and moving the soldiers and colonists to San Antonio to bolster defenses against the Indians. In addition, Rubi moved the presidio San Elizario north of the Rio Grande to defend the El Paso area and abandoned the San Saba mission and presidio, which were inactive anyway. Presidio La Bahia was strengthened, and a military way station was established at Arroyo del Cibola to protect the road between San Antonio and La Bahia. As a practical matter, however, much of Texas was not to be defended; it was, in a sense, "behind enemy lines."

Charles III's well-intentioned reorganization of New Spain took almost a decade. And in the interim, conflicting policies took their toll on good will and attempts to pacify the various Indian groups in Texas.

When Spain undertook the administration of Louisiana Territory, one of the terms of the cession by France was that the region would enjoy certain trading privileges denied to other Spanish dependencies. So although Texas and Louisiana were neighbors, trade between the two provinces was banned. The crown further complicated matters by placing the administration of Louisiana under authorities in Cuba, while Texas remained under the authorities in Mexico City. Officials often acted as if the two Spanish provinces were actually warring foreign countries. This was an intolerable burden on Spanish settlers in East Texas and on French traders who were being integrated into the effort to control the Nortenos, a term which covered a number of Plains Indians in Texas.

The Nortenos, who for a time were allied with the Comanches, warred intermittently against the Spanish after their victory at Spanish Fort in 1759. Nortenos resented treaties between the Spanish and their enemies, the Apaches. Punitive expeditions by the Spanish military only deepened the hostility and prompted retaliation. By the early 1770s, the Osage Indians were encouraged by renegade French traders and the British to raid the Nortenos, who in turn recouped losses of horses and livestock by sacking Spanish settlements.

Several attempts were made by Spanish officials in Texas to make peace with the Nortenos, but the prohibition of trade with Louisiana stymied the efforts. Often the Spanish were not able to produce annual gifts that were promised, and a strict ban on supplying the Indians with guns and munitions hurt the effort. The peace overtures to the Nortenos also damaged relations with the mission Apaches. Rubi's order to close the East Texas missions and forts was not executed until 1773, when Indian depredations again increased around San Antonio. On just a few days' notice, the settlers were ordered to gather up their personal belongings and leave. Many died on the trip across Texas to the new capital at San Antonio. Others were bankrupted when they had to leave behind many possessions acquired during a lifetime. And the incident emphasized another weakness in the Spanish colonial system: Unlike later American settlers, the Spaniards did not have control of their destinies. Too often geopolitical considerations were paramount in the government's colonial policy.

Although the East Texans were offered their choice of unsettled land around San Antonio, the good property had long ago been taken by early colonists. What good land was available was too exposed to Indian raids. The settlers, led by Antonio Gil Y'barbo and Gil Flores, petitioned officials for permission to move back to East Texas. They got approval to go as far as the Trinity River, where in 1774 they set up a fortified village, named Bucareli in honor of the viceroy, on the present-day Walker County line where the Camino Real crossed the river.

Without a listening post in Louisiana and with communications with the sister colony often officially banned, Texas officials were hard-pressed to keep up with the activities of the Nortenos. When settlers at Bucareli were frightened by Comanche raids in 1778 and 1779 and discouraged by continuing floods that washed away crops, they moved farther east to set up a community at the site of the old Nacogdoches mission. This marked the founding of present-day Nacogdoches. Although the move was not sanctioned initially, Y'barbo later was named lieutenant governor of the province at the settlement and established a clandestine trade and intelligence network with the French traders in Louisiana.

Jose de Galvez' survey of New Spain bore fruit in 1776, when as minister of the Indes he established the Internal Provinces to administer the defense of the northern frontier of New Spain. Under the new arrangement, Texas and Louisiana were ordered to cooperate, which temporarily eased many of the problems.

Not all the changes were welcome, however. Upon becoming commandant general of the Internal Provinces in 1776, Teodoro de Croix decreed that all unbranded livestock in Texas was the property of the crown. Ranchers and missionaries were furious. They complained that they had been unable to conduct semi-annual roundups of their stock for years because of the Indian hostilities. De Croix relented to the extent of giving the stockmen four months to brand and mark their cattle and horses, and thereafter they were required to pay fees on their animals. Texas' cattle and horse market improved in 1780 when a concession was granted by the king to allow legal livestock trade with Louisiana.

Bernardo de Galvez, the nephew of Jose and the namesake of Galveston County, was named acting governor of Louisiana in 1777. He had experience as an Indian fighter along the Rio Grande and had an insight into the colonial situation. During the American War for Independence, the younger Galvez occupied the British in Florida, preventing them from concentrating attention on the American revolutionaries. And Galvez had cattle driven from the Gulf Plains and South Texas to supply the Americans along the Mississippi River. The cattle drives were the forerunners of the later livestock movements that played so great a role in the development of Texas after the American Civil War.

During the last two decades of the 18th century, Spain reached the zenith of its power in the northern provinces of New Spain. Operating within Jose de Galvez' recommendations, Charles III reformed the administration of New Spain. Talented, experienced leaders were given control of the new provinces and improvements were made. Although maintaining amicable relations with the various Indian groups in Texas was difficult, the Spanish made accommodations with most of the aborigines. Some of the Apaches remained intractable, and groups within the Comanches sometimes failed to honor treaties made by other Comanche leaders. In 1791, Juan de Ugalde defeated Lipan and Mescalero Apaches in the Lower Rio Grande

Valley and brought peace for many years to that region. (Despite the difference in spelling, Uvalde County in South Texas is named for this soldier.)

One of the tragedies of the period was the untimely death of the promising young administrator, Bernardo de Galvez. His family had a long record of service to the Spanish crown, and Bernardo in 1785 succeeded his father, Matias, as viceroy of New Spain. Such was the crown's confidence in the new administrator that he retained control of Cuba, the Floridas and Louisiana and gained authority over the Internal Provinces in addition to his other responsibilities. Galvez conceived a policy that maintained peace with the Indians until the turn of the century. Very simply, he gave the Indians the choice between war and peace. Those that chose peace were given annual gifts and, in some cases, old firearms. Indians that chose war were mercilessly pursued. As long as the gifts were forthcoming and frontier-wise administrators were kept in the provinces, relative peace was maintained. But young Galvez died in an epidemic in 1786, and the great promise of his early administration was not fulfilled.

The death of Charles III in 1788 and the beginning of the French Revolution a year later also weakened Spain's hold of the New World dominions. Charles IV was not as good a sovereign as his predecessor, and his choice of ministers was poor. The quality of frontier administrators declined, and relations with Indians soured.

Charles IV's major blunder, however, was to side with French royalty during the revolution, earning Spain the enmity of Napoleon Bonaparte when he assumed control of the government. Spain also allied with England in an effort to thwart Napoleon, and in this losing cause, the Spanish were forced to cede Louisiana back to France. In 1803, Napoleon broke a promise to retain the territory and sold it to the United States. Spain's problems in the New World thereby took on an altogether different dimension. Anglo-Americans cast longing eyes on the vast undeveloped territory of Texas. The available land east of the Mississippi River was being quickly developed as the Americans drove the Indians of the American Southeast westward from their historic homelands.

With certain exceptions for royalists who left the American colonies during the revolution, Spain had maintained a strict prohibition against Anglo or other non-Spanish settlers in their New World territories. But they were unprepared to police the eastern border of Texas after removing the presidios in the 1760s. What had been a provincial line became virtually overnight an international boundary, and an ill-defined one at that.

Spain and France had never set a specific boundary between Texas and Louisiana, and during the colonial period from 1762 to 1803, only a general line was acknowledged. Thomas Jefferson initially tried to claim all of Texas to the Rio Grande as part of the Louisiana Purchase, based on weak French claims tied to La-Salle's explorations. For a period of time, Spanish and American authorities created a no-man's-land between the Sabine River and Arroyo Hondo, which became a refuge for renegades from both nations.

Anglo-Americans began to probe the Spanish frontier. Some settled in East Texas and were tolerated by authorities. Others, however, were thought to have more nefarious designs. Philip Nolan was the first of the American filibusters to test Spanish resolve. Several times, both authorized and unauthorized, he entered Texas to capture wild horses to sell in the United States. But in 1801, the Spanish perceived an attempted armed uprising by Nolan and his followers. He was killed in a battle near present-day Waco, and his company was taken captive to work in the mines of northern Mexico.

In 1806, Anglo-Americans were showing up in the El Paso area. Lt. Zebulon Pike, commissioned by President Jefferson to survey the newly acquired lands of the Louisiana Purchase, was taken into custody in the upper Rio Grande Valley. After a journey into the interior of Mexico, however, he was released and returned to the United States through Texas, becoming the first Anglo-American to write of the geographic features and economic potential of the region.

Spanish officials were beginning to realize that the economic potential of Texas must be developed if the Anglo-Americans were to be neutralized. In the late 18th and early 19th centuries, several attempts were made to find a short route to Sante Fe to open trade with that sister province. Later Moses Austin and Mirabeau Lamar would see the same economic potential in Texas-Santa Fe trade, although it was never realized.

On the Continent, Spain's fortunes were at a low ebb. Napoleon was pressuring Charles IV, whose abdication in 1808 the French ruler refused to accept. Ferdinand VII claimed the crown, and Napoleon in the same year placed his brother, Joseph Bonaparte, on the throne. Spain rebelled against this foreign intrusion, and the War for Independence on the Iberian Peninsula was on.

Resistance to Spanish rule had developed in the New World colonies. Liberal ideas from the American and French revolutions had grown popular, despite the crown's attempts to prevent their dissemination. And chaos reigned in the colonies. From the time of Philip II, Spain had been a tightly centralized monarchy with the crown making most decisions. But during the war on the peninsula, three sovereigns — Charles IV, Ferdinand VII and Joseph Bonaparte — often issued edicts simultaneously. The colonials rebelled. Father Miguel Hidalgo ignited the Mexican war for independence on Sept. 16, 1810. And a bloody, decade-long conflict ensued, taking on the trappings of a civil war in many respects. Native Spaniards were fought by Spaniards of Mexican birth. Mestizos — mixed-blood Mexicans — and Indians also joined in the fight for control of the government.

The French control of Spain reached its peak in 1810-1811. England entered the fray on the side of the Spanish, and in 1811, the Spanish parliament — the Cortes — wrote a liberal constitution providing for self-government once control of the peninsula was regained. But Spain was not ready for the liberal government designed by the Cortes, and more disturbances followed as Ferdinand VII regained the throne and dissolved the Cortes.

Mexico's war for independence was savage and bloody in the interior provinces, and Texas suffered, as well. In 1811, Capt. Juan Bautista Casas briefly seized Gov. Manuel de Salcedo and military commander Simon de Herrera in the name of King Ferdinand. But the revolt was quickly and bloodily repressed. Later that year, Jose Bernardo Gutierrez de Lara of Revilla (now Guerrero south of Laredo on the Rio Grande) was appointed the diplomatic agent of the Mexican revolutionaries and journeyed to Washington to seek recognition of the newly proclaimed nation. While Gutierrez was warmly received by U.S. officials, he received no formal recognition and no money or arms. In early 1812, the Mexican patriot traveled to Natchitoches, La., where, with the help of U.S. agents, an expedition was organized. Augustus W. Magee, a West Point graduate who had served in the neutral zone between the Sabine and Arroyo Hondo, commanded the troop, which entered Texas in August 1812. This "Republican Army of the North" easily took Nacogdoches, where it gathered recruits, and La Bahia. After withstanding a siege at La Bahia, the army took San Antonio and proclaimed the first Republic of Texas in April 1813. A few months later, the republican forces were bloodily subdued at the Battle of the Medina River. Royalist Gen. Joaquin de Arredondo executed a staggering number of more than 300 republicans, including some Americans, at San Antonio, and a young lieutenant, Antonio Lopez de Santa Anna, was recognized for valor under fire. The Green Flag of the first republic was never recognized by any foreign government. Thinly populated Texas was devastated, however.

Republican furor waned after Ferdinand VII regained the throne, and while Spanish officials in Texas accepted a return to the old order, they knew that more trouble would be forthcoming if the province continued to be neglected. Spain and the United States reached agreement on the eastern boundary of Texas in 1819 in a treaty that provided for the U.S. purchase of Spanish claims to Florida. But the relinquishing of claims to Texas was considered treasonous by some Americans who took matters into their own hands. Dr. James Long led two expeditions into Texas to claim the territory for Americans. The first was successful in capturing Nacogdoches, where many Anglo settlers joined his rebellion. The filibuster returned to the United States briefly, and re-entered Texas to complete his conquest. But while attempting to take La Bahia, he was captured by Mexicans, who had gained independence from Spain in 1821. Dr. Long was taken to Mexico City, where he died under mysterious circumstances. His wife, Jane, accompanied him on the second expedition and bore the first Anglo-American child to be born in the province, folklore holds. She was a popular figure in the early days of Anglo-American immigration into Texas.

Ferdinand VII was forced to re-assemble the Spanish Cortes in 1820, and a colonization law was passed that welcomed foreigners into Texas, if they pledged loyalty to the Spanish monarchy and to the constitution.

But Spain's role in the history of Texas was over. The Mexicans had gained their independence and would repel an attempted invasion by the king. After almost 300 years, the Spanish had changed the face of Texas, and the Latin nation's culture remains affixed to the state's history. The Anglo-American tide that would sweep across the Southwest was poised at the province's eastern boundary. In only a few years, it would surge across the former Spanish territory.

5 *The Mexican Period*

AS SPAIN'S grip on the New World slipped between 1790 and 1820, Texas was almost forgotten, an internal province of little importance. Colonization was ignored, and the Spanish government had larger problems in Europe and in Mexico.

Spain's mercantile economic policy penalized colonists in the area, working to charge them high prices for trade goods and paying low prices for products sent to markets in the interior of New Spain. As a result, settlers had no incentives to come to Texas. Indeed, men of ambition in the province often turned to illegal trade with Louisiana or to smuggling to prosper.

On the positive side, however, Indians of the province had been mollified through annual gifts and by developing a dependence on Spain for trade goods. Ranching flourished. A census in 1803 indicated that there were 100,000 head of cattle in Texas; in 1795, a census also found 69 families living on 45 ranches in the San Antonio area. But aside from a few additional families in Nacogdoches and La Bahia, the province was thinly populated.

When Spain returned the Louisiana Territory to France in the secret treaty of San Ildefonso in 1800, the vulnerability of Texas as a border province again became a concern. In Louisiana, Spain had relaxed its colonization policies. No attempt was made to use the mission system along the Mississippi River. Instead, an immigration policy was adopted that resembled later approaches in Texas. It provided for land grants, commercial privileges and religious toleration for colonists in exchange for a loyalty oath and actual settlement of land.

After Spain gave up Louisiana, Gen. Nemesio Salcedo, commandant-general of the Internal Provinces, allowed former Spanish subjects in Louisiana to settle in Texas. After 1805, other foreigners, under threat of death, were banned.

Several unsuccessful attempts also were made to attract colonists from the interior of Mexico. Gen. Salcedo improved the border defenses when the United States tried to press claims to the Rio Grande as the western boundary of Louisiana.

Texas' major problem was its isolation. Except for the threat of foreign immigration, the province was far removed from the political passions in Spain and Mexico City. The Spanish Cortes, for example, opened colonies to limited self-government in 1812, but the liberalization had little impact in Texas. Federalists and royalists battled for power in Mexico City, but except for a brief flirtation with republicanism after the Magee-Gutierrez expedition in 1813, Texas was unchanged and stagnated. But Spanish and Mexican officials knew that the province must be populated or lost.

Even worse, as the Spanish colonial government declined, Indians recognized its weakness. Annual gifts no longer were distributed. And as important, the Indians found an independent source of weapons and ammunition after American traders in Louisiana Territory began supplying guns and goods in exchange for horses and cattle. Frontier dangers were compounded after Father Hidalgo's 1810 uprising. The private ownership of firearms was prohibited. Indians stepped up raids, and settlers had fewer means of defense.

Therefore, Texas was in a state of suspension, only indirectly by the forces of political and social change that were gripping not only Europe and Mexico, but the North American continent as well. In the United States, currents of dissatisfaction were generated that made Texas very attractive. Federal land policy, agricultural practices and economic disruptions, along with population pressures, were steadily moving the Anglo-Americans westward.

Land policy was a long-standing point of contention between Eastern industrialists and frontiersmen. The industrialists favored high prices and tight credit policies on federal land sold to pioneers. The businessmen feared a reduction in their work force if land policies made settlement of the western lands too inviting. Until 1820, the government opened bidding on land at $2 an acre with a minimum purchase of 640 acres. The purchaser was required to pay down one-quarter of the price in cash, and the balance was due in four annual payments. And cash was scarce on the frontier.

Early in the 19th century, state banks began issuing scrip that was accepted by government land offices for purchases. With the financial panic of 1819, the nation's first major economic depression, these banks were among the first to fail. Many businessmen were ruined, and farmers saw prices drop below the cost of raising crops. The frontier was particularly hard hit.

After 1820, the federal government reduced land prices to $1.25 an acre with an 80-acre minimum purchase and credit policies were relaxed somewhat. Even in those days, Congress "primed the pump" of the nation's economy with a more lenient land policy that would stimulate financial growth. But the price was still high and the required cash was hard to come by.

The unstable economy made restless Americans look for fresh opportunities. The U.S.-Spanish boundary between the Americans and the rich agricultural lands of East Texas was no barrier to the energetic, nomadic pioneers. Early in the 19th century, they began to filter across the invisible dividing line to squat on New Spain's eastern frontier. Because the boundary was ill-defined until the Adams-Onis treaty of 1819, many Americans thought they were settling in the newly acquired Louisiana Territory of the United States. In 1815, for example, founders of the settlement of Jonesborough in present-day Red River County thought they were in Arkansas. (In fact, in 1824, the community was designated the seat of government of Miller County, Ark., and it was not until Texas attained statehood that the matter of jurisdiction was resolved.) Individual Anglos settled in Southeast Texas and were not disturbed by Spanish authorities. Nacogdoches attracted an undesirable element from the United States, in part because of its proximity to the neutral zone, the no-man's-land between the Sabine River and the Arroyo Hondo before the boundary settlement. As early as 1801 American traders had infiltrated East Texas. By 1804, Anglo families had become numerous enough around Nacogdoches for the Spanish military commander to attempt to expel non-Catholics.

East Texas was particularly attractive to farmers. Over the centuries the Caddo Indians — called Tejas by the Spanish — had cultivated hundreds of acres of land. When the Indians were hit hard by epidemics in the late 18th century, the rich farmland fell into disuse. But it was still cleared, and the open fields between the Sabine and Angelina rivers were quickly settled.

The largest group of early immigrants from the United States was not Anglo, but Indian. As early as 1818, Cherokees from the Southeast United States came to Texas, settling north of Nacogdoches on lands between the Trinity and Sabine rivers. The Cherokees had been among the first U.S. Indians to accept the federal government's offers of resettlement. As American pioneers entered the newly acquired lands of Georgia, Alabama and other areas of the Southeast, the Indians were systematically removed, through legal means or otherwise. The early U.S. policy of attempting to "civilize" and assimilate the Native Americans was changing. Pioneers wanted the Indians' land, and that meant that the native peoples must be moved. Some settled on land provided in Arkansas Territory, but others, like groups of Cherokees, came to Texas, seeking to escape the hostility of the Anglos. And these Cherokees were among the "Five Civilized Tribes" that had adopted agriculture and many Anglo customs in an unsuccessful attempt to get along with their new neighbors.

Alabama and Coushatta tribes had exercised squatters' rights in present Sabine County in the early 1800s, and soon after the Cherokees arrived, groups of Shawnee, Delaware and Kickapoo Indians came from the United States. All sought from the Spanish and Mexican governments title to some of the prime farmland in the region. The presence of the Indians became a factor in the Anglos' disputes with the Mexican government, which attempted, by promising land titles to the Indians, to play the two groups of U.S. immigrants against each other.

After 1820, the second wave of immigrants arrived, larger than the first and of different character. These Anglos were not so interested in agricultural opportunities as in other schemes to quickly recoup their fortunes.

The only group of immigrants expelled by Spanish authorities were Napoleonic exiles who in 1818 attempted to set up the French colony of Champ d'Asile on the present site of Liberty in Liberty County.

Spain, and later Mexico, recognized the danger represented by the unregulated, informal colonization by Americans. The Spanish Cortes' colonization law of 1813 attempted to build a buffer between the eastern frontier and Northern Mexico. The act served as the basis for later Mexican immigration policy through which it was hoped that European and Mexican colonists could be attracted to Texas to dilute the Anglo population. To prevent smuggling, which flourished because of a lack of legal ports, colonies were prohibited within 26 miles — or 10 leagues — of the coast. Also, special permission was required for Americans to settle within 52 miles of the international boundary, although this prohibition often was ignored. As initially envisioned, Americans would be allowed to settle the interior of the vast territory. European and Mexican colonists would be placed along the eastern frontier to limit contact between the Americans and the United States. The Americans already in Texas illegally would be stable if given a stake in the province through land ownership, officials felt.

Moses Austin, a former Spanish subject who had suffered a severe financial setback in the panic of 1819, applied for the first empresario grant from the Spanish government. With the intercession of Baron de Bastrop, a friend of Austin's from Missouri Territory, Gov. Antonio Maria Martinez approved the request in January 1821. Austin agreed to settle 300 families on land bounded by the Brazos and Colorado rivers on the east and west, by the El Camino Real (the old military road running from San Antonio to Nacogdoches) on the north and by the Gulf Coast, since his grant came before settlement in the area was prohibited. But Austin died in June 1821, leaving the work to his son, Stephen F. Austin.

The younger Austin was uniquely qualified for leadership of the colonial enterprise. Although born in Virginia in 1793, he moved with his parents to Missouri Territory at the age of five. Austin's experiences as a youth gave him an understanding of the disposition of the Spanish and Mexican administrators with whom he dealt. The 27-year-old empresario also was well educated, had served in the Missouri legislature and was appointed judge in Arkansas Territory before coming to Texas. Austin's problems began immediately upon entering Texas when he learned that Mexico had gained independence from Spain. Although his first colonists arrived in December 1821, Austin was told by Gov. Martinez that the provisional government would not recognize the Spanish grant. The new government had to approve the colonization program, Austin learned. So he spent a year in Mexico City, observing the organization of the new government and lobbying for his colonial authorization. On occasion he advised Mexican leaders on the creation of a federal system of government. Finally in January 1823, the Spanish grant was affirmed by the Mexican government.

Mexico's land policy, like Spain's, differed from the U.S. approach. Whereas the United States sold land directly to settlers or to speculators who dealt with the pioneers, the Mexicans retained tight control of the property transfer until predetermined agreements for development were fulfilled. But a 4,428-acre sitio — a square league — and a 177-acre labor could be obtained for only surveying costs and administrative fees as low as $50. The empresario was rewarded with grants of large tracts of land — but only when he fulfilled his quota of families to be brought to the colonies. Considering the prices the U.S. government charged, Texas' land was indeed a bargain — and a major attraction to those Anglo-Americans looking for a new start.

Austin had almost complete civil and military responsibility for his colony. He set up stringent requirements for his colonists, including requiring presentation of affidavits from community leaders at their previous home vouching for their good character and sober work habits. On several occasions, Austin had disreputable characters forcibly removed from his colony. As a consequence of these high standards, Austin attracted many financially stable colonists. And he made some enemies.

Austin was scrupulous in following the terms of his grant. He knew that Mexican officials, like the Spanish, distrusted the intentions of Americans, and the young empresario wanted to give no cause for suspicion. But despite Austin's efforts, the mistrust by officials persisted. They knew that whenever U.S. and Spanish boundaries had met, the Spanish boundaries receded. Florida had been lost in the agreement that set Texas' eastern boundary. Rights in Oregon Territory also had been given to the United States in the same treaty.

Under the Constitution of 1824, Mexicans reversed the U.S. approach to land distribution. The federalist government gave the states responsibility for developing public lands. And colonization policy became even more liberal as the government of Coahuila y Texas, which was the poorest of all the new Mexican states, sought to exploit the economic potential of the region and to build a buffer between Northern Mexico and both the United States and the Plains Indians. The state colonization law of 1825 brought explosive growth to Texas. More than 25 empresarios were commissioned to settle colonists. By 1830, Texas boasted an estimated population of 15,000, with Anglos outnumbering Mexicans by a margin of 4-to-1.

Austin was easily the most successful empresario. After his initial success, Austin was authorized in 1825 to bring 900 more families to Texas, and in 1831, he and his partner, Samuel Williams, received another concession to bring 800 Mexican and

European families. Through Austin's efforts, 1,540 land titles were issued to settlers, and the population of his colonies in 1831 was 5,665. The next two most successful empresarios were Green DeWitt and Martin De Leon.

Green DeWitt was authorized in April 1825 to bring 400 families to Texas in an area west of Austin's colony. Mexican officials felt that establishment of towns was important, and in 1825, Gonzales, in present-day Gonzales County, was laid out by surveyor James Kerr. The community was named in honor of Coahuila y Texas Gov. Rafael Gonzales. Because of the danger of Indian raids, many of DeWitt's colonists stayed in a small community called Old Station on the Lavaca River near the coast until 1827, when a peace treaty with the Karankawas was signed after a military campaign by joint American and Mexican forces.

DeWitt's colony suffered from other Indian attacks. First the Tonkawas raided because they were being pressed by the Comanches and Wichitas, who had moved into the South Plains. Later the Plains Indians found the horse and cattle herds of the colony lucrative sources of plunder.

DeWitt did not bring 400 families to the province, as he had contracted, but 166 land titles were issued to settlers who came to Texas through his efforts.

South and west of DeWitt's colony, Martin de Leon, a rancher in Tamaulipas who admired the region during a cattle drive, received a grant from the provincial delegation of San Fernando de Bexar for another colony. Because the Coahuila y Texas legislature was unaware of de Leon's grant, DeWitt's grant overlapped, and there were problems when the two empresarios tried to colonize the same region. De Leon won the dispute because his grant pre-dated DeWitt's and because Mexican citizens were given preference in colonization.

Forty-one Mexican families were settled in the region by de Leon, who in 1824 also founded the city of Guadalupe Victoria, named for the first Mexican president. By 1833, the city had a population of 200.

Austin's colony flourished, in part because of his understanding of the Mexican character and the necessity for strict adherence to Mexican law. Other empresarios were not so diligent.

In the early years of colonization, the settlers busied themselves by clearing lands, planting crops, building homes and fighting Indians. Many were successful in establishing a subsistence economy. One weakness of the Mexican colonial policy was that it did not provide the factors for a market economy. While towns were established, credit, banks and good roads were not provided by the government. Ports were established at Galveston and Matagorda bays after Mexican independence, but the colonists felt they needed more, particularly one at the mouth of the Brazos. And foreign ships were barred from coastwise trade, which posed a particular hardship since Mexico had few merchant ships.

One attempt to establish a bank failed. When Jose Felix Trespalacios was appointed the political and military chief of Texas in 1822, there was a limited amount of money in circulation in the province. Soldiers and officials were paid irregularly. So Trespalacios set up the Banco Nacional de Texas in San Antonio, which in November 1822 issued to soldiers and officials notes that could be redeemed at face value. Trespalacios had not received prior approval of the central government, which liked the idea. But in late 1822, the government decreed that only two-thirds of the face value of the notes would be redeemed in gold; the rest would be paid in government notes. The value of the Texas bank notes dropped, and the bank failed, leaving, in part, a residual distrust of banks that remained a part of the Texas heritage until the early 20th century.

In eastern Texas and the Austin colony, cotton was planted almost immediately by the new colonists. Four cotton gins were in operation in East Texas by 1826. In

1828, 500 bales of cotton were produced in the Austin colony alone. But in DeWitt colony, the basic crop was corn. Many settlers also raised cattle, hogs and goats for milk.

Although there were complaints about the administration of government, the colonists concentrated on establishing themselves in a new land. Most of the unrest was brought about through a lack of understanding of the Spanish language and an unfamiliarity with the institutions of the government of the fledgling Republic.

Mexican officials, however, distrusted the intentions of the colonists. Most disputes were settled amicably enough, although there undoubtedly was discontent. DeWitt's Old Station near Lavaca Bay was interpreted by some officials as an attempt to develop a way station for smugglers. In fact, James Kerr had misunderstood the 10-league setback requirement for settlements near the coast; he thought the distance began at the outer islands, not on the coast itself.

The first major conflict between the Mexican government and Anglo settlers arose through a misunderstanding. Hayden Edwards received a large land grant around Nacogdoches to be distributed to new colonists. But Edwards misunderstood his charter. He first tried to set himself up as a military commander for the area, which was interpreted by Mexican officials as an attempted revolt. Then the empresario attempted to take land away from long-time Mexican settlers who could not prove title to their property. Many of the families held land under informal grants made by Gil Y'barbo almost a half-century earlier, and others had not fulfilled the tedious requirements of Spanish land law to get full title. Others had simply lost the documents, of which there was no record in the Spanish archives. Acts more attributable to ignorance than guile were interpreted by Mexican officials as steps toward insurrection. Finally while Hayden Edwards was in the United States on business in 1826, his brother, Benjamin, declared the independence of the Republic of Fredonia and ejected a group of Mexican soldiers from the area.

Most Anglos did not support the revolt. So the Fredonians made a pact with a group of Cherokees to give the Indians the northern half of Texas in exchange for their support in the rebellion. The Mexican army, aided by a contingent of Austin's colonists, quickly put down the revolt. The rebellious leaders fled to the United States. But the insurgency sowed seeds of distrust with Mexican officials. As important in the long run, Anglos from the previously isolated colonies opened communication.

Mexican officials' hope of attracting large numbers of European immigrants never materialized. Government instability, stagnant economy and religious intolerance outweighed whatever attractions Europeans might find in Mexico, and the United States was a more popular place to relocate. Nevertheless, two small colonies of Europeans were settled. James Power and James Hewetson got a special concession to settle an area on the coast between the Lavaca and Nueces rivers. Despite many problems, the town of Refugio, located on the site of the old mission by the same name, was established and almost 200 land titles were issued under this grant. John McMullen and James McGloin got a grant just north of the Power-Hewetson concession and had 84 grants issued to their colonists, most of whom were from Ireland. San Patricio was settled in the McMullen-McGloin colony.

In late 1827, Gen. Manuel Mier y Teran, a soldier, statesman and intellectual, was dispatched by President Victoria on an apparent mission to locate the actual boundary line between the United States and Mexico. In fact, however, Teran was taking the pulse of Texas. Mexican officials could not ignore the nagging threat of American intentions in their northern state.

Although he found no overt rebellion, the tour only reinforced Teran's concern about the developing American influence in Texas. The farther east he traveled, the less Mexican influence he found in the society. In East Texas, only a few long-time

Mexican settlers remained, and he noted they were of the poorest classes. From this review of Texas, Teran made three major recommendations: a military occupation of Texas, to provide protection from Indians, but also to isolate the Anglo-American colonies; a counter-colonization program aimed at attracting European and Mexican settlers; and the opening of coastwise trade to develop closer economic ties with the interior of Mexico.

Austin had advocated more coastwise trade to Teran. Most Texas trade went through New Orleans, and Austin, along with Teran, understood that that could become a major problem.

In 1829, Gen. Teran became commandant general of the Eastern Interior Provinces and began to carry out his program, much of which was incorporated in the Law of April 6, 1830, which was obnoxious to most American colonists in Texas. The law went beyond Teran's recommendations by in essence barring further Anglo-American immigration into Texas. Also, it provided for Mexican convict-soldiers, and their families, to be sent to the area, with an option to stay at the end of their terms under favorable circumstances provided by the government.

Teran reinforced garrisons at San Antonio, La Bahia, Nacogdoches and Velasco. And five new garrisons, three with Nahuatl names to reinforce their Mexican character, were established: Anahuac on Galveston Bay, Tenoxtitlan on the Brazos, Lipantitlan on the Nueces River, Lavaca on the river of the same name, and Teran on the Neches River.

The moving of additional armed forces into Texas concerned the Anglo-Americans, and it was unrest caused by the 1828 election and the military occupation of the state a year later that led to revolution.

Prelude to Revolution 6

MEXICO'S war for independence had achieved little more than separation from Spain. Sensing that liberal reforms in Spain would reduce the authority of royalists in the New World, Mexican conservatives led the revolt against the mother country. And they achieved early victories in the debate over the form of government the newly independent Mexico should adopt.

The majority of Mexicans had little concept of self-government. The Spanish Constitution of 1812 had provided for election of local officials, but it was not universally implemented. Offsetting this brief experience was a 300-year tradition of authoritarian, centralized colonial government. Since the reign of Phillip II, administration of the Spanish colonies was tightly controlled and slow-moving.

An independent Mexico was torn between advocates of centralist and republican forms of government. Centralists wanted a strong central government with appointed officials at the state and local levels who would be under the direction of Mexico City. Federalists supported the election of officials at lower levels, who would run their own administrations. The former royalists won the opening debates, setting Emperor Agustin de Iturbide on the new Mexican throne. But he soon was overthrown and the Constitution of 1824 was adopted. Constructing a federal framework of government and making it function smoothly, however, are difficult for a people inexperienced in self-government. The fiercely independent character of the Mexican people often prohibited the acquiescence so necessary to democratic government.

The turbulence experienced in Texas as the Mexicans attempted to set up a representative government was not an isolated experience in the period. Within months after the rebellion in Texas, federalists in California and New Mexico also revolted. But the central government's reaction was not so harsh. Santa Anna's ruthless attempt to crush the Anglo-led rebellion in Texas was motivated as much by the fear of losing the colony to the United States as by the desire to punish the political dissidents. The uprisings in California and New Mexico were settled diplomatically, not with the sword as in Texas.

Friction between the two cultures was inevitable. To settle in Texas, pioneers had to become Mexican citizens and to embrace Roman Catholicism. Most of the

Americans were Protestants, if they adhered to any religion, and they were fiercely defensive of the right to religious freedom enjoyed in the United States. Although no more than one-fourth of the Americans ever swore allegiance to the Catholic church, the requirement was a long-standing irritation. Compounding the problem was the fact that to be legal, marriages had to be blessed by a priest. For a decade after the founding of the Austin colony, no priest regularly ministered to the people. A system of contract marriages evolved in which couples took out a bond to have their union blessed by a priest when one was available. Occasionally, couples who found they could not live together would simply destroy the bond to dissolve the marriage if no priest had blessed the union.

Slavery, too, was a point of contention. Mexico prohibited the introduction of slavery after December 1827. Nevertheless, many slaveholders in Austin's colony became nervous at the official rhetoric. Several efforts were made to evade the government policy. Austin got the state legislature to recognize labor contracts under which slaves were technically free but bound themselves to their masters for life. Often entire families were covered by a single contract. While many early Anglo colonists were not slaveholders, they were Southerners, and the ownership of slaves was a cultural institution that they supported. The problem was never settled during the colonial period despite the tensions it generated.

There also was a long delay in getting land titles after the settlers had made the required improvements. And the Mexican court system was cumbersome. Appeals in civil cases and pleadings in criminal cases had to go 700 miles to Saltillo for adjudication, causing interminable and expensive delays in the administration of justice.

Balancing these complaints, however, were many advantages. Taxes, tithes and excises were suspended for several years. Farm implements and household goods could be brought into the colony with no duty charged. Good land was cheap and available for those willing to turn a wilderness into productive farmland.

Austin kept attuned to the settlers' problems, seeking relief from the Mexican government when possible. Many Austin colonists left the United States with a burden of debt brought about by the economic recession. Austin sought relief from the legislature of Coahuila y Texas with the enactment in 1828 of a homestead law that prohibited a person's property from being taken for debt accrued outside Mexico. Based on early Roman and Spanish law, this statute was the forerunner of the homestead protection enjoyed by Texans today.

Mistrust was mutual between Mexican officials and the colonists. As the population grew, the settlers' complaints intensified. Mexican officials' alarm grew in proportion to the population. Hopes of attracting European and Mexican colonists to dilute the burgeoning number of Anglos were not realized. Only a few Irish settlers had been attracted to the San Patricio grant on the Gulf Coast.

Andrew Jackson's election to the American presidency in 1828 further fanned Mexican fears. Jackson was known to covet Texas. The new president reportedly once told a Mexican diplomat that "the United States should never have lost the opportunity to obtain Texas, and that the way to obtain a territory was first to occupy it and, after having possession, treat for it, as had been done in Florida." Indeed, several informal offers to purchase Texas were made by U.S. officials before and after Jackson's election.

The Mexican election of 1828 also was a turning point in the history of the young republic. Self-government had been in effect in parts of Mexico since 1812. Mexico had begun the difficult transition from being an appendage of an absolutist monarchy to a federal republic. Mexicans were transformed from subjects of a crown into citizens in a republic. But the transformation was incomplete. Democracy requires an acquiescence of strongly held individual opinions to the results of the ballot box. But the orderly transfer of power in Mexico was dealt a death blow in 1828 when the legally elected administration of Manuel Gomez Pedraza was overthrown by supporters of Vicente Guerrero, who in turn was ousted by his own vice president Anastasio Bustamante. Mexico's most chaotic political period followed. The pattern of military intervention, coup and countercoup would last a century. Between May 1833 and August 1855, the Mexican presidency changed hands 36 times. The average length of term was only seven and one-half months. As government replaced government and revolt followed rebellion, many Mexicans became disenchanted with the republican experiment. They understood their quality of life had declined without a strong, well-organized colonial administrative system. The centralist form of government eventually won out.

But the Americans who came to Texas were republicans to the core. On his tour of the state in 1827 and 1828, Gen. Manuel Mier y Teran noted that they "carried their constitutions in their pockets." And he feared the Americans' desire for more rights and liberties than the government was prepared to offer would lead to rebellion.

Most of the early Anglo colonists in Texas, however, intended to fulfill their pledge to become good Mexican citizens. But they had made the commitment with the understanding that they would live under a republican form of government as set forth in the Constitution of 1824. The political turmoil following the 1828 presidential election raised doubts in the Americans' minds about the ability of Mexicans to make that form of government function properly.

Unrest increased in Texas when Gen. Teran began reinforcing existing garrisons and establishing new ones. But a major factor in the discontent of Americans came with the decree of April 6, 1830, when the Mexican government in essence banned further Anglo-American immigration into Texas and tried to control slavery.

Austin protested that the prohibition against American immigration would not stop the flow of Anglos into Texas; it would stop only the stable, prosperous Americans from coming to the region. The great empresario had a firm image of the type of colonist he wanted — a Southern gentleman. Austin feared another type of settler: Those " . . . ardent, inexperienced, hot-headed youths piping from college, or ignorant, self-willed 'mobbish' mountaineers and frontiersmen who 'hold to lynch law' and damning those who are in office merely because they are in office would totally ruin us forever."

Austin's predictions about immigration were fulfilled. Legal immigration may have been barred, but illegal entry was not. By 1834, when the law was repealed, it was estimated that the number of Americans and their slaves in Texas totaled 20,700, double the number of four years earlier. By 1836, that number had reached 35,000.

The first two incidents that inflamed Anglo-American colonists, ironically, were instigated by Americans in the service of the Mexican government. George Fisher, a Serbian by birth but a naturalized American, was ordered by Gen. Teran to set up a customhouse at Anahuac on Galveston Bay and to appoint a deputy to a house at Brazoria at the mouth of the Brazos. Fisher tried to require ships leaving the Brazos to stop at Anahuac to pay duties, and in one case, a soldier was wounded when a ship failed to heed the order. In retaliation, Fisher tried to impound goods shipped into the Austin Colony until duties were paid. But Teran removed Fisher from office before further incident. Austin argued that the Americans were not being disloyal or attempting to avoid duties; Fisher's order was simply impractical. Nevertheless, the government abandoned attempts to collect duties in September 1832 and did not resume collection until the spring of 1835.

Col. John Davis Bradburn's problems were more serious. Teran gave him command of the newly established garrison of Anahuac, which was located near the settlement of Atascosito. The small community was one of many settled illegally by Anglo-Americans early in the 19th century. But Mexican authorities had promised to provide the settlers legal titles to their land. In 1831, Francisco Madero was appointed land commissioner to issue the titles. Bradburn detained Madero, arguing that his actions were illegal. The settlement, Bradburn asserted, was too close to the coast. The officer also disbanded a new ayuntamiento established by Madero at Liberty. Madero argued that the Americans settled the land before the Law of April 6, 1830, and the statute did not apply to them. Madero was freed and the titles issued, but complaints about Bradburn continued. He was charged with using the settlers' slaves without compensation to build military structures, with enticing slaves to escape and with arresting colonists and holding them for military trial. William B. Travis was jailed when he tried to represent the claims of a Louisiana slaveholder. An armed revolt ensued that resulted in Bradburn's removal from office. Mexican officials felt that Bradburn's actions had prompted the rebellion, and some ayuntamientos criticized the actions of the insurgents. Although Bradburn was removed from office as a gesture of appeasement, the incidents further kindled the emotions of the settlers — and deepened the concern of the Mexican government.

Thereafter, the colonists began a campaign to drive the Mexican soldiers from Texas, and except for the adroitness of Austin, the settlers would have brought upon themselves severe retribution from the government.

Events in 1830 ended the Texans' usual aloofness to the political maneuverings in Mexico. Gen. Bustamante had replaced Guererro as president and made himself dictator. Troops rebelled in Veracruz in January 1832, and, led by Santa Anna, were fighting to replace the dictator. Santa Anna, ever an opportunist, declared himself a friend of the republican cause, and Texans backed him. During the engagement at Anahuac, the insurgents who sought release of Travis and other prisoners had declared for Santa Anna. While the revolt at Anahuac was bloodless, Mexican soldiers were killed and injured at Velasco when Texans ran a blockade in an attempt to get aid to the other insurgents. Mexican troops at Nacogdoches also were ousted, although many soldiers were anxious to return to Mexico to fight with Santa Anna and the republic.

Upon hearing the reports of the insurgency in Texas in 1832, Gen. Jose Antonio Mexia brought 400 troops to the state by sea. He was lavishly feted by the Texans and was convinced that there was no rebellion against the government. A supporter of Santa Anna, Mexia returned to Mexico.

Heady with success and with Santa Anna's federalist campaign in Mexico going so well, the Texans felt it was time to petition the government for reforms and to explain their actions. A convention was called in San Felipe, the capital of Austin's colony, in October 1832. With Austin serving as president of the convention, several concerns were expressed to the government. Delegates wanted Texas separated from Coahuila, titles for land in East Texas, encroachments on Indian lands stopped, a militia to defend against Indian attacks, and government-donated land for schools. Mexican officials condemned the meeting, explaining that it was not the proper way to express grievances. Therefore, the concerns were not presented to the government.

Mexican officials, however, were concerned about the "illegal" convention. The proper method of addressing the government, under their system, was to function through the legally constituted ayuntamiento in each colony. For the Americans, the conventions were simply their traditional method of petitioning the government.

Despite the objections of the government, a second convention was called in April of 1833 at San Felipe. This time the radical faction of the colonists controlled, with William H. Wharton serving as president. Nevertheless, the requests of the delegates were essentially the same. They wanted the Law of April 6, 1830, repealed, and they wanted a separation from Coahuila. Serving in his first official capacity in Texas, Sam Houston, a former governor of Tennessee and former congressman, chaired the committee that wrote a sample state constitution. It was based on the Massachusetts constitution and incorporated few of the features usually found in the constitutions of Mexican states. Austin and two other delegates were selected to present the pleadings to the newly elected Mexican president, Santa Anna.

Austin alone reached Mexico City in October 1833 and presented the petition to Vice President Gomez Farias, who was running the government in the absence of President Santa Anna. A cholera epidemic swept Mexico City — and Texas — at the time, and Austin got no response from Farias. The acting president was preoccupied with other problems and also disagreed with the proposal that Texas be given independent statehood. Distressed by the delay, Austin wrote the ayuntamiento in San Antonio advising it to set up a state government. Upon his resumption of office, Santa Anna met with Austin and agreed with most of the reforms the Texans had requested, except the separation from Coahuila. On the return trip to Texas in December, Austin stopped in Saltillo, where he was arrested. The letter he had written in a huff to San Antonio was interpreted as a call for revolution. Austin was returned to Mexico City and imprisoned.

Under Farias' instructions, Col. Juan Nepomuceno Almonte toured Texas in 1834 with a twofold purpose: to assure settlers that the government was moving to implement reforms and to determine the attitude of the colonists. Almonte found no unrest in Texas and advocated most of the reforms that Austin had requested in Mexico City.

Indeed, despite the turmoil, Texas was prospering. By 1834, some 7,000 bales of cotton with a value of $315,000 were shipped to New Orleans. In the middle of the decade, Texas exports, including cotton and beaver, otter and deer skins, amounted to $500,000. Trade ratios were out of balance, however, because $630,000 in manufactured goods were imported. Almonte also found that there was little currency in Texas. Ninety percent of the business transactions were conducted in barter or credit, "which gives the country, in its trading relations, the appearance of a continued fair," he observed.

In 1833 and 1834, the Coahuila y Texas legislature also was diligently trying to respond to the complaints of the Texas colonists. The English language was recognized for official purposes. Religious toleration was approved (Gen. Teran in 1828 had noted that freedom of religion was better than no religion at all, which was the case in Texas at the time). And the court system was revised, providing Texas with an appellate court and trial by jury. Previously, the legislature had approved schools for the colonists, but this measure was not fully implemented because of a lack of funds and low population density. Texas also was divided into three departments, Bexar, Nacogdoches and Brazos, to facilitate administration.

In Mexico City, however, a different scenario was developing. Santa Anna had in essence shared the presidency with Farias, allowing the vice president to enact many federalist reforms that proved unpopular with the church, the wealthy and the military. Santa Anna assumed supreme authority in April 1834, exiled the vice president and began a program of dismantling the federalist government. By October 1835, a centralist government had replaced the federalist, and the Congress was subservient to Santa Anna.

Among the most offensive changes dictated by Santa Anna was the reduction of the militia to one man per each 500 population. The intent was to eliminate possible armed opposition to the emerging centralist government. But liberals in the state of

Zacatecas in Central Mexico rebelled. Santa Anna's response was particularly brutal, as he tried to make an example of the rebels. Troops were allowed to sack the state capital after the victory over the insurgents.

Trouble also was brewing closer to the Texans. In March 1833, the Coahuila y Texas legislature moved the state capital from Saltillo to Monclova. The Monclova legislature in 1834 gave the governor authority to sell 400 sitios — or 1.77 million acres of land — to finance the government and to provide for protection. Land speculators jumped at the opportunity to obtain land so cheaply.

A year later, the lawmakers criticized Santa Anna's repudiation of federalism. Seeing a chance to regain lost prestige, Saltillo declared for Santa Anna and set up an opposition government. But in the spring of 1835, Santa Anna sent his brother-in-law, Martin Perfecto de Cos, to break up the state government at Monclova.

Texans were appalled by the breakdown in state government, coming on the heels of so many assurances that the political situation was to improve. Texas politics were polarizing. A "war party" advocated breaking away from Mexico altogether, while a "peace party" urged calm and riding out the political storm. Most of the settlers, however, aligned with neither group. And it is said that the passion for rebellion was directly proportional to the stake the individual had in Texas. The long-time settlers wanted to maintain a status quo; newcomers favored revolt.

In January 1835, Santa Anna sent a detachment of soldiers to Anahuac to reinforce the customs office. But duties were being charged irregularly at various ports on the coast. William B. Travis, in an act not supported by all colonists, led a contingent of armed colonists against the Mexican soldiers, who withdrew without a fight.

Although some members of the peace party wrote Gen. Cos, stationed at Matamoros, apologizing for the action, he was not compromising. Cos demanded that members of the group be arrested and turned over to him. The Texans refused.

The committees of correspondence, organized at the Convention of 1832, began organizing another meeting. Because the term "convention" aroused visions of revolution in the eyes of Mexican officials, the gathering at Washington-on-the-Brazos in October 1835 was called a "consultation." But with the breakdown of the state government and with Santa Anna's repeal of the Constitution of 1824, the American settlers felt well within their rights to provide a new framework within which to govern Texas.

Help also came from an unexpected source. Austin was released from prison and arrived in Texas in September 1835. He immediately began agitation for a representative convention to deal with the developing crisis. Austin's long-standing support for patience was at an end. He urged war to protect Texas' rights in the Mexican confederation under the Constitution of 1824.

Fresh from brutally putting down the rebellion in Zacatecas, Santa Anna turned his attention to Texas. Gen. Cos was determined to regarrison the state, and the settlers were equally adamant about keeping soldiers out.

Col. Domingo Ugartechea, headquartered at San Antonio, became concerned about armed rebellion when he heard of the incident at Anahuac. And he recalled a six-pound cannon that had been given DeWitt colonists to fight Indians. Ugartechea ordered Cpl. Casimira de Leon with five men to Gonzales to retrieve the weapon. No problems were expected. But officials at Gonzales refused to surrender the weapon. When the Mexicans reinforced Cpl. de Leon's forces, a call was sent out for volunteers to help the Texans. Dozens responded. On Oct. 2, 1835, the Texans challenged the Mexicans with a "come-and-take-it" flag over the cannon. After a brief skirmish, the Mexicans withdrew, but the first rounds in the Texas Revolution had been fired.

Gen. Cos had entered San Antonio while the Texans were occupied with the affair in Gonzales. When the Mexicans left Gonzales, the volunteer force followed them to San Antonio.

The consultation in Washington-on-the-Brazos created a provisional government with Henry Smith as governor and with an executive council. Austin, despite a lack of military experience, was named commander-in-chief of the army. He immediately went to San Antonio.

Capt. George Collinsworth had captured Goliad and a large store of supplies, which was taken to the Texans besieging San Antonio. Austin remained at the head of the "Army of the People" until mid-November when he was sent to the United States to plead the Texans' cause for aid. Edward Burleson assumed command. In early December, a special force of Texans — led by Ben Milam, who died in the battle — assaulted the city, and five days later, Gen. Cos capitulated. The Mexican leader and his troops were furloughed with the understanding they would not fight against the cause of the Constitution of 1824 again, a pledge that Cos broke.

The Texans were euphoric with the string of victories over Mexican forces.It was a euphoria born of overconfidence, it turned out, and led to mistakes that claimed hundreds of lives.

But the Texas Revolution was under way.

7
End of the Beginning

AS 1836 opened, Texans felt in control of their destiny. The Mexican army had been driven from their soil. Winter was at hand. And the settlers were secure in their land and their liberties.

But tragedy loomed. Easy victories over Mexican forces at Anahuac, Nacogdoches, Goliad, Gonzales and San Antonio in the fall of 1835 had given them a false sense of security. Their frontier independence had served well in forcing Mexicans from their soil. Texans proved their unwillingness to take orders from the Mexican military, but they were not in a mood to take orders from each other either. That independent mood was their undoing, for no government worth the name coordinated the defense of Texas. Consequently, as the Mexican counterattack developed, no one was in charge. In November 1835, the Consultation failed to outline the duties and responsibilities of the provisional government it created. Henry Smith was named governor, and he and the provisional council — one representative from each of the 12 municipalities — were to run the administration. They were antagonists from the beginning. By mid-January the arrangement collapsed, but in the interim much damage was done. With the Mexican military out of Texas, the settlers' primary concern was relieved; the "war" was over. They had won. The victory's consolidation, however, was a point of contention. Smith supported complete independence for Texas. The council wanted to link up with Mexican liberals to restore the Constitution of 1824. Gen. Jose A. Mexia was to lead a rebellion against the dictator Antonio Lopez de Santa Anna at Tampico. If the Texans could attract the support of the liberal rebels, there was a chance to restore constitutional government in Mexico.

That was the sense of a resolution passed by the Consultation. And the council tried to implement the goal with disastrous results. Sam Houston was commander-in-chief of the Texas forces, but he had little authority. The council, pursuing its intention of gaining Mexican liberal support, conceived the idea of a campaign against Matamoros, the port city across the Rio Grande from present-day Brownsville. Dr. James Grant promoted the plan. He owned property in northern Mexico that had been confiscated by the government. If the dictator were overthrown, Grant could reclaim the land.

The so-called old settlers, however, had lost interest in the conflict. After Gen.

42

Martin Perfecto de Cos had been driven from San Antonio in December 1835, the Texan army had dwindled. Texas volunteers returned home to prepare for spring planting. Their places in the ranks were taken by Americans who flocked to Texas to fight Mexico. On Christmas Day, about 750 men, mostly American volunteers, made up the Texas army. Four hundred men were at San Antonio, 70 at Washington-on-the-Brazos, 80 at Goliad and 200 at Velasco. The provisional government's attempt to establish a regular army failed. It never had more than 80 soldiers, leaving most of the fighting to volunteers.

In late December, the provisional council authorized the Matamoros expedition with a round of comic-opera appointments. First Frank W. Johnson was appointed commander, and when he declined, James W. Fannin was named. Dr. Grant was given the post of commander of the volunteers. Shortly thereafter, Johnson changed his mind, and the council made him commander of the expedition again. Fannin retained his authority, however. Houston was not informed of any of the changes. So the Texas army had four commanders in chief.

Dr. Grant and Johnson soon took 300 men and supplies from San Antonio, heading south to set up a command post near Refugio. By Jan. 6, Col. James C. Neill had only 104 men — none Texans — and no clothing or supplies under his command at San Antonio. Fannin, one of the few Texas officers with West Point training, declined to participate in the Matamoros expedition after occupying the old fort at Goliad.

Houston initially planned a line of defense along the San Antonio River, which had strongly fortified positions at Goliad and San Antonio. But with the command split and none of the other three "commanders" willing to take orders, Houston's hands were tied. He visited Refugio but failed to convince Grant and Johnson to abandon plans for attacking Matamoros. Houston was successful in keeping many men from participating. When he left, Grant and Johnson had only about 150 men remaining under their command.

The status of the strongholds along the San Antonio River also was of concern. In mid-January, Houston sent James Bowie to San Antonio to determine if the Alamo was defensible. If not, Bowie had orders to destroy it and withdraw the men and artillery to Gonzales and Copano.

Houston took a furlough to travel to East Texas and meet with the Cherokees. Settlers were concerned about the Indians' intentions. Several chiefs of the Cherokees had met in September 1835 with Mexican officers in San Antonio. The Consultation had approved a "solemn declaration" to recognize Indian claims to ownership of land north of the San Antonio Road and between the Angelina and Sabine rivers. This pledge was repeated in the treaty Houston negotiated in exchange for the Indians' neutrality in the conflict with Mexico. (After the revolution, the treaty was rejected by the Texas Senate, and the Indians later were driven from the land.)

If the Texans' defense was disorganized, few settlers worried. Some thought the Mexicans would not try to re-enter Texas. Others felt the Mexican army would not mount an offensive until spring. The reasons were logical, if wrong. Mexico was experiencing financial problems, and the army was weakened by the continuing civil war between federalists and centralists. The government was disorganized. And the rich buffalo grass on the South Texas prairies was dead, denying fodder for invaders' horses and livestock.

Few Texans counted on the energy and determination of Gen. Antonio Lopez de Santa Anna, the dictator of Mexico. In August 1835, he proclaimed his intention of driving Anglo-American settlers from Texas and of executing any Americans found taking up arms or supporting the rebellion against Mexico. The campaign would be financed through the confiscation of the settlers' property. Preparations for the invasion began in the fall at San Luis Potosi. The army's depleted ranks were filled with conscripts. Forced loans were obtained from the church and other sources, and lenders were given outrageously beneficial terms for some funds. But arrangements were hurried and incomplete. Many of the soldiers were not properly clothed for the march in the cold winter weather. Mayan Indian recruits from the Yucatan, unaccustomed to the northers and other conditions in Northern Mexico, suffered pitiably, for example. Also the army, including officers, was put on half rations from the beginning. And no provision was made for physicans and field hospitals. Nevertheless, about 6,000 men were under arms as the army marched toward Texas.

Racial overtones permeated both sides of the developing conflict. Texans did not trust Mexican-Texans and usually stayed aloof from them. At Refugio, Mexican-Texans complained about abuse from Grant's and Johnson's men. And the Mexican-Texans were dubious about the motives of the Anglos. Many Mexican-Texans were willing to fight for restoration of the Constitution of 1824, but refused to take up arms for an independent Anglo Texas in which they would be a minority. Santa Anna held Anglo frontiersmen in contempt for many years.

As a 19-year-old lieutenant in the Royal Spanish Army, Santa Anna had served in Gen. Joaquin de Arredondo's campaign against republicans after the Gutierrez-Magee rebellion in 1813, which created the first Republic of Texas. Arredondo had been merciless in his retribution, killing more than 300 republicans at San Antonio alone. Santa Anna was revolted by the crude attempts of the Anglo frontiersmen to defend themselves against the best European tactics of the day. And he boasted that he would plant the eagles of Mexico on the banks of the Sabine River and even march to Washington, D.C., to teach the Anglos a lesson in the upcoming campaign.

If Santa Anna had been determined to punish Texas when he began the campaign, he became fanatical when his brother-in-law, Gen. Cos, crossed the Rio Grande with the remnants of his command, which was defeated at San Antonio. Santa Anna ordered Cos to ignore his pledge not to enter Texas again to fight against the Constitution of 1824.

On Feb. 12, Santa Anna's main force crossed the Rio Grande headed for San Antonio. The Mexican battle plan has been debated. But Mexico's national pride had been bruised by the series of defeats the nation's army had suffered in 1835, capped by Gen. Cos' ouster from San Antonio in December. The main body of the army moved northward to San Antonio, but Gen. Jose Urrea was ordered along the coast. Few Texans thought San Antonio — or Bexar as it was generally called — was worth defending. The direct route to the rich Anglo-Texan colonies on the Brazos and Colorado rivers was along the coast. Many strategists anticipated a quick thrust at San Felipe de Austin, the capital of Austin's colony and of Anglo Texas. Mexican strategists, however, did not want to leave a well-defended outpost to their rear during the campaign. And Santa Anna could not leave a pocket of Anglo-Americans behind him when he had pledged to sweep them all from Texas.

The grueling march took Santa Anna 11 days and cost many lives. The weather turned brutal and northers and rain took a heavy toll among the soldiers and animals. Texan scouts also had made the trek more difficult by burning large areas of grassland that the Mexicans had counted on as forage.

While the Mexicans prepared for war through the fall and early winter, the Texans' defensive preparations floundered. On Feb. 11, Gov. Smith sent Col. William Barret Travis to San Antonio to relieve Col. Neill. Immediately a split in command arose. Most of the American defenders were volunteers, who looked to Bowie as their leader. Travis had only a handful of Texas army regulars. So Bowie and Travis agreed to share the command. Almost immediately, Travis began asking for reinforcements. Only 150 men were available to fight, and Travis sought aid from Fannin, from Gov.

Smith, from Houston, from the provisional council and from the citizens of the United States. Only a plea to Gonzales was answered.

Aside from the pleas for help, however, activity around San Antonio was leisurely. Discipline was lax, and work on improving the fortifications of the Alamo moved slowly. Indeed, the defenders of San Antonio were fortunate not to have suffered a successful surprise attack on Feb. 22. Santa Anna ordered a surprise attack by Gen. Ramirez y Sesma's cavalry, but a rain-swollen creek scuttled the plan. The Texans would have had their hands full for they were enjoying a fandango celebrating George Washington's birthday at the time, and only 10 men guarded the Alamo. The following morning, however, the forward elements of the Mexican army were spotted by guards at San Antonio and their presence was confirmed by scouts. Quickly the Texans and Americans retreated to the Alamo, which soon was under siege by hundreds of Mexican soldiers whose ranks were being reinforced daily.

Santa Anna left no doubt regarding his attitude toward the Anglo defenders of the Alamo. Upon arrival, he had hoisted a blood-red flag, the traditional Mexican symbol of no quarter, no surrender, no mercy. Travis and Bowie defiantly answered the display with a cannon shot.

Immediately the Mexicans began surrounding the Alamo and bombarding it. Throughout the first night and nights to come, Santa Anna kept up a continual din to destroy the defenders' morale.

On Feb. 24, Bowie took ill and relinquished his share of command to Travis. That evening, Travis penned one of the most stirring appeals for help in the annals of history:

Commandancy of the Alamo—
Bejar, Feby. 24th,1836
To the people of Texas & all Americans in the world—
Fellow citizens & compatriots—

I am besieged, by a thousand or more of the Mexicans under Santa Anna — I have sustained a continual Bombardment & cannonade for 24 hours & have not lost a man — The enemy has demanded a surrender at discretion, otherwise, the garrison are to be put to the sword, if the fort is taken — I have answered the demand with a cannon shot, & our flag still waves proudly from the walls — I shall never surrender or retreat. Then I call on you in the name of Liberty, of patriotism & everything dear to the American character, to come to our aid, with all dispatch — The enemy is receiving reinforcements daily & will no doubt increase to three or four thousand in four or five days. If this call is neglected, I am determined to sustain myself as long as possible & and die like a soldier who never forgets what is due to his own honor & that of his country — VICTORY OR DEATH.

William Barret Travis,
Lt. Col. comdt.
P.S. The Lord is on our side — When the enemy appeared in sight we had not three bushels of corn — We have since found in deserted houses 80 or 90 bushels and got into the walls 20 or 30 head of Beeves.
Travis.

Within weeks, the plea for help was circulated up the Mississippi Valley and along the eastern seaboard of the United States. It is credited with generating hundreds of volunteers for the Texas cause. But they came far too late to help Travis and his little band of heroes at the Alamo.

The closest garrison of any size to the Alamo was at Goliad under Fannin's command. But Fannin refused several requests from Travis for aid. On Feb. 26, however, he began a relief march, only to have a wagon break down less than a mile from his fort. After a night's reflection on the tactical situation, he turned back.

Near Refugio on Feb. 28, Gen. Urrea fought with remnants of the Matamoros expedition under Johnson, killing several and taking 21 prisoners. The prisoners later were executed by Santa Anna's orders. Johnson escaped to carry word of the engagement to Fannin at Goliad. When news of this battle reached San Antonio, however, Mexican morale soared. The army had suffered nothing but losses, embarrassment and humiliation at the hands of the Texans for a year. Urrea's conquest was seen as a turning point. And on March 3, the general's troops ambushed another remnant of the Matamoros expedition at Agua Dulce Creek, and Dr. Grant and 15 others were killed.

Although the Mexican bombardment of the Alamo continued daily, none of the defenders was killed. In fact, they conducted several successful forays outside the fortress to burn buildings that were providing cover for the Mexican gunners and to gather firewood. Messengers also successfully moved through the Mexican lines at will, and 32 reinforcements from Gonzales under George Kimball and Albert Martin made it into the Alamo without a loss on March 1. But Santa Anna was tightening the perimeter. The last messenger got out on March 3, carrying, among other items, a letter to Jesse Grimes in which Travis asserted to the convention meeting at Washington-on-the-Brazos: "If independence is not declared, I shall lay down my arms, and so will the men under my command. But under the flag of independence, we are ready to peril our lives 100 times a day . . ."

Travis was unaware that the convention had declared Texas' independence from Mexico on March 2 and was engaged in writing a constitution and forming a government for the new republic. Historians disagree over which flag flew over the defenders of the Alamo. Mexican sources have said that Santa Anna was outraged when he saw flying over the fortress a Mexican tri-color, identical to the ones carried by his troops except with the numbers "1 8 2 4" emblazoned upon it. Texas historians have accepted this version because the defenders of the Alamo could not have known that independence had been declared. To the knowledge of the Alamo's defenders, the last official government position taken by Texans was in support of the Constitution of 1824, which the flag symbolized. But the only flag found after the battle, according to historian Walter Lord, was one flown by the New Orleans Grays.

By March 5, Santa Anna had 4,000 men in camp, a force he felt sufficient to subdue the Alamo. Mexican sources said he was furious that the Texans had held out through 12 days of bombardment and siege. The longer the small band held off the Mexicans, the less would be his glory. Other Mexican commanders felt that major losses in life were not necessary to take the fortress; the defenders could have been starved out eventually. But Santa Anna would not hear of it. His confidence rested in his troops' courage and their training in the best of Napoleonic military tactics. Crude frontiersmen, El Presidente thought, had little chance against this sort of sophisticated armed might.

Santa Anna overlooked the marksmanship of the frontiersmen behind the walls of the Alamo. To a man they had been raised with weapons and trained to hunt. With their long rifles, Davy Crockett and his Tennesseans prided themselves on regularly hitting targets at 200 yards or more. Mexican smooth-bore muskets could carry only 70 yards, and not accurately at that. Faced with the Mexicans' give-no-quarter policy, the defenders of the Alamo would be doubly lethal.

Historians disagree on the date, and in some cases whether the event took place. But legend holds that on March 3 or March 5, Col. Travis called his command together and explained the bleak outlook. He apologized if he had misled them into believing that reinforcements were on the way. But he explained that he had told them that in good faith; he had thought help was coming. Then the young colonel drew a line in the dirt and asked those willing to die for freedom to cross with him. Jim Bowie had his sick bed carried across. Only Louis Rose, a veteran of Napoleon's bitter retreat from Moscow, chose to fight another day. He slipped out of the Alamo that night.

Mexican troops were up well before dawn on March 6 preparing for the final assault on the Alamo. When reminded that there were no doctors or hospital facilities available, Santa Anna reportedly snapped that that was all the better. The troops would know, he said, that it was "not as bad to die as to come out wounded." Twenty-five hundred men in perfect formation surrounded the fortress and on command commenced their attack. During the action, the Mexican bands struck up the deguello, a traditional Spanish march dating back to the battles against the Moors. It signified a no-quarter, throat-cutting, merciless death. The first troops were cut down by the murderous cannon fire from the Alamo's guns and by the precision marksmanship of the frontiersmen's long rifles. Cannon loaded with scrap iron mowed down the Mexican regulars by the squad. There is no doubting the courage of the Mexican soldiers as they faced the lethal fire. At first they would fall back, regroup and attack again. Although the Mexicans were executing perfect Napoleonic maneuvers, they lacked the cannon to give the fortress an appropriate initial bombardment. Also, Mexican commanders were unaware that British army instructions at the time warned that frontal assaults on frontier riflemen behind breastworks could be conducted only with unacceptable casualties. Attempt after attempt at placing scaling ladders was thwarted by the Alamo's cannon and riflemen. But Mexican artillery finally began to have its effect. A wall was breached. The first few Mexican soldiers through the opening were killed. The number of skirmishers soon became too great. The Alamo's huge courtyard was filled with desperate hand-to-hand fighting. Mexicans were armed with bayonets; the defenders used rifle butts and Bowie knives. So frenzied had the Mexican soldiers become that the corpses of defenders were mutilated. Travis died of a bullet wound to the head. Bowie was killed in his sick bed, selling his life dearly with a brace of pistols left for his defense. Crockett's fate is still debated. Some sources say he died in a pile of Mexican soldiers, victims of his rifle and knife. One Mexican officer, Enrique de la Pena, held that Crockett was captured with a few other defenders and executed by Santa Anna.

When the fighting stopped between 8:30 and 9 a.m., all the defenders were dead. Only a few women, children and black slaves survived the assault.

But Travis and his men placed a heavy price indeed on the victory. Almost one-third of the attack force was killed or wounded. And these were the flower of the Mexican army, veterans for the most part. Their deaths in such number set back Santa Anna's timetable. Although recruits were available from the ranks of Mexican-Texans, they had to be trained. The Napoleonic tactics used by the army required highly trained soldiers, and training took time. The fall of the Alamo also brutally shook the old Texans out of their lethargy, and no doubt shamed them, too, for ignoring Travis' appeals for help.

Sam Houston, finally given command of all Texas' army, left the convention at Washington-on-the-Brazos on the day of the fall of the Alamo. On March 11, he arrived at Gonzales to begin organizing the troops. He found just over 370 men at the town, many of whom had been on their way to aid Travis. Two days later, Mrs. Dickinson, the wife of one of the victims of the Alamo, and two slaves arrived with the news of the fall of the fortress. Houston immediately began an evacuation of Gonzales, taking the inhabitants and leaving the town in flames to deny it to the Mexican forces he thought were close behind.

Houston ordered Fannin to abandon the old presidio La Bahia at Goliad and to retreat to Victoria. Fannin had arrived at the fort in late January with more than 400 men. As a former West Pointer, he had a background in military planning. Troops were drilled, and fortifications were reinforced. But Fannin had been indecisive. Travis' pleas for help were refused, and after receiving Houston's orders, Fannin waited for scouting parties to return. Finally, on March 19, he left, but too late. Forward elements of Gen. Urrea's troops caught Fannin's command on an open prairie near a wooded area. After a short battle, Fannin fortified his position around a broken-down ammunition wagon. Through the night, the Mexican troops were reinforced. After a brief skirmish the following morning, Fannin surrendered.

A controversy surrounded the capitulation. Survivors of Fannin's command later argued that they surrendered with the understanding they would be treated as prisoners of war. Documents indicate, however, that the surrender was unconditional, and the troops were thrown on the mercy of the Mexican commanders. The prisoners were marched to Goliad where they were kept under light restraint. So unconcerned were they that it is said that not one violated the pledge not to attempt an escape. Santa Anna was furious, however, when Gen. Urrea appealed for clemency for the captives. The Mexican leader issued the orders in triplicate for their execution. On March 27, a Palm Sunday, most of the prisoners were divided into groups and marched out of Goliad, thinking they were being transferred to other facilities. When the executions began, many escaped. But about 350 were killed.

In less than a month, Texas' military forces had lost almost 700 men in battle or by execution. Fewer than one in five of these were old settlers, most being American volunteers who had not been in Texas when hostilities began the previous fall. Houston spent almost two weeks on the Colorado River, and on March 26 began a retreat to the Brazos.

Santa Anna had not left San Antonio, but word of the losses soon reached the settlers who began leaving their homes, often in haste. When the Mexican army began pursuit of Houston's forces, Jose Enrique de la Pena, a young staff officer, lamented the fear that the war generated. He blamed the war on a group of promoters. These promoters, the young officer observed, "painted us as savages, as men more ferocious than beasts, to which belief the events of the Alamo, La Bahia and the mission at Refugio unfortunately contributed. No one will disagree with me that provisions should have been made to prevent the war, or that once begun in order to vindicate an injured nation, it should have been carried out in a less disastrous fashion."

But the old Texans finally faced the reality of the conflict. While many ran for safety, others joined Houston for the defense of the Republic. As one soldier noted, "We ask nor expect no quarter in the future." The Texans were on their way to San Jacinto.

San Jacinto and Beyond 8

SAM Houston spent only a short time at the convention that met March 1, 1836, at Washington-on-the-Brazos. But he may have been the most important man there, for he insisted that the Texans form a coherent government. The Alamo was besieged and in danger, he argued, because there had been no government in Texas.

Attempts to adjourn the convention so the delegates could rush to San Antonio were defeated. Long-winded oratory was discouraged. The convention quickly got down to the business of forming a government. Richard Ellis was named president, and a committee chaired by George Childress wrote a Declaration of Independence, patterned on the one that separated the United States from Great Britain. The declaration was adopted on March 2, and on March 6, the day the Alamo fell, Houston left the convention with full command of all the armed forces in Texas.

Upon arrival at Gonzales, Houston had quickly discerned the Texans' position was untenable. He had only a handful of men, the Alamo had fallen, the settlers were in chaos, and the position was far removed from the Anglo population that was so necessary for supplies and reinforcements. Near midnight, he began the long march to San Jacinto.

By March 17, Houston had reached Burnam's Crossing on the Colorado River, near the present city of La Grange. Two days later, the small army crossed the river and moved south to Beason's Ford near present-day Columbus. There he began to receive reinforcements. Within a week, the small force had become almost respectable with 1,200-1,400 men in camp.

At the same time Houston reached the Colorado, the convention at Washington-on-the-Brazos was completing work on a constitution for the new Republic. Only slightly did it differ from the U.S. Constitution. The Texas charter called for a unitary government, rather than dividing the territory into states. And from the Mexican constitution, it prohibited the president from succeeding himself after one three-year term. Ministers of the gospel also were prohibited from holding public office. David Burnet was named interim president of the new government and Lorenzo de Zavala was vice president. Thomas J. Rusk was secretary of war. Upon completion of the work, the new government moved to Harrisburg.

In the excitement of the period, however, important steps were not taken.

Stephen F. Austin, serving as Texas' agent in the United States, complained the group was never informed that independence had been declared. William Wharton and Branch T. Archer also were Texas' agents.

Close on Houston's heels was Gen. Joaquin de Ramirez y Sesma who had been dispatched from San Antonio by Santa Anna on March 11 to follow the Texans. Seven hundred and twenty-five men were in Ramirez y Sesma's command, and he sought reinforcements as soon as the Texans were spotted. Heavy rains swelled the river, preventing the Mexicans from crossing.

Houston was criticized for not fighting at this point. But the Texans' commander explained that he would have inevitably suffered casualties and had no means to transport them. Also, the Mexicans could easily be reinforced with numbers far exceeding the small Texan contingent. In addition, word of Fannin's loss had reached the area, and settlers were in full flight. On March 27, Houston moved his men to San Felipe on the Brazos, and left on the following day for Groce's Crossing 20 miles up river, which he reached March 31. The Texans were getting restless for a fight. Moseley Baker and Wylie Martin and their men, however, refused to follow Houston to Groce's, so they were ordered to defend the river crossings at San Felipe and at Fort Bend.

At Groce's Crossing, the Texans had a respite, offering Houston an opportunity to organize and drill his forces. Most of the volunteers had no military experience. In a battle against well-drilled forces, they would have been at a disadvantage. So Houston attempted to instill military discipline. Up to this point, one of the army's major responsibilities had been the protection of settlers involved in the Runaway Scrape, as the retreat was called. To reinforce discipline, Houston hanged four men accused of raping women and robbing settlers.

Santa Anna had divided his forces after the fall of the Alamo. Gen. Gaona had been ordered to Nacogdoches along a northern route, but he soon was diverted to San Felipe. Ramirez y Sesma had been in pursuit of the main force of the Texas army, and Gen. Jose Urrea was following a path along the coast from Goliad to Brazoria.

Santa Anna initially considered returning to Mexico City after the Alamo fell. The war was over in his mind, and the dictator, fully aware of the fickle political tides that rocked the Mexican government, wanted to consolidate politically his victories on the battlefield. But his general staff talked him out of leaving.

So Santa Anna joined Ramirez y Sesma on April 7, and the Mexicans entered San Felipe on that day. Mexican intelligence informed the dictator that the Texas government was in Harrisburg, and Santa Anna immediately conceived a plan of capturing the rebel leadership to end the war. But he could not cross the Brazos until April 10, when his troops finally gained control of the Fort Bend crossing from Texan sharpshooters. Three days later Ramirez y Sesma arrived, and the Mexicans reached Harrisburg on April 15. But the Texas government was gone, barely escaping advance units of Mexicans who watched them row to a schooner bound for Galveston. Settlers, however, told the Mexicans that Houston was marching toward Lynch's ferry on the San Jacinto River in an attempt to escape to Louisiana. Santa Anna burned Harrisburg and headed toward the ferry.

At Groce's Crossing, Houston was successful in organizing the army. On April 12, using the steamboat Yellow Stone, the army crossed the river, and orders were sent to outlying units to gather at Donoho's. Martin, who had refused to leave the Brazos, again ignored Houston's command to march and took his troops to Nacogdoches to defend against a feared Indian uprising.

The Texas army was impatient for a fight, and there was talk in the ranks that, if action did not develop soon, a new commander should be elected. So prevalent were the rumblings that Houston posted warnings that he would shoot any man who tried to mutiny. But the Texas government also was distressed with the commander-in-chief's tactics. On April 13, Houston received a message from President Burnet:

"This country expects something from you; the government looks to you for action. The time has arrived to determine whether we are to give up the country and make the best of our way out of it or to meet the enemy and make at least one struggle for our boasted independence."

Fifteen miles east of Donoho's was a fork in the road; one leg went to Nacogdoches and the other to Harrisburg. Here one of the great mysteries of the San Jacinto campaign rests. Critics long said that Houston had no intention of fighting the Mexicans, that his plan was to cross into Louisiana where protection of the U.S. Army was available.

Indeed, Gen. Edmund P. Gaines, commander of Fort Jessup near Natchitoches, La., had moved a large body of U.S. troops to the Sabine River by April 1836. Settlers in East Texas feared an Indian uprising while so many men were away fighting the Mexican army. The United States was under a treaty obligation to Mexico to maintain peaceful relations with the Indians. But Gen. Gaines' investigation found the Cherokees and others "more interested in planting corn" than in fighting. Nevertheless the U.S. troops remained on the Sabine until the fall of 1836.

When the Texas army reached the fork in the road, it marched toward Harrisburg, as Houston had indicated he planned to do in a letter written the previous night. Along the road, two Mexican couriers were captured and gave Houston the information he had hoped for. Santa Anna was leading the small Mexican force that in its haste had moved in front of Houston. Now the Texans had an opportunity to win the war. Throughout the war, Houston's intelligence system had operated efficiently. Scouts, commanded by Erastus "Deaf" Smith, kept the Texans informed of Mexican troop movements. Hendrick Arnold, a free black, was a valuable spy, posing as a runaway slave to enter Mexican camps to gain information.

On April 19, the Texans crossed Buffalo Bayou and made contact with an advance force of Mexican cavalry on April 20. A brief skirmish ensued, and the Texans were ready for more action. But Houston waited. So impressive was the performance of one private, Mirabeau B. Lamar, that Houston promoted him to colonel of the cavalry the next day.

Early on April 21, Gen. Martin Perfecto de Cos reinforced Santa Anna's troop with more than 500 men. Santa Anna complained later that they were recruits and not "picked" veterans that he had requested from Gen. Vicente Filisola, his second in command. Nevertheless, the new troops, who had marched all night, disrupted the camp's routine for a time, but soon all the soldiers and officers settled down for a mid-day rest. Curiously, no sentries were posted, although the Mexicans knew that the small Texas army was no more than a mile away across Peggy McCormick's ranch on the San Jacinto plain.

Houston held a council of war at noon on April 21, with the consensus being that the Texans should attack early the next day. But the men wanted to fight, so about 3 p.m., Houston ordered them to parade and the battle was launched at 4:30 p.m.

A company of Mexican-Texans, commanded by Juan Seguin, had served as the army's rear guard through much of the retreat across Texas and had fought many skirmishes with the Mexican army in the process. Perhaps fearing the Mexican-Texans would be mistaken for Mexican soldiers, Houston had assigned the company to guard duty as the battle approached. But after the men protested, they fought in the battle of San Jacinto.

Historians disagree widely on the number of troops on each side. Houston probably had about 900 while Santa Anna had between 1,100 and 1,300. But the Texans had the decided psychological advantage. Two-thirds of the fledgling Republic's army were "old Texans" who had family and land to defend. They had an investment of years of toil in building their homes. And they were just plain fighting mad about the massacre of men at the Alamo and Goliad. In less than 20 minutes — with strains of "Won't You Come to the Bower" and "Yankee Doodle" mingling with outraged cries of "Remember the Alamo" and "Remember Goliad" — they set the Mexican army to rout. More than 600 Mexicans were killed and hundreds more wounded or captured. Only nine of the Texans died in the fight. The killing frenzy of the Texans lasted until almost sunset.

Critics claimed that Houston tried to call a retreat and was guilty of other unworthy conduct during the battle. But the commander had two horses shot from under him and was severely wounded in the encounter. Thomas J. Rusk, secretary of war, however, probably was the most outstanding commander on the field.

But it was not until the following day that Santa Anna, who fled from his forces early in the fight, was captured. Houston had given patrols prophetic advice: "You will find the hero of Tampico, if you find him at all, making his retreat on all fours, and he will be dressed as bad at least as a common soldier." And that was the case. One Texan noticed that a grubby soldier his patrol found in the high grass had a silk shirt under his filthy jacket. Although denying he was an officer, the Mexican was taken back to camp by the patrol, where he was welcomed with cries of "El Presidente! El Presidente!" by other prisoners. Santa Anna introduced himself when taken to the wounded Houston.

Houston quickly got the Mexican dictator to agree to a truce and to order his armies to cease hostilities and withdraw to San Antonio and Victoria. Texas soldiers were ready to execute Santa Anna on the spot for the atrocities at the Alamo and Goliad. But Houston had no intention of killing him. Seeing the Texans' hostility, Santa Anna made quick conciliations, even offering to negotiate an immediate treaty with Houston. But the Texas commander refused, leaving that responsibility to the civil government. Houston soon left for New Orleans to have his wounded ankle treated.

Mexican critics of Gen. Filisola, Santa Anna's second in command, have argued that he should have ignored the dictator's orders, since they were given under duress, and attacked the Texans. The Italian-born officer had little choice, however, because he was almost out of supplies. The four-ship Texas navy, commanded by Charles E. Hawkins, kept the Gulf clear of Mexican shipping. Supply lines therefore were stretched hundreds of miles overland, and Houston's scorched-earth policy in retreat had denied the Mexicans forage from the land.

President Burnet took charge of Santa Anna, and on May 14 the dictator signed two treaties at Velasco, a public document and a secret one. The public agreement declared that hostilities would cease, that the Mexican army would withdraw to south of the Rio Grande, that prisoners would be released and that Santa Anna would be shipped to Veracruz as soon as possible. In the secret treaty, Santa Anna agreed to recognize Texas' independence, to give diplomatic recognition, to negotiate a commercial treaty and to set the Rio Grande as the new Republic's southern boundary.

Historian Eugene Barker has noted that "The Texas Revolution was not a spontaneous outburst of patriotic indignation against Mexican oppression. Few of the colonists were satisfied with all features of Mexican rule but few also were ready to go to the length of armed rebellion . . ." Some Texas settlers went so far as to oppose the rebellion. Gen. Urrea received almost an enthusiastic welcome when he entered Columbia on April 21. He observed that the settlers felt that many of the rebels were adventurers and were a greater threat to the colonists than the Mexican army. Houston found the names of many Texas Tories among Santa Anna's papers after San Jacinto. He never released the names, but a company of men commanded by Capt.

James Kokernot was sent to inform the Tories that they were then supporting a lost cause.

Texas soon faced another military threat, this one from its own army. One historian noted that the disagreement between the military and civilian government over policy and procedure after the revolution brought Texas near the establishment of the very type of military domination that it fought to avoid.

The character of the Texas army was changing rapidly after San Jacinto. Again, the old settlers, who provided two-thirds of the manpower for the fighting force at the time, were ready to go home. Almost immediately, some began drifting off to plant crops or to defend against anticipated Indian raids. These were not professional fighting men, but farmers and shopkeepers who had taken up arms in defense of family and home.

Rusk assumed command of the army when Houston left, and he was detailed to follow the Mexican army out of Texas. Further hostilities were to be avoided, however. But the army soon began to melt away, and neither reinforcements nor supplies were forthcoming. Rusk complained that between the Colorado River and Goliad and San Antonio "There is not a particle of corn or a hoof of cattle." Rusk's officers accused the government of neglecting the army. Burnet was informed by officers that he was to drop all other matters and give "particular attention" to the army or the army might find it necessary "to pursue at home our most sacred rights."

Burnet denied the charges of neglect and objected to the threat. "When the civil government of a country is compelled to receive a prescription of its duties from an armed force, that government is, if not virtually dissolved, in great danger of being lost in the blazonry of military misrule."

The government's problems deepened in early June when it attempted to release Santa Anna in compliance with the Velasco treaty. Gen. Thomas J. Green, a Texas agent in the United States, arrived with a group of volunteers he had raised. He took the Mexican leader off the ship and held him in army custody despite objections by President Burnet and the cabinet.

By July, the character of the army, and its attitude, changed substantially. Almost three-quarters of the 2,500 men under arms had not been in Texas when the battle of San Jacinto was fought. Most were American volunteers who came to Texas to seek vengeance against the Mexicans for atrocities at Goliad and the Alamo and to take advantage of the large land grants the Republic was giving for military service. But the new army was outraged that the Mexican leaders had not been hanged, although Burnet courageously pointed out that there was no precedent to try or punish a commander for official acts performed during war.

Because of the problems with the new army, Burnet ordered agents in New Orleans to send no more volunteers from the United States. Matters continued to deteriorate, however. Word was received that the Mexican Senate had repudiated Santa Anna's agreements in the treaty of Velasco. Texas agents sent to Matamoros were taken into custody, and it was rumored that Gen. Jose Urrea was marching into Texas with a new army.

In early July, Gen. Rusk sent Col. Henry Millard to Velasco to discuss various military matters with the president and the cabinet. While in the capital, Millard ordered Maj. Amasa Turner to arrest Burnet and to confiscate the cabinet's archives. Turner instead told Burnet of the order. The outraged president ordered Rusk to dismiss Millard from the rolls of the military and declared "the good people of Texas have been insulted and outraged in the person of the Chief Magistrate; a violent revolution has been attempted, involving the overthrow of the civil authorities and evidently intended to create a military supremacy in the government."

The crisis eased somewhat when attention became riveted on the rumored invasion by Urrea. Burnet ordered the army to prepare for an expedition against Matamoros, and that pacified the officers and men.

But Texas was in deep financial trouble. Debts from the revolution totaled $1,250,000 by the end of August 1836. So in July, Burnet called for an election on the first Monday in September.

Texas had won its independence from Mexico and from a threatened military dictatorship within its own army. But its future was far from assured.

Republic of Texas 9

SAM Houston was easily the most dominant figure through the nearly 10-year history of the Republic of Texas. While he was roundly criticized for the retreat across Texas during the revolution, the victory at San Jacinto endeared him to most of the new nation's inhabitants.

Houston handily defeated Henry Smith and Stephen F. Austin in the election called in September 1836 by President David G. Burnet and the interim government. Mirabeau B. Lamar was elected vice president, and voters approved the Republic's constitution and overwhelmingly expressed a desire for annexation to the United States.

Houston was inaugurated on Oct. 22 at the capital in Columbia, which was little more than a frontier village. The first cabinet appointed by the new president represented an attempt to heal old political wounds. Austin was named secretary of state; former provisional governor Henry Smith was secretary of treasury; Thomas J. Rusk, secretary of war; J. Pinckney Henderson, attorney general; Robert Barr, postmaster general, and J. Rhoads Fisher, secretary of navy. The First Congress of Texas, which convened Oct. 3, named James Collinsworth the chief justice of the Supreme Court.

A host of problems faced the new government. Gen. Santa Anna was still in custody, and public opinion favored his execution. Texas' leadership wisely kept Santa Anna alive, first to keep from giving the Mexicans an emotional rallying point for launching another invasion, which the leader's death would have represented. And second, the Texas leaders hoped that the dictator would keep his promise to work for recognition of Texas, as he promised in the secret Treaty of Velasco. Santa Anna was released in November 1836 and made his way to Washington, D.C. Houston hoped the dictator could convince President Jackson to recognize Texas. Jackson refused to see Santa Anna, who returned to Mexico, where he had fallen from power.

Texas suffered a major tragedy in late December 1836 when Austin, the acknowledged "Father of Texas," died of pneumonia after working long hours at the drafty capital at Columbia. The steamboat Yellow Stone ferried his body to Peach Point on the Brazos for burial. This historic steamboat played a major role in Texas history. In April the craft had been used to ferry Houston's army across the Brazos at Groce's Crossing; later the boat transported President Burnet and his cabinet to San

Jacinto and carried the government and Santa Anna to Velasco for treaty negotiations. The historic ship sank in Buffalo Bayou in late 1837.

Houston's second major challenge was even more vexing than the problem with Santa Anna. Felix Huston had assumed command of the Texas army when Rusk resigned to take a cabinet post. Huston favored an invasion of Mexico, and the army, made up now mostly of American volunteers, who came to Texas after the battle of San Jacinto, was rebellious and ready to fight. Houston tried to replace Huston as commander with Albert Sidney Johnston, but Huston seriously wounded Johnston in a duel. In May 1837, Huston was asked to Columbia to discuss the invasion. While Huston was away from the troops, Houston sent Rusk to furlough the army without pay — but with generous land grants. Only 600 men were retained in the army.

The Republic's other problems were less tractable. The economy needed attention; Indians still represented a menace; Mexico remained warlike; foreign relations had to be developed; and relations with the United States had to be firmed up.

The economy proved to be the most troublesome. Texas began its experience as a republic in a boom atmosphere. While most Texans existed in a subsistence economy, raising only enough crops to feed themselves, independence attracted land speculators. Everyone wanted to be in on the beginning of the new nation. But there was little currency in Texas. Some gold and silver Mexican coins were in circulation, but the principal medium of exchange was bank notes from the United States. These notes were in all denominations with no common base. Only the strength of the bank from which they were issued guaranteed the notes.

At the same time the United States also was experiencing an economic boom, but one based on speculation in canals, railroads and land. Foreigners invested heavily in these schemes. In the period 1835-37, nearly 40 million acres of federal land were sold, mostly to speculators, who borrowed from banks to make payments. The number of bank loans soared 500 percent between 1830 and 1837, and many of the institutions made loans without regard to reserves.

By 1836, revenue from federal land sales reached $24 million, and the U.S. Congress opted to distribute the federal surplus among the states on a population basis. The drain of cash from "pet banks" caused a hardship that was intensified when President Andrew Jackson in 1836 required that land payments be made only in hard currency or in notes from banks that paid specie (cash) for their outstanding notes. In May 1837, New York banks stopped paying hard money for their notes or other obligations, and this action precipitated a crisis that resulted in the failure of hundreds of banks. For the next five years, the United States was thrown into the worst economic depression in its history. The economic decline was aggravated when foreign investors withdrew their cash, and a series of crop failures reduced the purchasing power of the major segment of the agricultural economy.

Texas was not affected by the initial decline. But when the depression finally hit the new Republic, it was as devastating as in the United States and lasted longer.

Houston's first administration was plagued by a lack of money. Land was Texas' only asset, and conflicting policies were adopted for use of land. On one hand, land was to be used to back notes issued by the government. On the other hand, generous land grants were to be used to attract immigrants. But when vast amounts of land were given away, the resource was of little use as collateral because it would not hold its value. During the life of the Republic, more than 36.8 million acres of land were alienated by the congresses of Texas. The Republic's Constitution specified that white heads of families living in Texas on March 2, 1836, could receive a First Class headright of a league and a labor — 4,605 acres — of land. Single men could get 1,476 acres. Subsequent headrights were approved for newcomers, and additional grants were available for men who served in the army.

During his first administration, Houston issued $650,000 in interest-bearing notes — so-called "Star Money," because the star of Texas was printed on the backs of the notes — that held their value when redeemed in late 1838. This issue, redeemed before the Panic of 1837 reached Texas, was the only specie issued by the Republic that did not devalue immediately.

The Texas Congress tried to levy some direct taxes, but these were easily evaded. And the taxes were difficult to collect because there simply was little hard cash in Texas. The only source of real revenue was customs collections, and these were paid grudgingly by Texans. The tariffs ranged from one percent on breadstuffs to 50 percent on silk, and custom revenues represented between 50 and 80 percent of the government's income throughout the life of the Republic.

Standing armies are expensive to maintain, so to keep the cost of government down, Houston sought to maintain peaceful relations with the Indians and with Mexico. Frontier defense was to be maintained by local militia. The Congress authorized a line of block houses and trading posts along the frontier, and Houston met personally with the chiefs of several tribes in an effort to maintain peace. But the Texas Senate declined to ratify the treaty Houston had made with the Cherokees and other Indians in East Texas during the revolution, and this hurt the peace efforts. Also many of the trading posts promised to the Indians in agreements were never opened, damaging the government's credibility in the eyes of the Indians.

Houston's policy of frontier defense relied on ranging companies — the Texas Rangers. Since Stephen F. Austin personally financed a group of 10 men to protect his small colony in 1823, these organizations had been active in Texas. Before the Revolution in 1835, small groups of men had been commissioned to guard the frontier against Indians while other Texans were occupied with the Mexican army. The service of the historic Texas Rangers has been well-documented, and during this period, Capt. Jack Hays was the best-known of these frontier defenders. Also during this era, the six-shooter, one of the most important innovations in weaponry, was introduced into Texas.

Relations with Mexico were stagnant. Mexicans were too involved with internal politics to be concerned with Texas. But they also were adamant about refusing to recognize the independence of the Republic of Texas and about accepting the Rio Grande as any sort of boundary line.

Early attempts to gain recognition from England, France and other European countries also were stymied, as the nations waited to see if Texas could remain independent from Mexico.

The greatest disappointment in Houston's first term was the failure to have the Republic annexed to the United States. Henry Morfit, President Jackson's agent, toured the new Republic in the summer of 1836. Although impressed, Morfit reported that Texas' best chance at continued independence lay in the "stupidity of the rulers of Mexico and the financial embarrassment of the Mexican government." He recommended that annexation be delayed. Though U.S. Secretary of State John Forsyth recommended that diplomatic recognition be withheld until other nations led the way, U.S. recognition of Texas' independence came in March 1837, President Jackson's last official act in office. But in June 1837, John Quincy Adams led off the abolitionists' campaign against Texas by denouncing annexation on the floor of the U.S. House. Late that year, Houston withdrew the formal request for annexation. Texas' pride had suffered a severe blow.

Although immigrants were attracted to Texas, the Republic's economy was slow in developing. Almost all manufactured goods had to be imported throughout the history of the Republic, throwing foreign trade out of balance and aggravating the shortage of currency. Most Texans were farmers, eking out an existence for their families. Any surplus crops had to be sold in the immediate neighborhood because transportation facilities were nonexistent. The Republic left most road construction and maintenance to local government. And most of the roads were only cleared trails, muddy to the extent of impassability in wet weather and dusty in dry seasons. Goods had to be hauled by oxcarts or by horse, and fees were high.

The Republic's major rivers never fulfilled the promise of transportation arteries that early explorers expected. Although the Sabine, Red, Trinity and Brazos rivers had steamboat traffic at times, the waterways defied navigation very far inland. The water flow in most of the rivers was seasonal, and at many times, there was simply not enough water to float a craft. Snags, sharp meandering routes along with other obstacles also thwarted navigation, and sand bars at the rivers' mouths were hazardous.

In inland Texas, Preston, located on the Red River in present-day Grayson County, and Jefferson, located near Cypress Bayou in Marion County, were major points for river traffic, though much of it was seasonal. Several smaller communities on the lower reaches of other rivers also had water service. The Brazos, with heavy cotton farming along its lower reaches, was one of the most accessible rivers for water traffic. A small lumbering industry was developing on the rivers, too, with several sawmills in operation around Buffalo Bayou. The lumber was provided for local needs.

In addition to farming, cattle raising already was established in the Republic, and the animals were driven overland to markets in Louisiana. The Coastal Prairies, the Piney Woods and Northeast Texas were the principal centers of cattle ranching in the Republic, as well as South Texas.

San Antonio was the largest town in the Republic, but it was on the frontier and too near Mexico to play a leading role in affairs. The eastern rivers and the coast were the Anglo-American population centers. In April 1837, the capital of the Republic was moved from Columbia to the new city of Houston on Buffalo Bayou. The new capital was named for the hero of San Jacinto and was developed by the brothers A. C. and J. K. Allen near the previous capital of Harrisburg, which was burned by the Mexican army.

Houston's foreign policy achieved initial success when J. Pinckney Henderson negotiated a trade treaty with Great Britain. Although the agreement was short of outright diplomatic recognition, it was progress. In the next few years, France, Belgium, The Netherlands and some German states recognized the new Republic.

Under the constitution, Houston's first term lasted only two years, and he could not succeed himself. The Republic's politics already were dividing along lines of personalities. Houston was a controversial figure, and opponents roundly criticized his drinking habits, along with his policies as president. Lamar, an outspoken opponent of the first president, was the leading candidate to succeed Houston. And Lamar won the election handily when two opponents recruited by Houston's partisans committed suicide.

Lamar brought a different style of government to the Republic of Texas. He was a dreamer, a visionary. Texas, he felt, was in competition with the United States to see which would control the North American continent.

While Houston had been passive, partly out of frugality, in relations with Mexico and Indians, Lamar was more active. He thought Mexico could be forced to accept Texas' independence, and that the borders of the new Republic could be drawn with a sword. Lamar foresaw a Texas empire controlling all the territory to the Pacific Ocean and much of northern Mexico. Indians, the Republic's second president thought, were simply tenants in residence on the land they occupied and had no right to title if white settlers coveted the area.

While Lamar's visions may have been in keeping with those held by many Texans, his administration suffered from economic malaise. Houston was frugal, Lamar a spendthrift. Houston's first term cost Texas only about $500,000, while Lamar and the Congress spent $5 million in the next three years. During Lamar's administration, Texas became afflicted with the so-called "original sin of Americans," as one economist noted — the paper money disease. The government issued paper bills totaling more than $3.5 million in the next three years, leaving a debt of almost $6 million. The notes issued by the government during this period — called "Redbacks" because of the color of the back of the bill — carried no interest and soon depreciated. By the end of Lamar's administration the money was worth only two to three cents on the dollar.

Early in 1839, Lamar gained recognition as the "father of education" in Texas when the Congress granted each of the existing 23 counties three leagues of land to be used for education. Later the allotment was increased to four leagues. Fifty leagues of land also were set aside for development of a university. Despite the lip service paid to education, the government did not have the money for several years to set up a school system. Most education during the Republic was provided by private schools and churches.

Lamar's Indian policies, however, were the most dramatic departure from Houston's. One difference lay in the men's experience. Houston had lived with Cherokees as a child, was adopted as a member of a tribe and advocated Indian rights long before coming to Texas. He was one of the few Anglos who tried to give Indians title to their land rather than place them on reservations. Lamar more accurately reflected the frontier attitude toward the native Americans. His first experience in public life was as secretary to Gov. George Troup of Georgia, who successfully opposed the federal government's policy of assimilation of Indians at the time. Indians were simply removed from Georgia.

Texans' concern about Indian's intentions was raised in 1838 when Vicente Cordova, a former official at Nacogdoches, led an uprising of dissident Mexican-Texans, Anglos and Indians in East Texas. Cordova escaped, but Manuel Flores, a Mexican trader, was killed near Austin in 1839. Found on Flores' body were letters urging the Cherokees and other East Texas Indians to take up arms against the white settlers. Texans first tried to negotiate the Cherokees' removal from the region, but in July 1839, the Indians were forcibly ejected from Texas at the battle of the Neches River. Houston's close friend, the aging Cherokee chief Philip Bowles, was killed in the battle while Houston was visiting former President Jackson in Tennessee.

The most tragic miscalculation in Lamar policy came in March 1840 when a group of Comanches was invited to San Antonio to exchange prisoners. Chief Maguara led 12 other chiefs and dozens of warriors and their families to the city. But they brought only one white girl, who told of harsh treatment at the hands of the Indians. Texas' commissioners, Hugh McLeod and William G. Cooke, and militia commander, William S. Fisher, decided to hold the chiefs until more prisoners were returned. But the Comanches would not be taken prisoner, and the so-called Council House Fight ensued. Many chiefs and warriors were killed and their families captured. Word spread among the Indians of this treachery. In August 1840, an estimated 600 Indians raided Linnville and Victoria near the Gulf Coast in retaliation. Texas' militia under Ranger Ben McCulloch ambushed the raiding party at Plum Creek, killing several of the raiders and recovering horses, livestock and plunder. Later in the year, John H. Moore led a successful campaign against Comanches camped near the present town of Colorado City. The Comanches were Texans' implacable enemies until finally defeated in 1875.

Historians point out that while Lamar's Indian policy was expensive and of questionable morality, it was effective. Large regions of the Republic were cleared of native Americans for immigrants.

To demonstrate his intention to expand the boundaries of the Republic, Lamar wanted the capital moved from Houston. In early 1839, a commission was appointed to select a site to be located near the frontier and named for Stephen F. Austin. Lamar supported the selection of a site on the Colorado River the previous year while on a buffalo hunt. (Historian Eugene C. Barker also noted that Austin had once selected a site in the immediate area for a permanent home that was never built, although this was not connected to Lamar's choice.) Construction of government buildings began in the spring of 1839, and on Oct. 17, 1839, Lamar arrived with an official cavalcade to occupy Austin, the new capital of the Republic. Sam Houston and others never liked the site, feeling it was too vulnerable to attacks by Indians and the Mexican army.

Lamar's foreign policy bore fruit. In 1839, France became the first European nation to extend diplomatic recognition to the newest North American republic. The Netherlands and Great Britain followed suit in 1840, and Belgium joined the others in 1841. In exchange for Texas' promise to suppress the importation of slaves, Great Britain agreed to mediate Texas' discussions with Mexico. Lamar attempted to bludgeon Mexico into negotiations with the second Texas navy, which took to the seas under the command of Edwin Ward Moore, the "port captain of the Navy." The navy raided Mexican ports and shipping, and for a time it was "rented" to republican rebels in Yucatan, another Mexican state in revolt against the centralist government.

While Lamar was dreaming of empire, Texas' fragile economy collapsed. By the fall of 1840, the boom spirit had completely evaporated, and the economic depression that had swept the United States in 1837 was fully felt in the Republic. Its currency was almost worthless and its credit nonexistent. Lamar had long hoped for a major loan with which to establish a national bank to smooth Texas' economic problems. But most of the world was still gripped by the depression, and Texas could not obtain loans from either the United States or Europe.

Texas also was not attracting as many settlers as was hoped when generous land grants were offered to newcomers. The Fifth Congress revived the empresario program that had been successful for the Mexican government. Immigration companies would be chartered to bring colonists to the Republic. The newcomers would be given free land, and the company would receive blocks of land when immigration quotas were filled.

Several bills chartering companies were considered. The Peters Colony bill was passed in February 1841, setting aside large tracts of land in North Central Texas, running from about the present Dallas-Fort Worth area to the Red River. The Franco-Texiene bill, which would have brought several thousand European immigrants to the Republic, was defeated when concern arose about the impact on the country of such a conclave. Fear of the pro-abolitionist leanings of foreign colonists also may have been a factor.

In 1842, a general colonization law was passed. Henri Castro, a Frenchman, received two grants for settling 600 Europeans, and Henry Francis Fisher and Burchard Miller contracted to bring 1,000 settlers. In 1844, the Fisher-Miller grants were sold to the Adelsverein, a society for promoting German immigration.

Lamar's hopes for a $5 million loan were dashed in an incident that would be comical, if not so serious. The French charge d'affaires to Texas, Count Alphonse de Saligny, had many difficulties adjusting to life in frontier Austin. When he refused to pay his hotel bill, innkeeper Richard Bullock cursed him roundly. Saligny was offended, and to placate him, the Texas Congress passed a law against verbally abusing foreign emissaries. Troubles between the count and the innkeeper deepened when Saligny's servant killed some of Bullock's pigs, which were eating grain at the Frenchman's stable. When authorities failed to prosecute Bullock for again cursing him, Saligny demanded his credentials and left Texas. After that, a $5 million loan to Texas by the French government was cancelled. Saligny's brother-in-law was France's minister of finance.

Lamar tried several means of improving the government's finances. In 1839, the Congress authorized the opening of trade with Mexican merchants along the Rio Grande, but this soon soured because Texans were afraid that Mexican agents among the traders were stirring up trouble for settlers with the Indians. Lamar used the authority given in 1839 to launch the Santa Fe expedition in 1841. But this effort ended in disaster.

Lamar tried to reopen negotiations with Mexico. But Bernard Bee in 1839 was not allowed to land in Mexico. James Treat was received by Mexican officials in 1839, probably as a move to keep Texas from backing dissidents in Northern Mexico. In 1841, the Mexican government refused to accept James Webb. This region was almost forgotten by the Mexican government in the political chaos following the Texas Revolution. And the state of limbo was not acceptable to residents near the Rio Grande. In 1839, Antonio Canales, an attorney from Revilla (today's Guerrero), gained support for an independence movement. Canales envisioned a Republic of the Rio Grande separate from Mexico and composed of all the northern Mexican states. Cols. Jose Maria Gonzales of Laredo and Antonio Zapata of Revilla were prominent in the early military successes of Canales. In January 1840, the Republic of the Rio Grande was declared and Laredo the capital. The movement was short-lived as Mexican centralists defeated its army. Canales capitulated to offers of a commission in the Mexican army, and Gonzales and Zapata, for whom Zapata County in the Lower Rio Grande Valley is named, were executed. The Texas government stayed out of the fight, although many Texans fought in the independence movement.

From his seat in Congress, Houston had been a vocal critic of Lamar's administration. Texas' first president became the Republic's third chief executive when Lamar supporters, backing David G. Burnet, could not mount a serious campaign against the hero of San Jacinto.

Houston's second administration was even more frugal than his first. Government expenses were cut to the bone, and by late 1844, income almost matched expenditures. In 1842, Houston had to suspend — not repudiate — the Republic's debt, and he re-entered negotiations with Indian tribes in an attempt to quell the raids on settlements. A series of trading posts were opened along the frontier to pacify the Native Americans.

War fever reached a high pitch in Texas in 1842, however, and Houston grew increasingly unpopular because he would not launch an offensive war against Mexico. Texans were irate at the mistreatment of the members of the Santa Fe Expedition, who had been captured and marched to Mexico City. In retaliation for the expedition, Mexico, too, caused trouble. In March 1842, Gen. Rafael Vasquez launched guerrilla raids on San Antonio, Victoria and Goliad, but quickly left the Republic. Thirty-five hundred Texas volunteers quickly gathered at San Antonio, demanding that Mexico be punished. Houston urged calm, but the clamor increased when Gen. Adrian Woll with 1,400 men took San Antonio in September 1842. He raised the Mexican flag and declared the reconquest of Texas. Ranger Capt. Jack Hays was camped nearby and within days 600 volunteers had joined him, anxious to drive the Mexican invaders from Texas soil. Gen. Woll withdrew after the Battle of Salado.

Alexander Somervell was commanded by Houston to follow with 700 troops and harass the Mexican army, but Somervell was warned to observe the rules of civilized warfare. Houston wanted no retaliatory raids into Mexico. Somervell reached Laredo in early December 1842 and found no Mexican troops. The Texans sacked Laredo, but Somervell ordered them to return the plunder. Two hundred soldiers were sent home from Laredo, and Somervell continued the expedition, crossing the Rio Grande to find military targets. A few days later, the commander returned home, but 300 soldiers decided to continue the raid under the command of William S. Fisher. On Christmas day, this group attacked the village of Mier, only to be defeated by a Mexican force that outnumbered them 10-to-1.

On a march toward Mexico City, the survivors of the Mier expedition attempted a mass escape. Most were recaptured near Hacienda Salado and taken to Saltillo, the capital of Coahuila. An order to execute all the prisoners was refused by Commandant Gen. Jose Antonio Mejia. The Texans were returned to Hacienda Salado, where one in every 10 was ordered by Santa Anna to be executed in atonement for the attempted escape. The prisoners drew beans to determine who would be shot; bearers of black beans were executed. Texans again were outraged by the treatment of prisoners, but the war fever soon subsided. Two major defeats within a year were humiliating enough without attempting a poorly financed offensive war.

Never a fan of the new capital at Austin, Houston took the occasion of the Woll invasion of San Antonio to move the seat of government to Washington-on-the-Brazos, where the Seventh Congress convened in November 1842. Houston wanted to permanently move the capital away from the exposed frontier, and he gave confidential orders to Col. Thomas I. Smith and Capt. Eli Chandler to remove the Republic's records from Austin. The records were taken at night, but when Austin residents were alerted to the removal by a warning shot from a cannon fired by Mrs. Angelina Eberly, a party led by Mark B. Lewis caught the ox train on Brushy Creek in Williamson County. The so-called Archives War ended without a shot fired, and the records were returned to Austin.

Houston also had problems with the Texas Navy. His recall orders were ignored by Commodore Moore, and finally, Houston asked for international help in returning the "pirates" to Texas. Moore returned voluntarily and asked for a court-martial to clear his name. He was convicted on only two minor charges.

Many free blacks lived in Texas, and some fought in the revolution. The First Texas Congress had provided land grants for them, but in 1840, the Congress passed a punitive law designed to force free blacks to leave Texas. The law was not vigorously enforced, and the Congress approved many exemptions in individual bills. Houston went a step further in his second administration by issuing pardons in advance for free blacks convicted under the law.

While the Republic left most road construction to local government, the Congress did authorize construction of the Central National Road to tie Preston on the Red River in Grayson County to Austin. The road crossed the Trinity River near the confluence of its three forks, and a thriving community grew around a trading post opened by John Neely Bryan. The city is today's Dallas.

Galveston was the Republic's major port of entry, although the new community of Houston was making a bid for leadership. Many public works were considered by the congresses of Texas to facilitate trade and transportation. None was more bizarre than the suggestion of Houston's aggressive promoters to change the route of the Brazos River to empty into Buffalo Bayou. The bayou was Houston's lifeline to the Gulf, but it periodically ran low. Houston's leadership felt that rerouting the Brazos was reasonable, since the waterway had in ages past emptied into the bayou. The Congress rejected the idea.

As Houston completed his second term, the United States was becoming more interested in annexation. Texas had seriously flirted with Great Britain and France, and the Americans did not want a rival republic with close foreign ties on the North American continent. Houston orchestrated the early stages of the final step toward annexation. But his successor, Anson Jones, completed the process.

The Republic of Texas' main claim to fame is simply endurance. Its settlers, unlike other Americans who had military help, had cleared a large region of Indians by themselves, had established farms and communities and had persevered through extreme economic hardship. Adroit political leadership had gained the Republic recognition from many foreign countries. And although dreams of empire may have dimmed, Texans had firmly established an identity on a major portion of the North American continent. As Texas prepared to enter the United States, the frontier had been pushed to a line running from Corpus Christi through San Antonio, New Braunfels, Austin, Belton, Waco and Dallas to Preston.

The U.S. presidential campaign of 1844 was to make Texas a part of the Union.

10 *Annexation*

ANNEXATION to the United States was not a foregone conclusion for Texans once independence from Mexico was gained in 1836. American volunteers had shed much blood in the Texas Revolution, and patriotic passions flamed high as the Anglo-Texans battled the Mexican army across Texas.

Once the gun smoke settled and negotiations between Texas and the United States began, the road was not smooth. Indeed, on occasion, the Texans resorted to guile. Sam Houston noted that Texas "was more coy than forward" as the negotiations reached a climax.

William H. Wharton was Texas' first representative in Washington. His instructions were to gain diplomatic recognition of the new Republic's independence. After some squabbles, Congress appropriated funds for a minister in Texas, and President Andrew Jackson recognized the new country in one of his last acts in office in March 1837. Later that year, Memucan Hunt replaced Wharton, and although he pursued annexation, President Martin Van Buren rejected the appeal in September 1837. The president noted that annexation of an independent nation was of doubtful constitutionality and that Texas still was nominally at war with Mexico. Annexation could lead to a war between the United States and Mexico with Great Britain possibly siding with the Mexicans.

John Quincy Adams in 1837 argued that annexation was unconstitutional. The congressman mounted a campaign against annexation in the U.S. House in June and July 1838. He claimed the issue was a plan by the Southern slaveholders to strengthen their hand by annexing Texas and dividing it into several states. Texans revolted in 1836, Adams claimed, when Mexico tried to abolish slavery. In late 1838, Houston instructed Texas' minister in Washington to withdraw the annexation proposal, and the Texas Senate approved this action in 1839.

Annexation was in limbo during the presidential term of Mirabeau B. Lamar. He felt that the loss of freedom and independence as a nation was too high a price to pay for Texas to join the United States. Lamar held visions of empire in which Texas would rival the United States for supremacy on the North American continent. However, when Lamar was successful in gaining recognition for Texas by several European countries, the United States' interest in annexation was rekindled.

Great Britain maintained a close relationship with Texas and Mexico and made strenuous efforts to get Mexico to recognize Texas' independence and to develop normal diplomatic relations. This close relationship between Great Britain and Texas raised fears in the United States. Some Americans were concerned that Great Britain might attempt to make Texas part of its empire. Southerners feared for the future of slavery in Texas, which had renounced the importation of slaves as a concession to get a trade treaty with Great Britain. Newspapers noted that U.S. trade with Texas had suffered after the Republic received diplomatic recognition from European nations.

In Houston's second term, Texas began playing coy. Early, Houston suggested to the Texas minister in Washington that negotiations on annexation could be reopened if chances for success were good. Issac Van Zandt, Texas' minister to Washington, wrote that President John Tyler and the cabinet were anxious to annex Texas but worried about ratification in the U.S. Senate. Houston then suggested dropping the matter, hoping that he would be able to settle matters with Mexico.

U.S. Secretary of State Abel P. Upshur tried to reopen negotiations in October 1843, but Van Zandt said he had no instructions on the question. Texas wanted military protection while negotiations were under way, and this was not forthcoming. Upshur was killed in an accident, and John C. Calhoun replaced him. In the meantime, J. Pinckney Henderson was sent to Washington to help Van Zandt with the negotiations.

In January 1844, Houston again gave Van Zandt instructions to open negotiations, if chances of success were good. The president did not want another failure that could damage negotiations with other countries. Calhoun ordered a naval force to the Gulf and moved U.S. troops to the southwest border, which was the best he could do to provide Texas protection while negotiations were in progress.

On April 11, 1844, Texas and the United States signed a treaty for annexation. Texas would enter the Union as a territory, not a state, under terms of the treaty. The United States would assume Texas' debt up to $10 million and would negotiate with Mexico Texas' southwestern boundary. The treaty was sent to the U.S. Senate for ratification on April 22.

National politics intervened, however. The Whigs came down solidly against annexation and westward expansion. Abolitionists in the party apparently were more afraid of the slavery issue than expansion. The Senate rejected the annexation treaty on June 8 by a vote of 35-16. At least 15 of the opposition votes came from Southern Whig senators who had been counted on for support. Houston suggested to British agents that he was done with annexation after the rejection.

But the annexation of Texas and westward expansion became major issues in the 1844 presidential campaign. Through eight ballots at the Democratic convention, Van Buren failed to receive the necessary two-thirds majority for nomination. On the ninth ballot, his name was withdrawn from consideration, and the convention stampeded to James K. Polk, a supporter of expansion and the party's first "dark horse" nominee. In addition, the Democratic platform included a strong expansion plank, calling for the reoccupation of Oregon and the reannexation of Texas. Polk was elected president in November but would not take office until March 1845.

Great Britain and France increased pressure on Mexico to recognize Texas in hopes that independence would be more attractive to Texans than annexation. But Mexico delayed the decision.

In December 1844, President Tyler declared that the people had spoken on the issue of annexation and resubmitted it to Congress. Several bills were introduced in the U.S. House representing various proposals for annexation. In February 1845, the Congress approved a resolution that would bring Texas into the Union as a state. Texas would cede its public property — such as forts, barracks and customhouses — to the United States, but it could keep its public lands and must retain its public debt. The territory could be divided into four new states in addition to the original Texas. And the United States would negotiate the Rio Grande boundary claim. Texas had to present a state constitution for congressional approval by Jan. 1, 1846. These terms were much more beneficial to Texas than had been those of the treaty that the Senate rejected in 1844.

Political parties did not develop in the Republic of Texas, and annexation was not a partisan issue. But annexation did set the tone of Texas' politics for more than a century. One editor noted in January 1845, "We are all Democrats in Texas, since the glorious victory of that party, who fearlessly espoused our cause and nailed the 'Lone Star' to the top mast of their noble ship."

British officials asked the Texas government to delay consideration of the U.S. offer for 90 days to attempt to get Mexico to recognize the Republic. The delay did no good. Texans' minds were made up.

President Anson Jones, who succeeded Houston, called the Texas Congress into special session on June 16 and called a convention to write a state constitution into session in Austin on July 4. Mexico finally recognized Texas' independence, but the recognition was rejected. Texas voters overwhelmingly accepted the U.S. proposal and approved the new constitution in a referendum.

On Dec. 29, 1845, the U.S. Congress accepted the state constitution and Texas became a part of the United States.

State officials were elected in December 1845, and on Feb. 19, 1846, the flag of the Republic of Texas was lowered for the last time in Austin and was replaced by the stars and stripes of the United States. J. Pinckney Henderson was sworn in as the first governor of Texas by the speaker of the Texas House.

In an eloquent speech, President Jones reviewed the life of the Republic:

"The lone star of Texas, which ten years since arose amid cloud, over fields of carnage, and obscurely shone for a while, has culminated, and, following an inscrutable destiny, has passed on and become fixed forever in that glorious constellation which all freemen and lovers of freedom in the world must reverence and adore — the American Union. Blending its rays with its sister stars, long may it continue to shine, and may a gracious heaven smile upon this consummation of the wishes of the two republics, now joined together in one. 'May the union be perpetual, and may it be the means of conferring benefits and blessings upon the people of all the States' is my ardent prayer. The final act of this great drama is now performed. The Republic of Texas is no more."

Early Statehood 11

THE entry of Texas into the Union touched off the War with Mexico, a war that some historians now think was planned by President James K. Polk to obtain the vast American Southwest from Mexico.

Between J. Pinckney Henderson's 1845 election and inauguration as Texas' first governor, U.S. agents tried to get Republic of Texas President Anson Jones to send troops into the contested area between the Nueces River and the Rio Grande — the so-called Nueces Strip. The Republic had claimed the Rio Grande as its southern boundary, but no civil administration was established south of the Nueces River.

Many Texans supported the move, but President Jones flatly refused to initiate any military action after Mexico's attempted recognition of Texas as a nation. Jones was proud of the fact that at the end of his term Texas was at peace with its traditional enemies — the Mexicans and Indians. Jones also argued that if there was to be war with Mexico ". . . the United States Government must take all the responsibility, and all the expense and all the labour of hostile movements upon Mexico . . . Somebody else must break up the state of peace. It shall not be me."

U.S. Gen. Zachary Taylor was sent to Corpus Christi just above the Nueces River in July 1845. In February 1846, just after Texas formally entered the Union, the general was ordered to move troops into the disputed Nueces Strip and to the mouth of the Rio Grande. A month later, Gen. Taylor marched. Mexican officials protested the entry of U.S. troops into the territory, claiming that its status was under negotiation. But Gen. Taylor proceeded to set up a camp at Point Isabel (now Port Isabel) near Brazos Santiago and to fortify a position, under the command of Maj. Jacob Brown, across the Rio Grande from Matamoros. The young officer was killed in a bombardment of the facility in May 1846, and Brownsville is named in his honor.

The U.S. army was in a state of transition at the time. It had last engaged another organized army more than 30 years before during the War of 1812. The military's principal duties in the interim had been to move Indians from the eastern United States to new lands in the west and to fight Indians if they resisted the move. West Point had been under attack in the U.S. Senate, in which the question of the compatibility of a standing army with democratic freedom was debated. The performance of West Point graduates in the ranks of junior officers during the war may have saved the institution.

After Gen. Taylor refused to leave the disputed territory, Mexican President Mariano Paredes declared the opening of a defensive war against the Americans on April 24, 1846. Gen. Anastasio Torrejon crossed the Rio Grande above Matamoros and defeated a small force of U.S. dragoons shortly thereafter. The war with Mexico was under way.

On May 8, U.S. troops moving to relieve Maj. Brown's fort encountered a Mexican force under Gen. Mariano Arista at Palo Alto, about 12 miles from today's Brownsville. Although the Mexican contingent was twice as large as the American, the light artillery tactics of the West Point graduates gave the U.S. forces a victory. The next day the Mexican army was badly mauled at Resaca de la Palma and retreated across the river. Gen. Taylor waited two weeks before crossing the Rio Grande and occupying Matamoros. In the interim, however, he sent news of the military encounters to Washington, and President Polk persuaded Congress to declare war against Mexico on May 13, arguing that American blood had been spilled on American soil. After the initial encounters, the war was fought south of the Rio Grande.

President Polk devised a plan to raise 50,000 volunteers from every section of the United States to fight the war. Texans had long dreamed of carrying a war into the interior of Mexico, and more than 8,000 volunteered for service. About 5,000 Texans actually saw action in Mexico — including Gov. Henderson, who got permission from the Legislature to join the U.S. army during the war. When the Texas Rangers volunteered, they introduced the U.S. army to a new weapon — the six-shooter. The revolvers had been used for several years on the Texas frontier, and the Rangers demanded to be equipped with Colt revolvers when they joined the army. The initial contract to manufacture 1,000 of the weapons rescued Samuel Colt from bankruptcy, and he became a successful gun manufacturer.

Although the actual fighting took place in Mexico, some military activity continued along the lower Rio Grande as the army secured transportation points across the river. In July 1846, Capt. Richard A. Gillespie passed through Laredo and asserted Texas and U.S. sovereignty. For the first time, the American flag flew over the city. A few months later, Mirabeau B. Lamar, serving as a captain in the U.S. forces, established civil administration in Laredo, and for a time the city was in a huge Nueces County that included all of the Lower Rio Grande Valley with Corpus Christi the county seat. In July 1847, the first election in Laredo attracted 40 voters, 37 of whom were Mexicans. Lamar maintained discipline among his 150 troops by banning liquor sales, and regular patrols helped curb Indian activities in the region where 700 persons reportedly had been killed in the previous 20 years.

Steamboat transportation returned to the Rio Grande for the first time since 1831, when Henry Austin left with his ship Ariel. The paddlewheelers provided an important supply link for U.S. forces along the river and in Northern Mexico throughout the war. And important historical figures like Richard King, founder of the King Ranch, and Mifflin Kenedy, another regional rancher, businessman and leader, first came to the Lower Rio Grande Valley as steamboat operators during the war.

Much farther up the Rio Grande, the war was hardly noticed. Alexander Doniphan led U.S. forces south from Sante Fe, which had been secured by Brig. Gen. Stephen Kearny, in December 1846. After a minor skirmish with Mexican forces just north of present-day El Paso, Doniphan established American jurisdiction in this part of Texas.

U.S. Gen. Winfield Scott brought the war to a close in March 1847 with the capture of Mexico City. When the Treaty of Guadalupe Hidalgo was signed on Feb. 2, 1848, the United States had acquired the American Southwest for development. And in Texas, the Rio Grande became an international boundary, and the borderlands entered a turbulent period. One agreement required the United States to prohibit raids by Plains Indians — primarily the Comanches and Apaches— into the interior of Mexico.

Texas faced many old problems and a few new ones while embarking on the early days of statehood. George T. Wood was elected governor in 1847, succeeding J. Pinckney Henderson, who did not seek re-election. The state government, like the Republic, was short of cash. Although Texas kept its public lands, the United States got the customs receipts, which had been the Republic's major source of hard cash. And the state's claim to more than 105,000 square miles of land that included territory in New Mexico, Colorado, Wyoming, Kansas and Oklahoma was under attack in Congress. Wood threatened to go to war with the United States over the disputed land, and he also supported removal of all Indians from Texas' territory.

At the end of the Mexican War, most of Texas north and west of a line drawn from Preston on the Red River through Dallas, Austin and San Antonio to Laredo on the Rio Grande was unexplored territory controlled by Indians. One of the first orders of business in the new state was to explore the vast unknown territory.

The face of Far West Texas was to change rapidly. In early 1848, gold was discovered at Sutter's Mill in California and within a few months a gold rush across the continent was on. Jack Coffee Hays and a group of Texas Rangers tried to blaze a trail from San Antonio to El Paso in early 1848, but they got lost and almost died of thirst before returning to civilization.

In March 1849, Robert S. Neighbors, John S. Ford and Indian guides set out from Torrey's trading post near today's Waco to find an accessible route to El Paso. They blazed what was called the Upper Trail, which crossed the Pecos River at Horsehead Crossing, and reached El Paso on May 2. On returning along the estimated 500-mile trip, they met wagons already moving west. At the same time, U.S. Army Capt. William Henry Chase Whiting in late May opened the lower El Paso-San Antonio route that ran to the south of Neighbors' trail. Whiting also is the first writer to use the term "Big Bend" for that region of the state. Lt. Francis T. Bryan surveyed both trails.

Ports such as Galveston and Indianola, which was established in 1849 on the west shore of Matagorda Bay, dispatched pioneers along the western trails to California. Many went through San Antonio. By the end of the year, 4,000 people had traveled along the trails through El Paso, which was to develop into a way station for gold-seekers and other adventurers. For centuries, the El Paso region had been a major point along the trade route from the interior of Mexico to Santa Fe. The California gold rush established the area along two major trade routes.

U.S. Army Capt. Randolph B. Marcy led a third expedition through unexplored Texas in 1849, covering most of West Central Texas and tying into previously established routes. Marcy's trail later was used by the Butterfield Stage Line. Also during that year, the U.S. War Department established a string of frontier forts running from Fort Duncan at Eagle Pass on the south to Fort Worth on the north. Inexperience in fighting mounted Plains Indians led the army to station infantry at the forts. One Texas editor noted that "The idea of repelling mounted Indians, the most expert horsemen in the world, with a force of foot soldiers, is ridiculous."

One group of German settlers had little trouble with the Comanches, however. John O. Meusebach became leader of the German immigration movement in Texas in 1846. He led a wagon train of some 120 settlers to the site of today's Fredericksburg in May 1846, and a year later, Meusebach made a treaty with Comanche leaders on the San Saba River, which both sides kept. This was the only successful compact between white men and Indians in the state's history.

Germans, rather than Anglos, were the first whites to push into this frontier region after annexation. Germans also migrated to the major cities, like San Antonio and Galveston, and by 1850 there were more people of German birth or parentage in Texas than there were Mexican-Texans.

The eastern part of Texas was flourishing under statehood, as had been expected. The estimated population of 150,000 at annexation grew to 212,592, including 58,161 slaves, at the first U.S. census in 1850. Large plantations were blossoming in the valleys of the Brazos and Trinity rivers where steamboat transportation to Galveston and Houston was available. Leaders in these areas, however, were worried about the lack of railroad transportation and about a labor shortage. Texas was exporting 500,000 bales of cotton a year in the 1850s, but it was felt that the land could produce three million to five million bales if adequate labor — slave labor — was available.

Although Galveston was the state's major port, Jefferson in Marion County also was a shipping center. A huge log raft on the Red River backed water into Big Cypress Bayou, making Jefferson accessible by steamship. Goods from this northeast Texas city could be shipped to markets along the Mississippi River and to New Orleans.

As the state's population grew, the regions developed distinct population characteristics. The southeast and eastern sections attracted immigrants from the Lower South, the major slaveholding states. Major plantations developed in these areas. North Texas got more Upper Southerners and Midwesterners. These immigrants were mostly small farmers and few owned slaves.

Mexican-Texans had difficulty with the Anglo immigrants. The so-called "cart war" broke out in 1857. Mexican teamsters controlled the transportation of goods from the Gulf coast to San Antonio and could charge much lower rates than their competition. But a campaign of terror was launched by Anglo haulers, especially around Goliad, in an attempt to drive the Mexican-Texans out of business. Intervention by the U.S. and Mexican governments finally brought the situation under control, but it stands as an example of the attitudes held by Anglos toward Mexican-Texans.

Cotton was by far the state's largest money crop. But corn, sweet potatoes, wheat and sugar also were produced. Saw milling and grain milling became the major industries, employing 40 percent of the manufacturing workers.

In the 1849 election, Peter H. Bell defeated incumbent George Wood. Bell's administration was distinguished by settling the land disputes with the federal government. In the Compromise of 1850, Texas gave up claims to lands that are located outside the present borders in exchange for $10 million. The total settlement with the United States, including interest on some delayed funds and compensation for fighting some Indians, amounted to $12 million. That sum was used to pay off the debt of the Republic. Most of the state taxes for several years were remitted to local governments for constructing public buildings, and $2 million was set aside for a school fund during Gov. Elisha M. Pease's administration.

Gov. Bell was the first Texas governor to be elected to a second term, and he resigned in November 1853 to take a seat in Congress. Lt. Gov. James W. Henderson served as chief executive for less than a month before Gov. Pease took office. Henderson's tenure is the shortest of any Texas governor.

Although most Texans probably could be classified as Democrats, political parties were weak during the period of early statehood. Personalities dominated most elections, and Sam Houston was the state's major political figure. Candidates were judged as to whether they were pro-Houston or anti-Houston. Early attempts to formally organize the Democrats failed, and the party had no formal structure on the local level. Statewide conventions were held only to select delegates to national conventions.

After the mid-1850s, however, opposition party victories, particularly the Know-

Nothing Party, in local elections prompted Democrats to organize a more formal party structure. The Know-Nothings were a nativist group that arose during the decade. By 1859, the party had disappeared. For most Texans, however, politics were unimportant. Voter turnouts were low. National events began to bear more heavily on the state in the 1850s, and the movement toward support for secession from the Union gained strength.

12 *Secession*

TEXAS was far removed from the centers of authority and civilization in the 1850s. Settlers in the new state were more concerned with daily problems, but as the decade passed, the national debate over slavery became a factor in Texas' politics and economic and cultural lives.

Slavery had been a major issue in American politics for decades. The issue cooled somewhat by the Missouri Compromise of 1820 that barred slavery in territory north of a line drawn by the law. But the fear of slavery spreading into the Southwest was used by opponents of Texas' initial efforts to be annexed to the United States. The issue flared anew during the Mexican War. Rep. David Wilmot added a proviso to various fiscal bills in 1846 and 1847 in the U.S. House. It would have barred slavery in any territory gained by the United States by virtue of the Mexican War. Although the House approved the Wilmot Proviso, the Senate never did. Thereafter, however, slavery began to dominate almost all the actions of Congress.

In 1854, Sen. Stephen Douglas, D-Ill., sponsored legislation that in essence repealed the Missouri Compromise by allowing the residents of the territories of Kansas and Nebraska to decide whether they wanted slavery. Since both territories were north of the line drawn against involuntary servitude, abolitionists bitterly opposed the measure. Sam Houston, serving as one of the state's first U.S. Senators, won the undying hatred of Southern Democrats and many Texans by opposing Douglas' legislation. Always a strong Unionist, Houston's vote against the Kansas-Nebraska Act in 1854 cost him any chance of being reappointed to the Senate by the Texas Legislature five years later.

In addition, Texas' population almost tripled in the decade between 1850 and 1860 when 604,215 people were counted, including 182,921 slaves. (Indians were not counted.) Many of these new settlers came from the Lower South and had strong ties to the institution of slavery, even if they were not slaveholders. Population studies indicate that three-quarters of the Texas population and two-thirds of the farmers did not own slaves. But slaveholders controlled 60 to 70 percent of the wealth of the state and produced 90 percent of the cotton. The slaveowning farmers also tightened their grip on state politics during the decade. Studies indicate that in 1850, 41.4 percent of the state's officeholders were from the slaveholding class; a decade later, 51.1 percent of the officeholders also were slaveholders. Politics in antebellum Texas was a mix of democracy and aristocracy. But despite the lack of economic restrictions on free male suffrage, the slaveowning elite dominated politics.

In addition to the political power of the slaveholders, they also provided role models for new immigrants to the state. Land was cheap or free in Texas, as it always had been, and since land ownership was an element of social status, the state represented economic opportunity to newcomers. These new Texans saw slave ownership as another step up the economic ladder, regardless of whether they owned slaves or not. Slave ownership was an economic goal, for with slaves more land could be cultivated and more cotton grown. The attitude was prevalent in areas of Texas where slaveholding was not widespread or even practical. Against this background were the politics of Texas played and the passions for secession from the Union fanned through the 1850s.

Much of the decade of the 1850s was tranquil as Texans went about the business of developing the vast state. Even the frontier areas were relatively peaceful as the U.S. Army became more expert at handling the mounted Plains Indians. With more than 3,000 troops stationed in Texas by 1853, the Indians were quiet. The Texas Legislature even agreed to provide the U.S. government with up to 50,000 acres of land to set up reservations to pacify the state's Indian tribes. Two reservations were set up on the Clear Fork of the Brazos River in West Central Texas. One in Throckmorton County was set aside for the Comanches, and the other in Young County was to accommodate Indians from various other groups. By 1855, these reservations were in operation under the direction of Indian Agent Robert S. Neighbors. Camp Cooper was established near the Comanche Reservation and the Second Cavalry kept peace in the area. Several well-known officers commanded the small post, including Albert Sidney Johnston, Robert E. Lee and John B. Hood. When established, these reservations were in advance of the frontier settlement line. But the surrounding country soon was settled. Anglo hostility toward the Indians was fanned when raiding parties began to prey on settlers. Although there was no evidence that reservation Indians were involved, the frontier settlers began to demand removal of the Indians from Texas. By 1858, Neighbors was convinced that the move was necessary, and in August 1859, the reservations were closed and the Indians moved north of the Red River. Settlers quickly claimed the reservation land. The move did not end the Indian raids. Many of the transported Indians felt that the government had acted in bad faith and joined the attacks on settlements in Texas. As the decade drew to a close, the army became less effective in combatting the guerrilla tactics of the Indians, and the breakdown in defense had political repercussions.

In addition to the constant Indian problem, another fact of life was becoming apparent to settlers along the frontier. By 1860, the Texas frontier had moved westward to a line that ran irregularly from Henrietta on the north to Fort Belknap in Young County, Palo Pinto, Brownwood, Llano, Kerrville and Uvalde to Laredo. West of this line was a new land for the settlers from the woodlands of the South and the eastern United States. The treeless prairies and the marked reduction in rainfall posed a new barrier. New farming techniques would be needed to cope with the different environment, and the Indians must be subdued. Cattle ranching would prosper on the prairies, but the industry was in its infancy at the time. The frontier settlers found markets at the military forts and the communities around them. But development of the region had stalled.

In Austin, the 1850s were a relatively progressive period. Relieved of public debt, the state government began to debate economic issues. One of the most important was the development of railroads. One plan that was seriously considered would have made railroad construction a state responsibility. But in 1856, the Legislature decided that private corporations would build the railroad system with generous state aid. Grants of money were used, or the railway lines would be given 16 alternate sections of land (10,240 acres) for each mile of track built. Construction of the first railroad to move cotton and sugar to Galveston — the Buffalo Bayou, Brazos and Colorado Railway — began in 1851, and by 1853, 20 miles of track had been built. By 1860, almost 404 miles of railroad existed, mostly in the Houston-Galveston area.

In addition, other transportation was available. In North Texas, ox carts were the primary source of transportation for commerce. Although slow, the animals were reliable, especially in dry weather. By 1860, 31 stagecoach lines were operating in Texas, including some tied into intercontinental travel. The Butterfield Line began operation in the state in 1858 running from St. Louis and Memphis through Texas to San Francisco. Mail service between San Antonio and San Diego, Calif., commenced in 1857.

One economic problem that the state government could not and the federal government would not solve was the labor shortage. Cotton raising at the time was labor intensive, and in the minds of the plantation owners, that meant slave labor. Importation of African slaves had been prohibited in the United States in 1808 and in the early days of the Texas Republic. An illegal trade flourished in Texas, however, and hundreds, if not thousands, of the slaves in the state had been imported through this system. But some of the state's leadership saw the reopening of the slave trade as a solution to the labor shortage. More slaves also would bring the price down, and small landowners could afford to acquire involuntary labor. The view was hardly universal, however, because free laborers among the European immigrants saw it as a move to eliminate their jobs or to keep wages low. Support for reopening the slave trade also was light among the small farmers of North Texas and the frontier.

An outgrowth of the labor problem was strong private support in Texas for the filibuster expeditions to Cuba and Central America in the 1850s. Proponents of slavery thought it would be advantageous to have slave colonies in these areas to supply the labor needs of the state.

Politics quickened in the mid-1850s with the appearance of the Know-Nothing Party, which based its platform on a pro-American, anti-immigrant foundation. Because of the large number of foreign-born settlers, the party attracted many Anglo voters. In 1854, the Know-Nothings elected candidates to city offices in San Antonio, and a year later, the mayor of Galveston was elected with the party's backing. Also in 1855, the Know-Nothings elected 20 representatives and five senators to the Legislature. The successes spurred the Democrats to serious party organization. For the first time, the party nominated statewide candidates at a convention in 1857. Hardin Runnels, a former lieutenant governor and speaker of the Texas House, got the nomination at the convention held in Waco. Sam Houston returned to Texas to seek the governorship as an independent, but he also got Know-Nothing backing. Democrats were organized, however, and Houston was dealt his only election defeat in his political career.

Runnels was a strong states-rights Democrat and irritated many Texans during his administration by advocating reopening the slave trade. His popularity on the frontier also dropped when Indian raids became more severe, and neither the state nor federal governments could stop them.

Most Texans still were ambivalent about secession. The Union was seen as a protector of physical and economic stability. No threats to person or property were perceived in remaining attached to the United States. In 1859, Houston again challenged Runnels and based his campaign on Unionism. Combined with Houston's personal popularity, his position on the secession issue apparently satisfied most voters, for they gave him a solid victory over the more radical Runnels. In addition, Unionists

A.J. Hamilton and John H. Reagan won the state's two congressional seats. Texans gave the states-rights Democrats a sound whipping at the polls.

Within a few months, however, events were to change radically the political atmosphere in the state. The defense of slavery was the major concern. But other issues arose that secessionists could use in their arguments for withdrawal from the Union. Shortly after Houston's election, word of John Brown's raid on Harper's Ferry in Virginia reached Texas. States-rights proponents pointed out that it was an example of militant Northerners willing to resort to violence to impose their views on the South. On the frontier, the army could not control Indian raids, and with the later refusal of a Republican-controlled Congress to provide essential aid in fighting Indians, the federal government fell into disrepute. On the Texas border, Juan Cortina, a Mexican hero-bandit, captured Brownsville for a time, and rumor had it that he was backed by abolitionists.

Each breakdown in order or failure to provide adequate services, like frontier defense, threw the efficacy of the Union into doubt. Secessionists played on the growing distrust. Then in the summer of 1860, a series of fires in cities around the state aroused fears that an abolitionist plot was afoot and that a slave uprising might be at hand — a traditional concern in a slaveholding society. Vigilantes lynched blacks and Northerners across Texas, and a siege mentality developed. Texans who once viewed the Union as a beneficent protector now wondered if the institution was obsolete. When the election of Republican Abraham Lincoln — though he was not on the ballot in Texas — as president became apparent, secessionists went to work in earnest. Pleas were made to Gov. Houston to call the Legislature into session to consider a secession ordinance. Houston refused, hoping the passions would cool. They did not. Finally, Oran M. Roberts and other secessionist leaders issued a call to the counties to hold elections and send delegates to a convention in Austin to consider the secession ordinance. Ninety-two of 122 counties responded, and on Jan. 28,1861, the convention convened. Houston called the Legislature into session to try to thwart the convention, but the lawmakers legalized the meeting, noting that the state constitution delegated to the citizens the power to "alter, reform or abolish" their government in any manner they felt expedient. Houston then insisted that any action of the convention must be ratified by voters.

Roberts chaired the secession convention, and it quickly passed the secession ordinance on Feb. 1. Only eight delegates voted against it, while 166 supported secession. An election was called for Feb. 23, 1861, and the ensuing campaign was marked by intimidation, intolerance and violence. Opponents of secession were often intimidated — except Gov. Houston, who courageously stumped the state opposing withdrawal from the Union. Houston argued that the convention had overstepped its authority by joining Texas to the Confederacy. The governor declared that if Texas was to leave the Union, it should revert to its status as an independent republic. Only one-fourth of the state's population had been in Texas during the days of independence and the argument carried no weight. On election day, 76 percent of 61,000 voters approved secession, which would become official March 2, 1861, exactly 25 years after Texas had proclaimed its independence from Mexico. However, only Edwin Waller had the distinction of signing both the secession ordinance in 1861 and the Declaration of Independence in 1836.

President Lincoln reportedly sent Gov. Houston a letter offering 50,000 federal troops to keep Texas in the Union. But after a meeting with other Unionists, Houston declined the offer. "I love Texas too well to bring strife and bloodshed upon her," the governor declared. On March 16, Houston refused to take an oath of loyalty to the Confederacy and was replaced in office by Lt. Gov. Edward Clark.

Texas then embarked on one of the darkest periods in its history.

13 *Civil War*

TEXAS fared fairly well through the Civil War. The state did not suffer the devastation of its Southern colleagues. Only on a few occasions did Union troops occupy territory in Texas, except in the El Paso area. A manpower shortage did develop as so many men joined the Confederate army or served in the ranks of state troops.

Texas' cotton was important to the Confederate war effort, for it could be transported from Gulf ports when other Southern shipping lanes were blockaded. Some goods became difficult to buy, but unlike other Southern states, Texas still received consumer goods because of the trade that was carried on through Mexico during the war. Public order did break down, particularly during the latter part of the war. Army deserters often passed through on the way to Mexico, and with so many men in military service, some communities were left poorly defended or policed. These hardships hardly compared to the damage done by military operations and by the complete social disruption in other states. Texas was virtually without manufacturing facilities prior to the war, however. Several small munitions factories were set up in the state. Bullets were made at the State Land Office in Austin, for example. And the state penitentiary became a major manufacturer of cloth for the Confederacy.

After the secession ordinance was approved by voters, the convention reconvened on March 2, 1861, in Austin. Although the question of joining the Confederacy was not on the ballot, most Texans felt approval was implied. So the convention accepted the provisional government of the Confederacy, and delegates to Montgomery were instructed to apply for statehood. The action was unnecessary since the Confederate Congress already had passed a law admitting Texas as a state.

Military operations began in Texas even before voters approved the secession ordinance. The secession convention appointed a public safety committee to see to preparations for war. The initial goal was to take charge of U.S. army facilities in the state.

Ben McCulloch led a contingent of Texas troops to San Antonio. After brief negotiations, U.S. Maj. Gen. David E. Twiggs surrendered U.S. forces — about 2,700 men scattered across the state — and facilities to the Texans on Feb. 15, 1861. Twiggs was later court-martialed for his action. Like many U.S. army officers, the commander of the Department of Texas was a southern sympathizer and later was given a commission in the Confederate army. On the other hand, Col. Robert E. Lee refused to take an oath of allegiance to the Confederacy before leaving Texas and did not leave the U.S. army until he reached Washington and properly resigned.

Col. William C. Young and Lt. Col. James W. Throckmorton secured three federal posts north of the Red River in May 1861 without firing a shot. Throckmorton, a future governor, was one of many Unionists who opposed secession but fought for Texas in the Confederacy.

Secessionists had argued that the North would not contest the dissolution of the Union. They felt that the great commercial nations of Europe would not allow the North to disrupt the important cotton trade. Therefore early in the war, the Confederate government did not think a large army would be needed. Even if hostilities broke out, it was felt that any war would be short. Most of these arguments were overturned shortly after the firing on Fort Sumter, South Carolina.

Thousands of Texans volunteered for service in the Confederate army as soon as hostilities broke out between the North and South. And after Francis R. Lubbock was elected governor in 1861, he worked to see that the state also fulfilled its manpower quotas under the Confederate conscription law of April 1862. Texans fought in every Confederate campaign in the war. Confederate President Jefferson Davis was highly complimentary of the prowess of Texas soldiers in an address to the troops in Virginia, noting that "The troops from other states have their reputations to gain. The sons of the defenders of the Alamo have theirs to maintain." Units like Hood's Brigade and Terry's Texas Rangers became legendary. Sul Ross, a future governor, fought in more than 130 battles, entering the war a private and emerging as an officer. Although accurate figures are not available, historians estimate that between 70,000 and 90,000 Texans fought for the Confederacy, and between 2,000 and 3,000, including some former slaves, saw service in the Union army.

Texas was important to the Confederacy for several reasons. It had a great reservoir of men with some military experience. With more than 400 miles of shoreline, the state could provide important ports, and as the most westerly of the Southern states, Texas held the key to Confederate expansion to the west.

Texas also had some unique problems. It had to defend three of its borders from hostile forces: from the Union on the Gulf coast, from the Mexicans in the borderlands, and from the Indians on the frontier, including along the Red River. Consequently there were tensions between the state and Confederate governments at times during the war. Some Texas governors, like Pendleton Murrah, felt that more manpower should be devoted to frontier defense, and consequently he was not always cooperative with demands from Richmond for additional troops.

Texas' coastline was completely without defenses when the Civil War broke out. Slave labor was used to fortify Sabine Pass, Galveston, Matagorda Island, Aransas Pass and Port Isabel. The work was speeded up when the Union blockade of the Gulf ports reached Texas in July 1861.

On land, Texans participated in one of the war's most ambitious early campaigns. Col. John R. Baylor had taken Union posts in southern New Mexico soon after the war broke out. In late 1861, Gen. Henry H. Sibley was ordered to conduct in the upper Rio Grande Valley a major campaign designed to cut the Union off from California. With 3,000 men, Sibley captured Santa Fe and Albuquerque in early 1862. But the campaign failed when Union soldiers captured the Texans' supply train during the battle of Glorieta Pass in northern New Mexico. Sibley's forces left New Mexico in complete disarray. After the Texans straggled through the El Paso area, Union Col. E.E. Eyre, leading the California Column, occupied the Far West Texas outpost for the remainder of the war. If Gen. Sibley had been successful, the Civil War might have turned out differently. Subsequent campaigns against Union forces in California would have been necessary, but there was support for the Confederate cause in Southern California. And defenses against counterattacks by the Union would have had to be maintained. But with Confederates in control of California's gold, lumber and ports, many of the South's difficulties could have been avoided. The gold would have supported Confederate money; the lumber would have provided ships, and the ports would have opened trade, since the Union could not have blockaded ports on both the Gulf and Pacific coasts. With Sibley's defeat, these opportunities were lost.

One of the most important unsung battles of the Civil War may not have been fought by Americans at all, but by Mexican troops under the command of a native of Texas, Ignacio Zaragoza, at Puebla near Mexico City on May 5, 1862. The French were attempting to place Maximilian on the throne of Mexico. But Gen. Zaragoza defeated the French army at Puebla, delaying the conquest of Mexico for more than a year. Some historians think the French would have supported the Confederate cause if they had gained full control of Mexico at the time. If so, more ports would have been open to Confederate trading, and the character of the Civil War might have changed. Mexico's annual Cinco de Mayo celebration commemorates Zaragoza's victory. He was born near Goliad in 1829.

Texans became disenchanted with the Confederate government early in the war. Gov. Lubbock had to levy direct state taxes for the first time since the Compromise of 1850, and by war's end, the Confederacy had collected more than $37 million in the state. But most of the complaints about the government centered on Brig. Gen. Paul O. Hebert, the Confederate commander of the Department of Texas. In April 1862, Gen. Hebert declared martial law without notifying state officials. Opposition to the South's new conscription law, which exempted persons owning more than 15 slaves among other categories of exemptions, prompted the action. In November 1862, the commander prohibited the export of cotton except under government control, and this proved a disastrous policy. And the final blow came when Gen. Hebert failed to defend Galveston and it fell into Union hands in the fall of 1862.

Maj. Gen. John B. Magruder replaced Hebert and was much more popular. The new commander's first actions were to combat the Union offensive against Texas ports. Sabine Pass had been closed in September 1862 by the Union blockade, and Galveston was in Northern hands. On Jan. 1, 1863, Magruder retook Galveston with the help of two "cotton-clad" gunboats, the Bayou City and Neptune. Decks of the two steamboats were lined with cotton bales for protection, and sharpshooters proved devastating in battles against the Union fleet. Three weeks later, Magruder used two other cotton-clad steamboats to break the Union blockade of Sabine Pass, and two of the state's major ports were reopened.

Late in 1863, the Union launched a major offensive against the Texas coast that was partly successful. On Sept. 8, however, Texas Lt. Dick Dowling and 42 men fought off a 1,500-man Union invasion force at Sabine Pass. In a brief battle, Dowling's command sank two Union gunboats and put the other invasion ships to flight.

Gen. N.J.T. Dana was more successful at the mouth of the Rio Grande. On Nov. 1, 1863, he landed 7,000 troops at Brazos Santiago, and five days later, Union forces entered Brownsville, which had been set on fire by the retreating Confederate Gen. Hamilton Bee.

Union control of Brownsville and the Lower Rio Grande Valley forced the rerouting of the cotton trail across Texas. Brownsville and Matamoros were major shipping points for Southern cotton. The Rio Grande was declared an international river in the Treaty of Guadalupe Hidalgo in 1848, and it could not be legally blockaded by the Union. Texas shippers operated under the Mexican flag, and the region boomed economically from the trade. After the Union took the mouth of the Rio

Grande, the cotton trail was shifted up river to Laredo and Eagle Pass, where the river could be crossed. Then the cotton was transported overland to Matamoros.

Texas Unionists led by E.J. Davis were active in the Valley, moving as far up river as Rio Grande City. Col. John S. "Rip" Ford, commanding state troops, finally pushed the Union soldiers out of Brownsville in July 1864, reopening the important port for the Confederacy. Most of the Union troops were withdrawn, however, to be used in an invasion of Texas along the Red River through Louisiana.

Union Maj. Gen. Nathaniel Banks conceived the invasion, planning to mass troops in Louisiana to march into Texas. The plan was thwarted with Confederate victories at the battles of Mansfield, La., and Pleasant Hill, La., in April 1864. Most of Texas never saw a Union soldier during the war. And the ones they might have seen were in the prisoner-of-war camps operated in Kerr County, at Hempstead or the largest, Camp Ford, near Tyler, which could accommodate 5,000 prisoners.

There was considerable fighting, however, on the Texas frontier. Early in the war, the Confederates tried to man some frontier forts, but the troops were transferred to East Texas in 1864. State attempts to patrol the frontier were not successful in stopping Indian raids. As the defenses grew weaker, the Indians became bolder, raiding in groups numbering in the hundreds rather than in the traditional small bands. Many settlers moved to more secure areas, and the state's frontier receded up to 100 miles eastward in some areas. In many cases, the settlers who remained on the frontier "forted up" in private facilities. Several families would band together for protection, and crude stockades and other breastworks were constructed. Probably the largest of these private forts was Fort Davis in northwest Stephens County, where more than 100 people gathered.

As the war dragged on, the mood of Texas changed. Despite the lack of devastation, many families had sacrificed on the home front. With the manpower shortage, many women had to operate plantations and farms with little help. There also was a shortage of consumer goods and prices were greatly inflated. Slaveholders had been exempt from service in many cases, and the homefolks began to feel that they were sacrificing loved ones and suffering hardship so cotton speculators could profit. Public order broke down as refugees flocked to Texas. And slaves from other states were sent to Texas for safekeeping. When the war ended, there were an estimated 400,000 slaves in Texas, more than double the number counted in the 1860 census.

Morale was low in Texas in early 1865. Soldiers at Galveston and Houston began to mutiny. At Austin, Confederate soldiers raided the state treasury in March, and found only $5,000 in specie. Units broke up, and the army simply dissolved before Gen. Lee surrendered at Appomattox in April 1865.

A month earlier, Texas had an opportunity to enter into a separate peace. U.S. Maj. Gen. Lew Wallace, an unofficial representative of Gen. Ulysses S. Grant, met with Confederate Brig. Gen. John E. Slaughter and Col. John S. Ford at Port Isabel on March 10, 1865. Gen. Wallace offered Texas and the Trans-Mississippi Department a separate peace, so Union and Confederate forces could unite in a show of force to the French in Mexico. The offer was presented to the Confederate command in Houston, where it was rejected. U.S. officials were concerned that they would have to enforce the Monroe Doctrine in Mexico, where both the French and English had interests. If the offer had been accepted, Texas possibly could have been spared the agonies of Reconstruction.

The last battle of the Civil War was fought more than a month after Lee's surrender. Col. Ford led a troop of Confederates in the battle of Palmito Ranch near Brownsville on May 11, 1865. After the victory, the troops learned of the surrender.

On June 19, 1865, Gen. Gordon Granger, under the command of Gen. Philip M. Sheridan, arrived in Galveston with 1,800 men to begin the Union occupation of Texas. Gen. Granger proclaimed the emancipation of the slaves. And A.J. Hamilton, a Unionist and former Texas congressman, was named provisional governor of Texas by President Andrew Johnson. Gov. Pendleton Murrah, elected in 1863, fled to Mexico with other Confederate officials, who feared prosecution for their part in the rebellion. Texas was embarked on Reconstruction.

Reconstruction 14

TEXAS was in turmoil when the Civil War ended. Although thousands of the state's men had died in the conflict, the state was hardly touched by the war. Indian raids had caused as much damage as the skirmishes with the Union army along the Gulf coast and in the Lower Rio Grande Valley.

Even worse, confusion reigned. No one knew what to expect from the conquering Union army. Gov. Pendleton Murrah had tried to call the Legislature into special session to repeal the secession ordinance and to ease Texas' re-entry into the Union. But it became apparent that federal authorities would not accept the actions of the Confederate government as legitimate.

As the Confederate army dissolved in April and May 1865, lawlessness prevailed across the state. Confusion seemed to paralyze authorities.

Upon landing at Galveston on June 19, 1865, Union Gen. Gordon Granger dispatched troops to the population centers of the state to restore civil authority. But only a handful of the 50,000 federal troops that came to Texas was stationed in the interior. Most were sent to the Rio Grande as a show of force against the French in Mexico. Clandestine aid was supplied to Mexican President Benito Juarez in his fight against the French and the Mexican royalists.

Texas' frontier, which had suffered an increasing number of Indian raids at the end of the war, got no relief. The federal government banned local militia, fearing that the Confederates would continue to fight a guerrilla war. But the frontier forts were not remanned, and the prohibition against a militia denied settlers a means of self-defense. Provisional Gov. A.J. Hamilton, however, did allow some counties to organize local police forces to work with the military.

The emancipation proclamation issued by Gen. Granger added to the confusion. Thousands of former black slaves were freed. The Union had no plan for providing direction for the freed men. Some stayed on the plantations, but others left immediately, eager to exercise their new freedom. Many blacks migrated to the cities where they felt the federal soldiers would provide protection. Still others traveled the countryside, seeking family members and loved ones from whom they had been separated during the war. Unaccustomed to free blacks, white Texans feared a breakdown in law and order. The status of the newly freed slaves in society also was not defined. And not the least of the problems was the failure of slaveholders to plan for emancipation.

The Freedman's Bureau, authorized by Congress in March 1865, began operation in September 1865 under Gen. E.M. Gregory. It had the responsibility to provide education, relief aid, labor supervision and judicial protection for the newly freed slaves. The bureau was most successful in opening schools for blacks. Education was a priority because 95 percent of the freed slaves were illiterate. The agency also was partially successful in getting blacks back to work on plantations under reasonable labor contracts. But because it was perceived as being involved in partisan politics, many Texans disliked the bureau. It was disbanded in 1870 when President Ulysses S. Grant declared Reconstruction at an end.

Some plantation owners harbored hopes that they would be paid for their property loss when the slaves were freed. In some cases, the slaves were not released from plantations for up to a year. To add to the confusion, some former slaves had the false notion that the federal government was going to parcel out the plantation lands to them. These blacks simply bided their time, waiting for the division of land.

In Washington, President Andrew Johnson tried to pursue Lincoln's ideas for reconstruction. The rebellious states would be brought back into the Union as quickly as possible. As Johnson executed the plan, Congress became enraged. Public opinion in the North required the rebels to be punished for secession.

A.J. Hamilton assumed the provisional governorship on June 22, 1865. He planned to restore civil government as quickly as possible, and soon a series of meetings was held with unionists. Then Hamilton set up a statewide system of voter registration. Prospective voters had to take loyalty oaths to the Union, and former Confederate officials and wealthy planters had to get presidential pardons to regain full civil rights.

Voter registration went slowly, and violence was common. Hamilton interpreted these actions as acts of disloyalty to the Union and delayed calling a constitutional convention as long as possible.

Adding to the confusion was the fact that unionists were split over how the state should be readmitted to the Union. Some unionists who had stayed in Texas during the war had suffered discrimination and intimidation from Confederates, and they wanted revenge. Other unionists had fought for the Confederacy and wanted Reconstruction to be as quick as possible. And a third group had been forced to leave and live in the North. This group had a good idea of what the victors had in mind for the South and Texas.

Under pressure from President Johnson, Hamilton called for an election of delegates to a constitutional convention in January 1866, and the convention convened on Feb. 6, 1866. Hamilton told the parley what was expected: Former slaves were to be given civil rights; the secession ordinance had to be repealed; Civil War debt had to be repudiated; and slavery was to be abolished with the ratification of the Thirteenth Amendment.

Many delegates to the convention were former secessionists, and there was little support for compromise. J.W. Throckmorton, a unionist and one of eight men who had opposed secession in the convention of 1861, was elected chairman of the convention. But a coalition of conservative unionists and Democrats controlled the convention. As a consequence, Texas took limited steps toward appeasing the victorious North. Slavery was abolished, and blacks were given some civil rights. But they still could not vote and were barred from testifying in trials against whites. No action was taken on the Thirteenth Amendment, which abolished slavery, because, the argument went, it already had been ratified. Otherwise the constitution written by the convention followed closely the Constitution of 1845. President Johnson in August 1866 accepted the constitution and declared insurrection over in Texas, the last of the Southern states so accepted under Presidential Reconstruction.

Throckmorton was elected governor in June, when other state and local officials were selected by voters under the new constitution. However, Texans had not learned a lesson from the war. When the Legislature met, a series of laws limiting the rights of blacks was passed. In labor disputes, for example, the employers were to be the final arbitrators. The codes also bound an entire family's labor, not just the head of the household, to an employer. Many of the laws later were overturned by the Freedman's Bureau or military authorities. Funding for black education would be limited to what could be provided by black taxpayers. Since few blacks owned land or had jobs, that provision effectively denied education to black children. The thrust of the laws and the attitude of the lawmakers was clear, however: Blacks simply were not to be considered full citizens.

In addition, the Legislature appointed O.M. Roberts and David G. Burnet, both ardent secessionists, to the U.S. Senate. Neither was seated by Radical Republicans in the upper house.

Radical unionists, led by Hamilton, felt that the constitutional convention had not gone far enough in providing full rights of citizenship to blacks. They appealed to federal authorities in Washington, and the Congress in March 1867 responded with a Reconstruction plan of its own. The Southern states were declared to have no legal government, and the former Confederacy was divided into districts to be administered by the military until satisfactory Reconstruction was effected. Texas and Louisiana made up the Fifth Military District under the command of Gen. Philip H. Sheridan.

The freeing of the slaves threw the Texas economy into a crisis. Plantation owners were hard-pressed to attract adequate field labor, especially for harvesting. And since the state's cash economy depended on cotton production, a recession resulted. But in South and West Texas a new industry was developing. In 1866, an estimated 260,000 head of cattle were driven to market outside the state, primarily to Sedalia, Mo. Cattle raising had been basically a hide and tallow industry before the war. But the North and Midwest had developed a taste for beef, and there were thousands of head of wild cattle in Texas for the taking. During the war, herds had not been tended, and unbranded cattle were common across the state. South Texas and the coastal prairies had a long tradition of cattle raising, dating from the Spanish colonial period. Other traditions had come to Northeast Texas and the Piney Woods of East Texas from the eastern United States. And West Central Texas was among the major source areas for cattle for the emerging business.

The great trail drives moved northward to Kansas in 1867 after Texas drovers encountered resistance from farmers in Missouri and Kansas. "Texas fever," which afflicted cattle in these areas, became a problem, killing the native animals although not affecting Texas cattle. The opening of railheads at Abilene, Kan., and other locations gave Texans alternate markets for their herds. But growth of the cattle industry helped offset some of the problems brought on by the labor shortage in the cotton industry.

Gov. Throckmorton clashed often with Gen. Sheridan and Gen. Charles Griffin, commander of the Texas subdistrict of the military district. The governor thought the state had gone far enough in establishing rights for the newly freed slaves and other matters. One federal official noted that Texas resisted Reconstruction so strenuously because it "had not been whipped" in the war. Finally in August 1867, Throckmorton and other state officials were removed from office by Sheridan because they were considered an "impediment to the reconstruction." E.M. Pease, the former two-term governor and a unionist, was named provisional governor by the military authorities.

A new constitutional convention was called by Gen. Winfield S. Hancock, who replaced Sheridan in November 1867. For the first time, blacks were allowed to participate in the elections selecting delegates. Stricter regulations also disenfranchised between 7,000-10,000 former Confederates. A total of 59,633 whites and 49,497 blacks, however, registered for the election. Many whites stayed away from the polls on election day, but the convention call was approved. Delegates gathered on June 1, 1868. The Constitution of 1869 granted full rights of citizenship to blacks, created a system of education, delegated broad powers to the governor and generally reflected the views of the state's unionists. Deliberations got bogged down on partisan political matters, however, and the convention spent $200,000, an unheard-of sum. At one point, Radical Republicans, arguing that parts of Texas were ungovernable because of the continuing violence, tried to create a State of West Texas, west of the Colorado River, but Congress would not accept dividing the state.

Gov. Pease, disgusted with the convention and the military authorities, resigned in September 1869, and Texas had no chief executive until January 1870, when E.J. Davis took office. The new constitution was approved by voters in November 1869, and Davis was elected governor.

The Republican Party formally organized in Texas in April 1867. Despite internal problems, Radical Republicans, with almost 100 percent support from black voters, controlled the Legislature. Meeting in February 1870, the Legislature passed a series of so-called "obnoxious acts." These created a state militia under the governor's control; created a state police force, also controlled by the governor; postponed the 1870 general election to 1872; enabled the governor to appoint more than 8,500 local officeholders, and granted subsidized bonds for railroad construction at a rate of $10,000 a mile. For the first time, however, a system of public education was created. The law required compulsory attendance of school for four months a year, set aside one-quarter of the state's annual revenue for education and levied a poll tax to support education. Schools also were to be integrated, which enraged many white Texans.

Heavy-handed tactics were used by Radical Republicans in the Senate, where they held only a slim majority. When Democrats and some moderates walked out to break a quorum while considering the militia bill, the Senate leadership had them arrested. Four senators were returned to the capitol to give the Senate a quorum, and 10 were jailed for several days while the upper house considered many of the controversial parts of Gov. Davis' program.

Violence was rampant in Texas. One study found that between the close of the Civil War in 1865 and June 1868, 1,035 were murdered in Texas, including 486 blacks, mostly the victims of white violence. Gov. Davis argued that he needed broad police powers to restore order. And despite their unpopularity, the state police and militia — blacks made up 40 percent of the police and a majority of the militia — brought the lawlessness under control in many areas.

The Davis administration was the most unpopular in Texas' history. In fairness, historians have noted that Davis did not feel that whites could be trusted to assure the rights of the newly freed blacks. Therefore many of the governor's actions that have been interpreted as abuses of power were, in the governor's view, his constitutional responsibility. Davis personally was a man of integrity. But he made some bad appointments. His adjutant general, James Davidson, absconded with $37,000 in state funds in 1872, and other officials and legislators were accused of corruption.

State taxes also skyrocketed during the Davis administration and gave moderate Republicans and Democrats a major issue to use against him. E.M. Pease chaired a taxpayers' convention that met in Austin in September 1871 to protest the levies. A.J. Hamilton pointed out that in 1866, state taxes had amounted to 15 cents per $100 worth of property; by 1871, the tax rate had risen to $2.175 per $100 evaluation. Local taxes also rose because communities would offer grants to attract railroads.

Democrats, aided by moderate Republicans, regained control of the Legislature in the 1872 elections — at which Austin also was designated the permanent capital of Texas. In 1873, the lawmakers set about stripping the governor of many of the powers the Radical Republicans had given him.

Through the turbulent period, Texas' economy rebounded. Cotton production had dropped more than 80,000 bales between 1859 and 1869 to 350,629 bales. But by 1873, Texas re-emerged as the leading cotton-producing state. Manufacturing increased with production at 2,399 plants increasing to $11.5 million in 1870 from $6.6 million at 983 plants in 1860. The cattle business that sprang up after the war moved 700,000 head to Kansas in 1871 in the greatest drive in history. So despite the political dissension, Texas was progressing economically.

Gov. Davis also was a champion of frontier defense, which was often neglected by the federal government. Ranger companies were authorized for patrol, but when that proved too expensive, local militia were used by the state. The federal government was slow to re-establish frontier forts. One reason was that Congress was working on a new Indian policy. Another apparently was that federal authorities did not know the situation on the frontier. Gen. Sheridan once answered critics of frontier defense with the charge that more unionists and blacks were being killed by Confederates than were dying at the hands of Indians. He may have been right. An incomplete report from county judges found that between May 1865 and July 1867, 163 persons had been killed by Indians on the frontier, 43 captured and 24 wounded.

But attempts to pacify Indians on reservations did not ease Texas' plight. The Comanches and Kiowas in particular did not look on Texans as Americans. Texas was a place apart from the rest of the United States in their minds. One Comanche chief insolently told an Indian agent that, if the Great Father did not want the young reservation Indians raiding Texas, Texas should be moved.

The ferocity of the raids was vividly brought home to Gen. William T. Sherman, general in chief of the army, in May 1871. He and a small party were inspecting frontier facilities and traveled from Fort Belknap to Fort Richardson. Shortly after reaching Fort Richardson, survivors of a wagon train that had followed the military party reached the fort. They told a story of brutal murder and torture during an Indian attack at Salt Creek in Young County. Gen. Sherman immediately ordered Col. Ranald Mackenzie to launch a vigorous campaign against the Indians. Three Kiowa chiefs, Satank, Satanta and Big Tree, were arrested on the reservation for the crime, and Satanta and Big Tree were tried in state court. At the request of Indian authorities, Gov. Davis pardoned them after a short time in prison.

Cols. Mackenzie and Nelson A. Miles conducted a vigorous campaign against the Comanche and Kiowa, breaking their backs in the Red River campaign. For the first time, the army pursued the Indians to their previous sanctuaries on the Texas Plains. And in a September 1874 engagement in Palo Duro Canyon, the Indians' horses were killed. Without the animals for transportation, the braves soon reported to the reservations. Texas' Indian problems were at an end.

The political turmoil also ended with the gubernatorial election of 1873 when Richard Coke easily defeated Davis. Davis tried to get federal authorities to keep him in office until April, but President Grant refused to intervene. And in January of 1874, Democrats were in control of state government again. The end of Reconstruction concluded the turbulent Civil War era, although the attitudes that developed during the period lasted well into the 20th century.

15 *Retrenchment*

WHEN Gov. Richard Coke and conservative Democrats regained control of state government in 1874, they had power but little else. Texas' economy, unlike that of the rest of the defeated South, was not in ruins. Although there were labor problems, railroads expanded, manufacturing grew and cotton production returned to pre-war levels by 1873. But the economic Panic of 1873 slowed recovery.

Pre-Civil War Texas' economy was based on two factors: slaves and land. After the war, the slaves were free, and land values dropped precipitously. And little hard currency was to be had. Confederate money was worthless, and few Texans had acquired much gold during the war.

Gov. E.J. Davis' administration also was accused of extravagance. But Texans bore a tax burden much lighter than other Southern states.

Railroad construction had resumed after the war, and the total mileage tripled to almost 1,500 miles before the economic panic curtailed work in 1873.

Coke and the Legislature therefore had little choice in financing state government. The Democrats chose to cut state spending dramatically. Although the Davis administration was accused of profligate spending, many Democrats had supported the appropriations. With Davis out of office, however, public education was cut to the bone, the prison system was put on a pay-as-you-go basis by continuing a tragic policy initiated under Davis of leasing convicts to private contractors.

A constitutional convention was called in 1875 to rewrite the state constitution, a hated vestige of Radical Republican rule. Again, every avenue to cutting spending at any level of government was explored. Salaries of public officials were slashed. The number of offices was reduced. Judgeships, along with most other offices, were made elective rather than appointive. The Legislature was prohibited from assuming debt beyond $200,000 without a statewide vote. The state road program was curtailed, and the immigration bureau was eliminated. State-chartered banks also were prohibited, as they had been in every Texas constitution but one since 1836. Perhaps the worst change was the destruction of the statewide school system. The new charter created a "community system" without a power of taxation, and schools were segregated by race. The constitution, which was approved by voters on Feb. 15, 1876, reflected the public attitudes of the day. Almost half the delegates to the convention were members of the Grange, a new organization that had come to Texas in 1873 to relieve the plight of the farmer. Under Reconstruction, Texans felt they had experienced what government could do to them, not for them. They had borne what they considered a burden of heavy taxation for programs that they neither supported nor approved. And they wanted no repeat performances. Though the United States was in the middle of the Industrial Revolution, the basic law of Texas reflected a world view more in line with 1836.

Despite the basic reactionary character, the charter also was visionary. Following the lead of several other states, the Democrats declared railroads to be common carriers and subject to regulation. But consistent with the desire for keeping government at a minimum, no method for regulation of railroads was provided, and the omission was to fire political debates for a decade and a half.

Another major challenge was the re-establishment of law and order across the state. Since before the Civil War, respect for civil authority had been on the decline in Texas. After the war, the situation deteriorated as thousands of disillusioned and embittered soldiers returned home to suffer under Reconstruction. Indians remained a problem, although the U.S. Army was making progress in taming the frontier. And in the long troublesome Nueces Strip — the land between the Nueces River and the Rio Grande — the Mexican bandit-hero Juan Cortina was again causing trouble. The enigmatic Cortina had served both the Union and the Confederacy during the Civil War, and at one time, the Texas Senate approved a pardon for him before the House bowed to a public outcry and let the matter drop. While serving as an official of the Mexican government, however, Cortina also operated a thriving cattle theft business north of the Rio Grande, stealing stock to fulfill meat contracts with Cuba. Anglo ranchers were not safe from the marauders, and many settlers took the law into their own hands, victimizing Mexican-Texans in the process.

To meet the dual challenge of lawlessness and Indian insurrection, Gov. Coke in 1874 re-established the Texas Rangers. Major L. H. McNelly was to lead the Special Force to clean up the borderlands, and Maj. John B. Jones commanded the Frontier Battalion, consisting of six companies of 75 Rangers each.

McNelly's force of only 40 men was controversial because it took few prisoners.The Rangers were ordered to kill captives if any attempt was made to free them. But McNelly also developed an excellent intelligence system that kept him a step ahead of the bandits. One of his first acts was to remove the Anglo posses from the field, for many had been used as cover for individuals to settle personal grievances. After a few months in the field, McNelly's force killed 13 Mexican bandits in a running gun battle, and the bodies were displayed on the square at Brownsville as an example for future cattle thieves. Soon the situation was under control, and McNelly moved his operations farther up the Rio Grande to clean out American outlaws operating around Eagle Pass.

Major Jones' task was more difficult. His Frontier Battalion was divided into small groups that continually patrolled the edges of settled Texas to discourage Indian raids. The U.S. Army also put a severe crimp in raids. Cavalry units, under Ranald Mackenzie, relentlessly pursued Indians across the plains. Jones and a group of Rangers fought the last battle against Indians in northern Texas in June 1875 at Lost Valley on the Jack-Young County line. Twenty-seven Rangers, commanded by Jones, engaged 100 Indians for a full day before getting help from Fort Richardson.

Thereafter most Indian raids were concentrated in Far West Texas where U.S. Army Lt. John Bullis and his Negro Seminole Indian Scouts waged a relentless campaign against the Apaches. The last Indian battle in Texas was fought in January 1881 when Capt. George Baylor and a group of Rangers ambushed the remnants of Chief Victorio's Apaches in the Sierra Diablo Mountains.

Also by 1881, every part of Texas had felt the presence of the Rangers. The day of the professional outlaw was coming to an end. Major Jones had quelled feuds in several counties and had reduced the list of wanted criminals in the state. Rampant lawlessness had been reduced to mere sporadic outbursts.

Gov. Coke was re-elected in 1876, but he left office in December of that year for a seat in the U.S. Senate. Lt. Gov. Richard Hubbard replaced him.

Though Texas' population grew substantially after Reconstruction, transportation remained a major problem. The state's rivers were not navigable except for a few miles from the Gulf. Counties were given responsibility for creating and maintaining a road system, and in East Texas, the most populous part of the state, a "firstclass road" was one in which tree stumps were no more than six inches in height. To facilitate construction of much-needed railroads, the Legislature in 1876 established a land-grant system. Railroad companies got 16 alternate sections of land for each mile of track completed, with payment beginning after completion of 10 miles of track. Between 1875 and 1885, one-half of the total railroad mileage built in the 19th century in Texas was completed. In 1877, Texas led all states in railroad construction, and the following year, the construction in Texas exceeded the aggregate for all other states and territories combined. But embarrassed state officials discovered in 1881 that the Legislature had given away eight million more acres of land than was available, and the land-grant law was repealed. More than 32 million acres of land were granted to railroads during the period, however.

As railroads extended across the state, the character of the economy began to change. Farmers began to move from self-contained subsistence agriculture to commercial production. But this meant that they had to purchase many household goods and supplies that they once provided by their own labor. Cash, rather than barter, became the medium of exchange, and in the war-ravaged Confederacy, the need for hard money compounded many problems.

In addition, the construction of railroads spurred other industries. In 1880, Texas & Pacific Railroad alone purchased 500,000 crossties to stimulate lumbering, which became the state's largest manufacturing industry.

Emancipation of the slaves brought about a major realignment of the division of labor in the state. Many owners of large plantations were financially ruined by the loss of slaves and by the drop in land prices. At first, landowners feared there would be a labor shortage, because it was felt that the former slaves would not work for wages. Within a decade, however, most blacks were either employed on farms, had entered into share-cropping agreements or had acquired land. White landowners often would not sell land to blacks or would charge high interest rates for the purchase. Like all small farmers, blacks also got caught in the crop-lien system in which they had to mortgage future crops to buy supplies on credit. Often they still owed money after selling their crops, and a cycle of permanent indebtedness developed. Wage demands of the blacks and a basic prejudice against the former slaves also prompted efforts to attract immigrants into the state. The effort was successful, but landowners also found that many new immigrants worked for others only briefly before acquiring land for themselves. By 1876, 62 percent of the workers were white, with blacks making up only 38 percent. Unlike some other states, Texas did not develop a class of black artisans during the slavery period, so after the war, those blacks not engaged in agricultural work held only menial jobs in either rural or urban areas. A class of independent black businessmen developed only slowly, and most were in service industries like cafes, barbershops and funeral parlors.

Conservative Democrats maintained a firm grip on state politics for almost 20 years after Reconstruction, although dissident political groups arose periodically. The thrust of the Democratic administrations was economy in government and white supremacy. Despite heroic efforts, the state government remained in debt, which served as a continual reminder of the failure of the Confederacy. Texans could not divide the quest of blacks for full civil rights from full social equality. And most white Texans continued to expect subservience from blacks. Efforts had been made to legally discriminate against blacks after the Civil War. In 1866, the Legislature required railroads to provide separate accommodations for black passengers, and the law was not repealed until 1871. Later the lawmakers eliminated state licensing for many businesses in an effort to avoid the antidiscrimination thrust of the federal Civil Rights law of 1875.

In statewide politics, race was not a major question because the percentage of blacks in the population was declining, although the number of blacks in the state grew. In local politics, however, particularly in East Texas, race was a major factor. Blacks were in the majority in several counties in the so-called Black Belt. Here blacks, along with white Republicans, often controlled local offices. Often white Democrats would use intimidation and violence to discourage black voter participation. As often, black politicians would bend the law. In some counties, specially colored ballots were used for black-supported slates of candidates so illiterate voters could more easily vote a straight ticket. The practice was ended by an 1879 law that required certain types of ballots. As early as 1874 some local Democratic clubs conceived the all-white primary as an instrument for denying blacks participation in local government. Although initial efforts were unsuccessful, the approach continued and finally became state Democratic policy after the turn of the century.

Violence against blacks often was fatal. One source estimates that 500 blacks died in mob violence between 1870 and 1900. Many were victims of lynching after being accused of crimes. On occasion, the victims proved to be innocent.

For 15 years after Reconstruction ended, Texas Democrats could campaign against the Civil War and expect success. During this period, most statewide officeholders and local officials were Confederate veterans. O. M. Roberts, chief justice of the state supreme court, became a compromise candidate for governor when the Democratic convention deadlocked. Roberts, who chaired the secession convention of 1861, was elected for the first of two terms in 1878 and pursued a strict policy of fiscal austerity. He cut spending for public education from one-quarter to one-seventh of state revenues one year and supported a law providing for the sale of stateland at 50-cents an acre. Despite the intent of providing cheap land for immigrants,the law actually encouraged widespread speculation, driving land prices up for farmers.

John Ireland succeeded Roberts as governor and continued the tight fiscal policies. Ireland opposed the liberal land policies of his predecessors and is credited with saving much public land for the state schoolchildren. But cracks were developing in the Democratic dominance of state politics. G. W. (Wash) Jones, a former Democratic lieutenant governor, contested Ireland as an independent in 1882 and polled more than 100,000 votes. It was an impressive showing by a dissident candidate against the entrenched Democrats.

Economic and social problems that began in the 1870s became the major political issues in the 1880s. Democrats were hard-pressed to maintain control of the state government in the turbulent final 20 years of the 19th century.

16 *Economy in Transition*

HOLLYWOOD distorted the picture of the Texas economy. While the cowboy and cattle drives are romantic subjects, the fact is that the simple cotton farmer was the backbone of the state's economy well into the 20th century.

But neither the farmer nor the cattleman prospered throughout the last quarter of the 19th century. At the root of their problems was federal monetary policy and the lingering effects of the Civil War.

To finance the war, the Union had gone off the gold standard and had issued paper money — or greenbacks. Throughout the war, paper money could not be redeemed for specie from the national government. The prevailing monetary theory, however, held that this paper was only fiat money without real value. Only a gold-backed currency had intrinsic value. At the end of the war, there were almost $500 million in national bank notes in circulation. Northeastern bankers began to lobby for a return to the gold standard and to hard money. Although the issuance of paper money had brought about a business boom in the Union during the war, inflation also increased. Silver was demonetized in 1873. Congress passed the Specie Resumption Act in 1875 that returned the nation to the gold standard in 1879. Almost immediately a contraction in currency began. Between 1873 and 1891, the amount of national bank notes in circulation declined from $339 million to $168 million.

The reduction in the money supply was devastating in the defeated South. Of the region's major fiscal assets, slaves had been lost altogether and, because of the lack of money, land values plummeted. In 1870, Texas land was valued at an average of $2.62 an acre, compared with the national average of $18.26 an acre. Confederate money was worthless, and gold was scarce. Massachusetts alone had five times more national bank currency in circulation than the entire South.

With the money supply declining and the national economy growing, farm prices dropped. In 1870, a bushel of wheat brought $1, but by 1885, it had dropped to 80 cents. And in the 1890s, wheat was 60 cents a bushel. Except for a brief spurt in the early 1880s, cattle prices followed those of agricultural products.

Credit became an important commodity. And Texas was ill-equipped to meet the challenge. State-chartered banks were prohibited by the constitution, and there were hardly enough national banks to service the state's growing population. To compound the farmers' problems, national banks would not loan money with land as a collateral. The credit problem was exacerbated in Texas by growth. In 1870, there were 61,125 farms in the state; 30 years later, the number spiraled to 352,190.

The transition from a self-sufficient agricultural economy to commercial agriculture that the state experienced also strained the farmers' need for credit. Efficient commercial farms needed more land and mechanized equipment. Both were expensive. The war had stripped Texas of its farm implements, and it took time to replace them. In 1860, the value of Texas farm implements per farm was $24 above the national average. For the remainder of the century, however, Texas' average per farm was $50-$60 below the national average, and other regions surpassed the state. Bad weather and poor prices often forced land-owning farmers into tenancy. Between 1880 and 1890, the number of farms in Texas doubled, but the number of tenants tripled. By 1900, almost half the state's farmers were tenants.

The much-criticized crop-lien system was developed following the Civil War to meet the credit needs of small farmers. Merchants would extend credit to farmers throughout the year in exchange for liens on their crops. In most cases cotton was the major cash crop. Critics have blamed the creditors for prohibiting farmers from diversifying. But that is only partly true. Many farmers faithfully planted cotton because it seldom had a complete failure. Through almost any type of bad weather, some cotton would be produced when other crops failed completely. But the result of the crop-lien system, particularly when small farmers did not have enough acreage to operate efficiently, was a state of continual debt and despair.

Furnishing merchants also have been criticized for charging high interest rates for goods that carried premium prices when sold on credit. But many small farmers were not good businessmen, and the merchant's risks were high.

Cotton was a physically demanding crop to raise. One estimate was that it took 168 man-hours of labor to raise one acre of cotton a year. But many small farmers toiled long hours and then found at the end of the year that their labor had yielded no return. In some cases, they had gone further in debt to the furnishing merchant.

The work ethic held that a man would benefit from his toil. When this apparently failed, farmers looked to the monetary system and the railroads as the causes. Their discontent hence became the source of the agrarian revolt that developed in the 1880s and 1890s.

Farmers, on the other hand, were criticized for thinking of themselves as laborers, rather than investors or capitalists. Across the South, land traditionally had been looked on as a tool, not an investment. Once a piece of land was worn out, the farmer discarded it by moving to the next frontier. But in Texas the familiar land use pattern broke down as the frontier reached the arid plains. Farmers were slow in understanding that new techniques would be needed for dry-land farming, and the periodic droughts, originally thought to be aberrations in the weather, wrought considerable misery before settlers solved the problems of successfully farming land beyond the 98th meridian.

With the defeat of the Indians and the buffalo kill that began in 1874-75, West Texas was opened first to cattlemen and later to farmers. Cattlemen traditionally practiced open-range grazing from Spanish colonial days until the early 1880s. Livestock was allowed to roam over wide areas and was rounded up twice a year. Huge cattle drives following the war had proved successful, and when the High Plains of Texas were cleared of Indians and buffalo, cattle thrived on the rich grasses. Large cattle operations developed. Charles Goodnight established the JA Ranch in the Palo Duro Canyon in the Panhandle in the 1870s, and others soon followed. The huge cattle drives ended about the same time that many states quarantined Texas cattle because of the "Texas Fever" they carried — which was fatal to other domestic livestock. Railroads snaked across Texas in the 1880s, establishing shipping points and eliminating the need for the long drives to out-of-state markets.

Cattle prices improved between 1880 and 1885, but other problems faced stockraisers. In 1883, the Legislature required that stockmen pay grazing fees for state land that their cattle used. Previously this grazing had been free, and many cattleraisers ignored the law or circumvented it by fixing bids to keep fees low. Attempts to prosecute ranchers for conspiring against the law failed because most public officials and jurors in western Texas were either cattlemen or employees of the ranches.

The introduction of barbed wire in the early 1880s brought a revolution to ranching. Texas had long needed a cheap form of fencing. Stone and wooden fences were expensive, and in West Texas the materials simply were not available. Without fences, however, the quality of cattle herds could not be improved. Farmers also needed fences in cattle-raising regions to keep stock from ruining their fields. The new wire was introduced into Texas at Denison in the late 1870s, and in less than 10 years, it had spread across the state. John W. "Bet a Million" Gates, one of the most successful barbed-wire salesmen, dramatically demonstrated the new product by building a corral in downtown San Antonio and wagering that a steer could not break out. The animal didn't, and ranchers bought the wire.

Small range wars developed between open-range cattlemen and fencers as barbed wire moved across the state. Often landowners would block public roads and seal off water holes with their new fences. Fence-cutters would simply snip the wire to remove the barriers. The battles became particularly bitter during droughts when cattle were cut off from water. Finally, Gov. John Ireland called a special session of the Legislature in 1883 to make fence-cutting and the fencing of public lands illegal. Estimates are that more than $20 million in property damage was done by fencecutters, and the adverse publicity surrounding the battles discouraged immigration and land development for a time.

The cattle boom of the 1880s also attracted foreign investment to the state. Thirteen British corporations — five from England and eight from Scotland — invested an estimated $25 million in Texas and controlled between them 15 million to 20 million acres of land, primarily on the High Plains and the Rolling Plains. The operations proved generally unprofitable for investors when cattle prices dropped. Drought, bitter winters, cattle thieves and public animosity also took their toll. But the foreign investors are credited with introducing barbed-wire on a large scale, bringing windmills to the region and with improving cattle herds.

One of the largest ranches was created after a disaster in Austin. The state capitol burned in 1881, and the following year, the Legislature gave the Capitol Syndicate three million acres of land to construct a new building. The project was completed in 1888. With the land, the XIT Ranch in the Panhandle was established in 1885, covering parts of nine counties: Dallam, Hartley, Oldham, Deaf Smith, Parmer, Castro, Bailey, Lamb and Hockley. More than 1,500 miles of fence enclosed the ranch, which was operated until 1901 when tracts were sold by the syndicate.

The breakup of the large ranches began in the 1880s and continued after the turn of the century. Small farmers entered the region and purchased the large estates piecemeal. The immigration proved more profitable to the large ranches than cattleraising.

As bleak as the picture was, there were bright spots. After 1860, cottonseed, which had been a waste and a nuisance, developed commercial value. Previously it had been burned or dumped into streams and rivers to the dismay of other Texans. But it was discovered that cottonseed cake could be sold to stock raisers for feed, and the oil became valuable. Cotton presses could be easily moved, and a thriving industry developed. By 1900, cottonseed processing became the second largest industry in Texas, behind lumbering.

Lumbering continued to grow, and by 1890 became the state's largest industry. Improved transportation also allowed wood products to be shipped outside the state as well as to be used within Texas.

In December 1887, the Texas League of Professional Baseball Clubs was organized, and in its inaugural season, Austin, Dallas, Fort Worth, Galveston, Houston and San Antonio fielded teams.

Railroad expansion also continued at a brisk pace. In 1880, there were 3,025 miles of track in operation, and a decade later, the mileage more than doubled to 8,667. In hand with railroad expansion, coal production was initiated in the late 1870s. A mine in Stephens County in West Central Texas produced coal for Fort Griffin and shipped to Fort Worth at a price of $11 a ton, $2 below the eastern price. As coal became available in quantity, the railroads abandoned wood as fuel. In the 1880s, commercial coal production began in Palo Pinto County, and Thurber, near the Palo Pinto-Erath county line, became a major coal production center for the Texas & Pacific Railroad. On the border, Eagle Pass became a coal production center for the Southern Pacific.

Galveston and San Antonio were important trade centers in the last quarter of the century. Galveston was a major cotton-shipping center, and San Antonio was a supply center for the frontier forts. Along the border, El Paso and Laredo became major international trade centers. The Southern Pacific reached El Paso from the west in 1881, and shortly thereafter a northern railroad tied into the Mexican system. Maintenance shops were established at El Paso, and nearby coal mines provided fuel for trains visiting the trade center. Entrepreneur Uriah Lott completed a rail line to Laredo in November 1881, and a few days later, Jay Gould's International and Great Northern Railroad arrived, tying the border community to San Antonio and northern markets. Laredo and its sister city, Nuevo Laredo, marked the arrival of the railroads with a month-long celebration.

Railroad towns blossomed in the wake of construction. Many grew from crew camps. As Jay Gould's Texas & Pacific Railroad moved west from Fort Worth, the cities of Gordon, Eastland, Baird and Abilene were laid out in 1880, and the following year, Sweetwater, Colorado City and Big Spring were established along the route. T&P and Southern Pacific met at Sierra Blanca about 90 miles east of El Paso on Jan. 1, 1882, completing connections with the East and West coasts for Texas.

In 1887, the Fort Worth and Denver City Railroad began a diagonal extension across West Texas and the Panhandle. It crossed Childress, Donley, Armstrong, Potter, Hartley and Dallam counties in the Panhandle and reached Texline on the New Mexico-Texas state line in 1888. The cities of Childress, Clarendon, Amarillo and Dalhart became terminal points for farmers and ranchers. With this extension, most areas of Texas had railroads. But Lubbock on the South Plains and the Lower Rio Grande Valley did not receive rail service until after the turn of the century.

The entry of the Texas & Pacific and the Missouri-Kansas-Texas railroads from the northeast changed trade patterns in the state. Since the days of the Republic, trade generally had flowed to Gulf ports and primarily at Galveston. Jefferson in Northeast Texas served as a gateway to the Mississippi River, but it never carried the volume of trade that was common at Galveston. The earliest railroad systems in the state also were centered around Houston and Galveston, again directing trade southward. With the T&P and Katy lines, North Texas had direct access to markets in St. Louis and the East.

Some problems developed with the railroads, however. In 1882, Jay Gould and Collis P. Huntington, owner of the Southern Pacific, entered into a secret agreement that amounted to creation of a monopoly of rail service in Texas. They agreed to stop competitive track extensions, to divide under a pooling arrangement freight moving from New Orleans and El Paso, to purchase all competing railroads in Texas, and to share the track between Sierra Blanca and El Paso. Railroads owned by the pair soon organized the Texas Traffic Association with its goals of increasing revenues and doing away with abuses and losses. When the courts ordered the association dissolved, the railroads simply reorganized associations based outside Texas.

The Legislature made weak attempts to regulate railroads, as provided by the state constitution. Gov. Coke had recommended creation of a railroad commission in 1876, but was ignored. Gould thwarted an attempt to create a commission in 1881 with a visit to the state during the Legislative debate. The railroad tycoon subdued the lawmakers' interest with thinly disguised threats that capital would abandon Texas if the state interfered with railroad business. In 1879, the lawmakers did set a maximum rate that railroads could charge for freight and made it unlawful for a rail carrier to discriminate against any person or place. But the laws were loosely enforced.

With the railroads came Texas' first militant labor organizations. The state's traditional agrarian society had little need for unions. Some workers had organized during the days of the Republic. Journeyman printers struck a Houston newspaper in 1839, and groups of artisans organized loosely to seek legislation. Texas' mechanics lien law of 1839 was one of the first protections for workers of its type in North America. Workingmen's associations organized occasionally prior to the Civil War, but they were weak and often did not last long. Only two unions existed in Galveston at the outbreak of the war. Prior to 1870, no outside unions provided aid to Texas workers. In the self-sustaining agricultural economy, unions also were looked upon as "Yankee innovations" and "abominations." After the Civil War, unions became more numerous. The Screwmen's Benevolent Association of Galveston organized in 1866 and lasted into the 20th century after affiliation with a national union. Black dock workers also organized in Galveston, and skilled workers, such as carpenters and bricklayers, struck in major cities.

With the railroads, however, came the militant Knights of Labor. In 1885, the union struck and gained concessions from T&P Railroad, but a year later, another strike turned violent. Troops were called out to protect railroad property, and the strike failed. The unions were heavily criticized for the job action, and the labor movement in Texas remained weak until the state's industrial base developed in the 20th century.

As the 19th century closed, Texas remained an agricultural state, albeit commercial agriculture and not family farms. But the industrial base was growing. Between 1870 and 1900, the per capita value of manufactured goods in the United States rose from $109 to $171. In Texas, these per capita values increased from $14 to $39. But manufacturing values in Texas industry still were only one-half of the annual agricultural values.

But Texas was definitely a state in transition, and there was no better evidence than the tumultuous political upheavals of the last quarter of the 19th century.

The Agrarian Revolt 17

CONSERVATIVE Texas Democrats maintained control of the state government throughout most of the last quarter of the 19th century. Their ascendancy was based on white supremacy and on the strong emotional rejection of the Radical Republican Reconstruction era. As across most of the United States, Texans had no attraction to burning national issues. Regional and local interests prevailed.

But as the plight of the farmers worsened, strong passions were unleashed that overrode the issues of secession and the Civil War on the national level. A series of third parties with national affiliations arose in Texas that seriously threatened to break the Democrats' grip on the state house and the Legislature.

Texas farmers were not alone in their poverty. The entire South suffered, and the condition was noted by O.H. Kelley, a clerk in the Agricultural Bureau in Washington, on a trip through the region. He was appalled by the Southern farmers' poverty and apathy. To give voice to their plight, he organized the National Grange — the Patrons of Husbandry — in the nation's capital in 1867. The first Texas Grange was established in 1872 at Salado in Bell County. At its peak membership in 1877, the state organization claimed 45,000 members, including 6,000 women, in more than 1,200 local chapters. It had a threefold purpose: to improve the home life of its members; to foster social intercourse to the mutual benefit of all, and to provide economic benefits in dealing with the business world. Grangers were encouraged to participate in politics as citizens, but the organization was not directly involved. Many local Granges and the state organization petitioned the Legislature on various issues, and members felt they had a voice in government through the organization. About half of the 90 delegates to the state constitutional convention of 1875 were Grangers, and they left their mark on the state charter that provided for limited government, restrictions on taxation and debt, and provided a framework for railroad regulation.

The Grange's lasting contribution came through its educational programs. Many of the local meetings were agricultural schools, teaching farmers how to be more efficient. The founding of Texas Agricultural & Mechanical College (now Texas A&M University) in 1876 received strong support from the organization.

But the Grange foundered on two issues. First, it established the Texas Cooperative Association in an effort to circumvent the furnishing merchant who held so many farmers in debt. The goal was to eliminate the middle man and to provide merchandise wholesale to farmers. The state cooperative was to be associated with local cooperatives sponsored by the organization. And this effort attracted many members. Unfortunately, it did not work. The cash-only Grange stores were of no help to farmers who had no cash. And in 1883 and 1884 both the state and local cooperatives suffered severe financial losses because of bad crops and many closed their doors. In addition, as time passed, farmers became more militant and wanted an organization that was more directly involved in politics. State Grange leaders would not abandon the original nonpolitical policy. While most farmers were emotionally tied to the Democratic Party and wanted to work within its framework, others were becoming disenchanted with the "party of the fathers." The Grange's membership began to fall.

The Greenback Party was attractive to many farmers, although the Grange leadership remained loyal to the Democratic Party. The monetary devaluation that was damaging farmers also took its toll on the wages of workers in the industrialized parts of the nation. On the national level, the Greenback Party began activity in 1876 and reached Texas two years later. Although the party supported issues like woman suffrage and an income tax, its basic goal was to provide a greater money supply. Greenbackers opposed the return to the gold standard, supported remonetization of silver and demanded repeal of the national bank law. First and foremost, the party supported an expansion of the currency to eliminate the growing economic hardship of many Americans. In four gubernatorial elections between 1878 and 1884, Greenbackers supplanted Republicans as runners-up to the winning Democrats. In 1882, Greenbacker G.W. "Wash" Jones polled 102,501 votes, the most ever attracted by a dissident party in the state up to that time. In local races, Greenbackers occasionally were successful, as in the case of the party candidate who was elected mayor of Dallas. The Greenback movement failed, however, when the Democrats usurped some of its platform planks. Farmers also became uncomfortable with some of the radical socialists who gained control of the national party. There was little cultural affinity between the farmers and the socialists of the industrial world. Farmers looked elsewhere for a political champion.

In 1877, another farm organization was established. On the J.R. Allen farm in Lampasas County, a group of farmers banded together in the Knights of Alliance with its purpose "to assist the civil officers in maintaining law and order." This group was primarily concerned with curbing livestock thefts. But it had a simple ritual, and its literary program was borrowed from the Grange. The Alliance was reorganized in 1879 in Poolville in Parker County, and in the next few years, it provided the impetus for the radical politics of the 1890s.

By 1886, the Alliance, led by S.O. Daws and William Lamb, became more radical. At a meeting in Cleburne, the organization issued a list of 17 "demands" — in contrast to the Grange's simple petitions — addressed to the state and federal governments. These included demands for fiscal reform, railroad regulation, changes in land policy and the recognition of labor unions. Though some conservative Alliance members were distressed at the apparent split with the Democratic Party, the organization's membership grew tremendously after the meeting. The demands struck a welcome note for many farmers. By the time a second meeting was held in Waco in January 1887 to heal the rift that developed, the Alliance claimed 200,000 members in 3,000 chartered suballiances in Texas.

In Waco, Dr. Charles W. Macune struck a compromise between the divergent elements and took a major step toward spreading the Alliance's influence. He proposed a national system of cooperatives to market farm products and to serve as a purchasing medium for farmers. Within five weeks, Texas lecturers were sent to other states throughout the South. When a national convention was held in Shreveport, La., in October 1887, 10 states that had been organized in eight months were represented.

Democrats easily weathered the early third-party challenges in Texas. Democratic governors continued their policies of fiscal austerity. John Ireland successfully coped with the fence-cutting wars and reversed some of the liberal land policies that were fueling speculation. Lawrence S. "Sul" Ross, elected in 1888, was a popular Confederate veteran who benefited from a large monetary settlement with the federal government. Texas was compensated for its costs in fighting Indians and guarding the Mexican border. Ross cut taxes and improved state services.

In 1886, a new breed of Texas politician appeared. James Stephen Hogg was not a Confederate veteran, although his father was, and he was not tied to the party policies of the past. As a reform-minded attorney general, Hogg had actively enforced the state's few railroad regulatory laws. Through the experience, he became convinced that the state must have a railroad commission. With farmers' support, Hogg was elected governor in 1890, and at the same time, a debate on the constitutionality of a railroad commission was settled when voters amended the constitution to provide for one. Hogg led a group of young Democrats who were a step removed from Reconstruction and ties with the Confederate past. These young Democrats launched a brief reform era in state government.

Nationally, the growing power of the emerging corporate interests had become a major political issue. In 1887, Congressman John Reagan of Texas won a 10-year fight to establish the Interstate Commerce Commission to regulate railroads. Two years later, the Texas Legislature passed an antitrust law, just weeks after Kansas had approved the first such statute in the nation.

Hogg was bitterly opposed in his campaign, but the reform mood of the state was evident. Voters returned only 22 of the 106 members of the Texas House in 1890. The Legislature created the Railroad Commission of Texas in 1891 after an extended debate. A compromise was reached that allowed the first commission to be appointed by the governor, but beginning in 1894, the panel would be elected. Hogg accomplished one of the great political moves of the century by luring Reagan out of the U.S. Senate to serve as the first chairman of the commission, along with commissioners L.L. Foster and William P. McLean. Reagan's long battle to create the ICC gave him an intimate knowledge of railroad operations, and, as the former postmaster general of the Confederacy, he was well-respected by all Texans.

Despite his reputation as a reformer, Hogg accepted the growing use of Jim Crow laws to limit minority access to public services. In 1891, the Legislature responded to public demands and required railroads to provide separate accommodations for blacks and whites.

The stage was being set for one of the major political campaigns in Texas history, however. Farmers did not think that Hogg had gone far enough in his reform program, and they were distressed that Hogg had not appointed a farmer to the railroad commission.

In 1889, Charles Macune, now editor of the Farmers Alliance's national newspaper, the National Economist in Washington, had proposed a radical new monetary system. Under his plan, the federal government would eliminate the farmers' credit pinch, underwriting cooperatives by issuing greenbacks to provide credit for farmers' crops. A more flexible national currency would be created in the process. In addition, the government would store the crops until time for sale and issue "subtreasury" certificates that would serve as legal tender. While the plan contained elements of a modern crop insurance program, it was wildly radical at the time. Texas Democrats had refused to endorse either the subtreasury plan or free silver in their 1890 platform, and to many farmers this was a signal of the party's insensitivity to their plight. Many began to look elsewhere for the solutions to their problems.

The Kansas Farmers Alliance provided the answer in 1888: direct political action through sponsoring slates of candidates. Kansas' success prompted the formation of the People's Party in Texas in August 1891.

The 1892 general election was one of the most spirited in the state's history. Conservative Democrats, after Gov. Hogg's supporters shut them out of the so-called roundhouse convention in Houston, bolted and nominated railroad attorney George Clark for the governorship. Populists for the first time had a presidential candidate, James Weaver, and a gubernatorial candidate, T.L. Nugent.

Texas Republicans also broke ranks. The party's strength centered in the black vote. After the death of former Gov. E.J. Davis in 1883, Norris Wright Cuney, a black, was the party leader. Cuney was considered one of the most astute politicians of the period, and he controlled federal patronage. White Republicans revolted against the black leadership, and these so-called "Lily-whites" nominated Andrew Jackson Houston, son of Sam Houston, for governor. Black Republicans recognized that, alone, their strength was limited, and throughout the latter part of the 19th century, they practiced fusion politics, backing candidates of third parties when they deemed it appropriate. Cuney led the Republicans into a coalition with the conservative Democrats in 1892, backing George Clark.

The election also marked the first time that major Democratic candidates courted the black vote. Gov. Hogg's supporters organized black voter clubs, and the governor got about one-half of the black vote. Black farmers were in a quandary. Their financial problems were the same as those small farmers who backed the Populists. White Populists varied in their sympathy with the racial concerns of the blacks. On the local level, some whites showed sympathy with black concerns about education, voting and law enforcement. Minority farmers also were reluctant to abandon the Republican Party because it was their only political base in Texas.

Hogg was re-elected in 1892 with a 43 percent plurality in a field of five candidates.

During his second term, Hogg continued to try to correct abuses by the railroads. Transportation rates were based in part on railroads' investments. The governor charged during the campaign that railroads had watered their stock, meaning more was sold than necessary for operation. In the previous seven years, Hogg argued, railroad construction had been negligible, but railroad obligations had increased at a rate of $30 million a year. In addition, for rate purposes, railroads claimed outstanding stocks and bonds valued at $455,520,744, while for tax purposes, these same properties were valued at $63,000,000. In 1893, the Legislature gave the railroad commission authority to review new stock sales and to regulate the sales.

Populists continued to run well in state races until 1898. But historians have placed the beginning of the party's demise in the 1896 presidential election in which national Populists fused with the Democrats and supported William Jennings Bryan. This fusion weakened the demand for Macune's subtreasury plan, which would have created a new monetary system, in favor of the Democrats' "free silver" platform plank. Although the Populist philosophy lived on, the party declined in importance after the 1898 elections. Following a depression in the early 1890s, farm prices began to rise after a European crop failure in 1897, and gold discoveries in South Africa, Australia and Alaska helped relieve the currency shortage. Farmers remained active in politics, but most returned to the Democratic Party, which usurped many of the Populists' issues.

But Texas was on the brink of another revolution — an economic revolution that would forever change the face of the state.

Spindletop 18

SELDOM can a people's history be traced to a single event on a single day. But Texas' entrance into the industrial age can be linked directly to the discovery of oil at Spindletop, three miles from Beaumont, on Jan. 10, 1901. From that day, Texas' progress from a rural, agricultural state to a modern industrial giant has been steady.

The presence of oil near the salt domes along Texas' Gulf Coast had been suspected for many years. Patillo Higgins drilled wells near Spindletop for a decade before his resources were exhausted. In 1900, Higgins leased land to Anthony Lucas to prospect for oil.

Quicksand in the area presented a serious engineering problem to Higgins and to Lucas. But Lucas had experience with similar problems in Louisiana before coming to Texas. A telescoping system of casing, ranging from 12-inch pipe at the surface to four-inch pipe at the bottom of the hole was devised to keep the sand from filling the hole as it was dug. The Lucas No. 1 was spudded-in with a rotary rig in October 1900, and on the afternoon of Jan. 10, blew in. Initial production was estimated between 75,000 and 80,000 barrels of oil per day. Lucas was hardly prepared for the quantity of oil the well produced, and for several days, the oil flowed freely before the drilling crew could bring it under control. Oil was stored in earthen tanks when possible, but much simply was wasted.

Within days, the area was engulfed in Texas' first oil boom. Investors and con men from across the nation descended to enrich themselves in the hysterical activity that followed. Land values skyrocketed. Hundreds of wells were drilled as close together as possible. Little effort was made to stem the flow of oil until a disastrous fire struck the field in March 1901.

Spindletop was not the first oil strike in Texas. Even before Europeans came to the area, oil from seeps had been used by Indians for medicinal purposes. Early Spanish explorers used it as a lubricant and to caulk boats.

Lyne Barret drilled the first commercial well near Nacogdoches in 1866. But there were few uses for his product. Oil was used to settle dust on public roads. But it was principally used as a lubricant and occasionally as a fuel. Barret's well at Oil Springs was 106 feet deep and produced 10 barrels of oil a day. The field was abandoned and reopened in 1887, though it was never commercially profitable.

Wells also were made in Brown County in 1878 and in Bexar County in 1886 before the first major commercial well was completed at Corsicana in 1894, when oil was struck while the city was drilling a water well. The first well was abandoned, but others soon were drilled. By 1898, Corsicana had 342 wells producing 500,000 barrels of oil a year. Joseph S. Cullinan, a former employee of Standard Oil, arrived in Corsicana in 1897 and developed an integrated oil operation. He constructed the state's first pipeline to serve a refinery he also built. Cullinan also was a champion of conservation, supporting an 1899 law that required abandoned wells to be plugged. He also demonstrated the value of petroleum as a locomotive fuel.

With the development of the Corsicana wells, Texas' oil production in 1900 was 836,000 barrels a year, about one-nineteenth of the total U.S. production.

Spindletop exceeded that production within a few days. In its first year of operation, the well produced 3.2 million barrels of oil. But the price also dropped to three cents a barrel. Desperately needed new markets for oil were soon forthcoming. Railroads were the first to recognize the advantage of the new, inexpensive resource. They soon began converting locomotives from coal to oil. Steamship lines followed suit, and many industries found great cost-saving advantages in fueling boilers with inexpensive oil rather than more expensive coal. Cattlemen even experimented with oil as a possible dip to rid cattle of the ticks that carried so-called Texas Fever, although it caused the animals to get too hot in the summer. These customers supported the industry until automobiles were in widespread use.

Railroad tank cars at first were used to haul oil, but by January 1902, a pipeline had been completed from Spindletop to the Neches River. Soon lines were constructed to points on the Gulf.

Several major oil companies also got their start with Spindletop. Cullinan came from Corsicana and with partners organized the Texas Fuel Co. in 1902 and erected a refinery at Port Arthur. The company grew into Texaco. Likewise, Gulf and Mobil trace their beginnings to Texas' first major oil strike.

Oil strikes soon followed at Sour Lake and Humble, near Houston. In North Texas, W.T. Waggoner discovered oil in 1904 while drilling for water in Wichita County. The Petrolia Field also opened in 1904, and a few years later, the Electra Field was opened. In 1917, oil was discovered at Ranger in Eastland County. The boom days of Ranger were depicted in the movie "Boom Town," and it is probably the best known of the boom towns. Discoveries followed at Burkburnett, Breckenridge, Mexia and in West Texas.

Texas' oil production grew steadily until it reached 28 million in 1905 and then declined until 1910. Thereafter the growth resumed.

Until 1928, Texas vied with California and Oklahoma for oil production leadership in the United States. But Texas gained a lead that was never relinquished after the discovery of the East Texas Field by C.M. "Dad" Joiner in October 1930. Joiner's Daisy Bradford No. 3, drilled near Kilgore, was the first of 1,000 wells drilled in the field in a six-month period. In the first year, the East Texas Field yielded 100 million barrels of oil. When it was finally defined, the field proved to be 42 miles long, four to eight miles wide and covered 200 square miles. Virtually every acre produced oil.

Natural gas, which was often considered a nuisance and wasted, also was recognized as an important resource. In 1909, Lone Star Gas was organized and ran a pipeline to carry natural gas to Dallas and Fort Worth a year later. Within a few years, the state's major cities had access to this important fuel.

Progressivism 19

AFTER Jim Hogg left the governor's office in 1895, the reform movement waned. The flurry of passionate political activity during the late 1880s and early 1890s left Texans ready for a respite. Hogg's successor, Charles A. Culberson, was moderately progressive, but the character of the Legislature was changing. In 1890, about half the members were farmers, but by the turn of the century, two-thirds of the lawmakers were lawyers and businessmen. Also, the reform movement had almost brought the railroads to heel, and these were the most obvious extensions of growing corporate power in Texas.

Gov. Culberson's successors, Joseph D. Sayers and S.W.T. Lanham, the last Confederate veteran to serve as governor, were more conservative than Culberson. In 1901, Sayers had to cope with the tragic hurricane that destroyed Galveston in September, killing 6,000 people. In rebuilding from that disaster, Galveston's civic leaders fashioned the commission form of municipal government that was widely copied nationally. Amarillo later refined the system into the council-manager organization that is widely used today. And the great Galveston storm also reinforced arguments by Houston's leadership that an inland port should be built for protection against such tragedies and disruptions of trade. The Houston Ship Channel was soon to be a reality.

The reform spirit in government was not completely dead, however. In 1901, the Legislature prohibited the issuing of railroad passes to public officials. More than 270,000 passes were issued to officials that year, and farmers claimed that the free rides increased their freight rates and influenced public policy as well. In 1903, State Sen. A.W. Terrell got a major election reform law approved, a measure that was further modified two years later. A primary system was established to replace a hodge-podge of practices for nominating candidates that had led to charges of irregularities after each election. And the state, for the first time, imposed the poll tax as a requisite for voting. Historians differ on whether the levy was designed to keep blacks or poor whites from voting. Certainly the poll tax cut election turnouts. Black voter participation dropped from about 100,000 in the 1890s to an estimated 5,000 in 1906. The Democratic State Executive Committee also recommended that county committees limit participation in primaries to whites only, and most accepted the suggestion.

Also in the reform spirit, the Legislature in 1903 prohibited abuse of child labor and set minimum ages at which children could work in certain industries. The action preceded federal child-labor laws by 13 years.

The election of Thomas M. Campbell as governor in 1906 introduced the progressive period in Texas politics. Interest revived in controlling corporate influence. Under Campbell, the state's antitrust laws were strengthened and a pure food and drug law was passed. Texas took the lead of states with similar statutes, and the Robertson Insurance Law of 1907 also had a major impact. Life insurance companies were required to invest in Texas 75 percent of their reserves on policies in effect in the state. Less than one percent of the reserves had been invested in Texas prior to the law. Some companies left Texas. But the law was beneficial in the capital-starved economy. Texas' officials also vigorously prosecuted antitrust cases, notably the Waters-Pierce Oil Co. suit, and the state was developing an anti-business reputation.

In 1904, voters amended the constitution to allow the state to charter banks for the first time in history, and this eased some of the farmers' credit problems. And in 1909, the Legislature approved a bank deposit insurance plan that predated the federal program of the 1930s.

The discovery of oil sparked an economic revolution. And other industries flourished. Lumbering entered a period of exceptional growth. In 1901, John H. Kirby organized the Kirby Lumber Co., capitalized with $10 million. The firm's mills developed a capacity to process more than 300 million board feet of lumber a year. By 1900, Texas mills processed one billion board feet of lumber a year, and three times in the next 20 years production topped two billion board feet annually. The peak year was 1907, when almost 2.2 billion board feet were produced. By 1930, 18 million acres of Texas pineland had produced 60 billion board feet of lumber over a 50-year period.

The growth in lumber production, however, brought problems. Conservationists warned of overcutting as early as the 1880s. W. Goodrich Jones, called the "Father of Texas Forestry," organized the Texas Arbor Day and Forestry Association in 1889, and in 1914, Jones founded the Texas Forestry Association. Its successor, the Texas Forest Service, today is operated by Texas A&M University. After a boom during World War I, lumbering declined in Texas. Only 354 million board feet were produced in 1932. The state's 14 million to 16 million acre virgin pine forests had been depleted to one million acres.

In addition, lumber companies also operated much like feudal barons. Isolated company towns were built around mills, and workers, about 40 percent of whom were black, were paid in merchandise checks that could be redeemed only at company stores. Union attempts to organize lumber workers were thwarted until the 1930s. Because lumbering was far removed from most of the state's population centers, little interest was aroused by the companies' practices.

With Campbell's election, the progressive era in Texas government was underway. The era is characterized by the attempt to improve both individuals and society through government action. In Texas, with the small corporate influence under acceptable control, attention turned to the moral issue of prohibition. Progressives and prohibitionists joined forces against the conservative establishment to exert a major influence in state government for the next two decades. The period also was dominated by the personality of Joseph W. Bailey, who served as U.S. Senator from 1901 to 1913. Bailey's ethics were called into question when he served as a counsel for oil companies while in the Senate. Although he was cleared of wrongdoing by a legislative investigation, Bailey did not seek re-election in 1912. And voters split along pro-Bailey and anti-Bailey lines for many years thereafter, depending on which side of a political issue the former senator took.

Prohibitionists had long been active in Texas. They had the local-option clause written into the Constitution of 1876, which allowed counties or their subdivisions to be voted dry. In 1887, a prohibition amendment to the constitution had been defeated by a 2-to-1 margin, and public attention had been turned to other problems. In the early 20th century, the movement gathered strength. Most of Texas already was dry because of local option. When voters rejected a prohibition amendment to the constitution by a slim margin in 1911, the state had 167 dry counties, 61 partially wet ones and 21 totally wet counties. The heavily populated counties, however, were wet. But prohibition continued to be a major issue.

In 1910, Oscar Colquitt, a wet, won a hard-fought campaign. His administration was progressive, but turbulent.

A quiet but significant event also occurred when Lt. Benjamin D. Foulois arrived in San Antonio in 1910 with a crated biplane. The young officer had three orders: assemble the plane; learn to fly it, and teach others to fly the machine. Foulois' arrival in the Texas city marks the beginning of American military aviation. In 1911, he flew the first military mission from Laredo to Eagle Pass in record time, and by 1919, regular patrols of the border were flown.

Problems along the U.S.-Mexico border escalated in 1911. The regime of Mexican President Porfirio Diaz became increasingly unpopular. Francisco Madero challenged Diaz for the presidency in 1910 and was imprisoned for a time during the campaign. He decided that only revolution would remove the unpopular dictator from office. Madero plotted his revolution from hideouts in San Antonio and Dallas and launched his rebellion in early 1911. Soon the revolutionaries controlled some northern Mexican states, including Chihuahua. Juarez and El Paso were major contact points. El Paso residents would stand on rooftops to observe the fighting between revolutionaries and government troops. And some Americans were killed.

A thin line often divided the true revolutionaries and outright bandits. The Lower Rio Grande Valley was particularly hard hit by renegades. After pleas to the federal government got no action, Gov. Colquitt sent state militia and Texas Rangers into the Valley in 1913 to protect Texans after Matamoros fell to the rebels. Unfortunately, the Rangers killed many innocent Mexican-Texans during the operation. In addition to problems caused by the fighting and raids, thousands of Mexican refugees flooded Texas border towns to escape the violence of the revolution.

Texas progressives became prominent nationally in the presidential election of 1912. Several Texans had quietly urged New Jersey Gov. Woodrow Wilson to seek the presidency, and in the precinct caucuses of 1912, progressives gained control of the party. Texas' delegation to the national Democratic convention in Baltimore was instructed to vote for Wilson as long as his name was in nomination. Through 46 ballots, the "Immortal Forty" stuck with Wilson until he received the Democratic nomination. And Texas overwhelmingly supported Wilson at the polls. E. M. House, who had been active behind the scenes in Texas politics since Jim Hogg's second campaign in 1892, became a close personal adviser to President Wilson, and three Texans served in the cabinet: Postmaster Albert Sidney Burleson, Attorney General Thomas Watt Gregory and Secretary of Agriculture David Houston.

Also in 1912, Texans selected a U.S. Senator at the ballot box for the first time. The Terrell Election Law required a preferential primary for all offices, although the Legislature still officially appointed U.S. Senators. In 1906 and 1910, incumbents had not been opposed. But when Joseph Bailey declined to seek re-election in 1912, Morris Sheppard received a plurality of the popular vote. Runoffs were not required at the time. In early 1913, Gov. Colquitt recommended that the Legislature honor R.M. Johnson, a newspaper publisher and long-time conservative Democrat, by appointing him to Sen. Bailey's unserved term. Johnson was appointed senator, but served only 26 days. Sheppard's supporters argued that he should get the early appointment to gain valuable seniority over other freshmen senators, and the Legislature agreed.

In 1914, James E. Ferguson entered Texas politics, and for the next three decades,"Farmer Jim" was one of the most dominating and colorful figures on the political stage. A banker in Temple, Ferguson entered the 1914 gubernatorial campaign after a friend turned down the race. Ferguson skirted the prohibition issue by pledging to veto any legislation pertaining to alcoholic beverages. His strength was in the farming community, however. Sixty-two percent of Texas' farmers were tenants, and the candidate pledged to back legislation to limit tenant rents. Ferguson also was a dynamic orator. He easily won the primary and rolled over three opponents in the general election.

Ferguson's first administration was successful. The Legislature passed the law limiting tenants' rents, although it was poorly enforced. And aid to rural schools was improved. In early 1915, the border problems heated up. A Mexican national was arrested in Cameron County carrying a so-called "Plan of San Diego." The document outlined plans to create a rebellion of Mexican-Americans, Indians, Japanese and blacks in Texas and the Southwest. Once all Anglo males over age 16 were eliminated, a new republic controlled by blacks would be created to serve as a buffer between the United States and Mexico. Authorship of the plan has never been determined, but whatever its intent, it started a bloodbath in the Lower Rio Grande Valley. Mexican soldiers participated in raids across the Rio Grande, and Gov. Ferguson sent in the Rangers. Historians differ on the number of people who lost their lives, but a safe assessment would be "hundreds." Tensions were raised so high that Gov. Ferguson and Mexican President Venustiano Carranza met at Nuevo Laredo in November 1915 to improve relations. But the raids continued.

Pancho Villa raided Columbus, N.M., in early 1916, and two small Texas villages in the Big Bend, Glenn Springs and Bouquillas, also were attacked. In July, President Wilson determined the hostilities were critical and activated the National Guard. Soon 100,000 American troops were stationed along the border. Fort Bliss in El Paso housed 60,000 men, and Fort Duncan near Eagle Pass was home to 16,000 more.

With the exception of Gen. John J. Pershing's pursuit of Villa into Northern Mexico, few American troops crossed into Mexico. But the service along the border gave soldiers basic training that was put to use when the United States entered World War I in 1917.

Gov. Ferguson was easily re-elected in 1916, and he worked well with the Legislature the following year. But after the Legislature adjourned, the governor got into a dispute with the board of regents of the University of Texas. The disagreement culminated with the governor vetoing all appropriations for the school. As the controversy swirled, the Travis County grand jury indicted Gov. Ferguson for misappropriation of funds and for embezzlement. In July 1917, Speaker of the Texas House F. O. Fuller called a special session of the Legislature to consider impeachment of the governor. Although the state constitution provides that only the governor can call special sessions, the attorney general said that it was appropriate for the speaker to call a session on impeachment. The Texas House voted 21 articles of impeachment, and the Senate in August 1917 convicted Ferguson on 10 of the charges. The Senate's judgment not only removed Ferguson from office, but barred him from seeking office again. Ferguson resigned the day before the Senate rendered the decision in an attempt to avoid the prohibition against seeking further office.

Lt. Gov. Will Hobby of Houston became governor. His first order of business was to mobilize Texas to fight in World War I.

War and Reaction 20

WILL Hobby immediately turned his attention to Texas' war effort after assuming the governorship following Ferguson's removal. Ferguson had appointed a Council of Defense to guide the state's war activities. It helped the Red Cross, conducted war-bond drives and aided in drought relief. The council also became involved in some anti-German and anti-pacifist activities that developed.

Texas participated actively in the war. Almost 200,000 young Texans, including 31,000 blacks, volunteered for military service, and 450 Texas women served in the nurses' corps. Five thousand lost their lives overseas, either fighting or in the influenza epidemics that swept the military. Texas also was a major training ground during the conflict, with 250,000 soldiers getting basic training in the state.

On the negative side, the war frenzy opened a period of intolerance and nativism in the state. German-Texans were suspect because of their national ancestry. A law was passed to prohibit speaking against the war effort. Persons who failed to participate in patriotic activities often were punished. Gov. Hobby even vetoed the appropriation for the German department at the University of Texas.

Ferguson's removal from office was a devastating blow to the state's anti-prohibitionists. It was learned that the former governor had received a $156,000 loan from members of the brewers' association while in office. And this provided ammunition for the progressives. Here was an industry that had not been brought under control. With so many young men receiving military training in the state, prohibitionists proposed to prohibit saloons within a 10-mile radius of military posts to protect the soldiers from the temptations of alcohol and vice. One critic said that step alone would dry up 90 percent of the state. The measure was approved in a special session in February 1918, and at the same time, the national prohibition amendment, which had been introduced in Congress by Texas Sen. Morris Sheppard, was ratified by the lawmakers. Women also were given the right to vote in the state primaries at the same session.

Hobby easily won election to a full term as governor in 1918, and progressives and prohibitionists gained control of the Legislature.

Although national prohibition was to become effective in early 1920, the Legislature presented a prohibition amendment to voters in May 1919, and it was approved, bringing prohibition to Texas earlier than to the rest of the nation. At the same time, a woman suffrage amendment was defeated.

Although World War I ended in November 1918, it brought many changes to Texas. Rising prices during the war had increased the militancy of labor unions. Open Shop Associations were organized in many cities. And in 1921, Gov. Hobby declared martial law and called out state troops to end a dock strike in Galveston. Blacks also became more militant after the war. Discrimination against black soldiers led in 1917 to a riot in Houston in which several people were killed.

Federal courts stripped the Texas Railroad Commission of its authority to regulate interstate rates in the "Shreveport case" in 1914. The commission had set up a rate structure for goods entering Texas from Louisiana that had been detrimental to Shreveport merchants. The commission was given additional regulatory responsibility with the approval of a constitutional amendment in 1917 authorizing the state to regulate natural resources. The state also changed a long-standing policy that prohibited companies from operating in more than one field in their industry. Major oil companies needed integrated operations in which they could produce, transport,refine and sell petroleum products, and they lobbied to have the restrictive laws repealed. Finally the lawmakers agreed, and in another move, the Legislature in 1919 also prohibited the waste of natural resources, especially oil, and authorized the railroad commission to regulate pipelines, which carried petroleum. Although the commission approved a rule in 1920 that regulated the spacing of oil wells (Rule 37), little more was done. The oil industry was doing well in Texas, and everyone concerned left well enough alone.

With the election of Mexican President Alvaro Obregon in 1920, the fighting along the U.S.-Mexican border subsided. Although mistrust between the Mexicans and Texans remained for many years, a cohesive social intercourse developed. In 1919, State Rep. J. T. Canales of Brownsville instigated an investigation of the Texas Rangers' role in the border problems. As a result of the study, the Rangers' manpower was reduced from 1,000 members to 76, and stringent limitations were placed on the agency's activities. Standards for members of the force also were upgraded. Later the Rangers were merged with the highway patrol to form the Department of Public Safety.

Pat M. Neff won the gubernatorial election of 1920, beating former Sen. Bailey. Neff visited 152 counties and made 850 speeches in his campaign. As a former prosecuting attorney in McLennan County, Neff made law and order the major thrust of his administration. Like many governors of the period, Neff was more progressive than the Legislature, and his program often fared poorly. During his administration, however, the state took full responsibility for developing a highway system. And a gasoline tax was imposed. A state park board also was established, and Neff's mother donated 10 acres of land near McGregor for the state's first park. In 1921, a group of West Texans threatened to form a new state because Neff vetoed the creation of a new college in their area. Two years later, Texas Tech College was authorized in Lubbock and opened its doors in 1925.

Neff had problems with the Legislature. Since 1907, it had become the lawmakers' practice not to pass an appropriations bill in the regular session. They were paid $5 a day for the first 60 days of the session, and only $2 a day thereafter. But they received $5 a day in special sessions. In addition, they got travel allowances when returning home between sessions. Neff called the lawmakers into special session the day after the regular session ended in March 1923, but the lawmakers met for only one hour and adjourned, ending what may have been the shortest legislative session anywhere.

Although still predominantly a rural state, Texas cities were growing. In 1900, only 17 percent of the population lived in urban areas; by 1920, that figure had almost doubled to 32 percent. A discontent developed with the growth of the cities. Rural Texans had long seen cities as hotbeds of vice and immorality. Simple rural values were cherished, and it seemed that these values were threatened in a changing world. After World War I, this transition accelerated. In addition, "foreigners" in the state became suspect; nativism reasserted itself. The German-Texans were associated with the enemy in the war, and Mexican-Texans were mostly of the Roman Catholic religion and likened to the troublemakers along the border. Texas was a fertile ground for the new Ku Klux Klan that entered the state in late 1920. The Klan's philosophy was a mixture of patriotism, law-and-order, nativism, white supremacy and Victorian morals. Its influence spread quickly a cross the state, and reports of Klan violence and murder were rampant.

Prohibition had brought a widespread disrespect for law. Peace officers and other officials often ignored speakeasies, gambling and other vice. The Klan seemed to many Texans to be an appropriate instrument for restoring law and order and for maintaining Victorian morality in towns and cities. By 1922, many of the state's large communities were under direct Klan influence. Between 1922 and 1924 in Dallas, for example, the Klan controlled every public office in city and county government. Opposition was raised, but it was ineffective in the early stages of the development of the Klan.

In 1922, a Klan-backed candidate, Earle Mayfield, was elected to the U.S. Senate from Texas, and the state gained the reputation as the most powerful Klan bastion in the Union. Hiram Wesley Evans of Dallas also was elected imperial wizard of the national Klan in that year.

Gov. Neff never denounced the Klan by name, although he did deplore violence in any form. Once when the governor was out of the state, Lt. Gov. T. Whitfield Davidson ordered the Rangers to investigate a Klan murder. Neff concurred in the order, but soon the investigation was dropped.

After 1922, the Klan became more directly involved in politics and planned to elect the next governor in 1924. Judge Felix Robertson of Dallas got the organization's backing in the Democratic primary. Former governor Ferguson filed to run for the office, but the Texas Supreme Court ruled that he could not because of the impeachment conviction. So Ferguson placed his wife, Miriam A. Ferguson, on the ballot. Several other prominent Democrats also entered the race.

As soon as Mrs. Ferguson entered the race, she was dubbed "Ma" from the initials of her first and middle names. And she ran a vigorous campaign, although it was her husband's oratory that attracted the crowds, particularly in rural areas. The Fergusons made no secret that Jim would have a big influence on his wife's administration. One campaign slogan was, "Two governors for the price of one." Mrs. Ferguson surprised most observers by finishing second to Robertson in the first primary. And she easily won the runoff when many Texans decided that "Fergusonism" was preferable to the Klan in the governor's office.

Minorities began organizing in Texas to seek their civil rights. The National Association for the Advancement of Colored People opened a Texas chapter in 1912, and by 1919, there were chapters in 31 Texas communities. Similarly, Mexican-Texans formed Orden Hijos de America in 1921, and in 1927, the League of Latin-American Citizens was organized.

The Klan also dominated the Legislature in 1923, and a law passed that year barring blacks from participation in the Democratic primary had been passed. Although blacks had in fact been barred from voting in primaries for years, this law gave Dr. Lawrence A. Nixon, a black dentist from El Paso, the opportunity to go to court to fight the all-white primary. In 1927, the U.S. Supreme Court overturned the statute, but that was only the beginning of several court battles — which were not resolved until 1944, when blacks were allowed to vote in Democratic primaries.

Disgruntled Democrats and Klansmen tried to beat Mrs. Ferguson in the general election, but she was too strong. Voters also sent 91 new members to the Texas House, purging it of many of the Klan-backed representatives. After the 1924 election, the Klan's power ebbed rapidly in Texas.

Mrs. Ferguson named Emma Grigsby Meharg as Texas' first woman secretary of state in 1925. The governors Ferguson administration was stormy. Jim was accused of cronyism in awarding highway contracts and in other matters. And "Ma" returned to her husband's practice of liberal clemency for prisoners. In two years, Mrs. Ferguson extended clemency to 3,595 inmates.

Although Jim Ferguson was at his bombastic best in the 1926 Democratic primary, young Attorney General Dan Moody had little trouble winning the nomination and the general election. Texas Republicans in a unique twist held their first primary in 1926 because of Butte's showing against Mrs. Ferguson two years earlier. Political parties were required to hold primaries if they polled more than 100,000 votes in the previous general election.

At age 33, Moody was the youngest person ever to become governor of Texas. Like many of the state's governors, he was more progressive than the Legislature, and much of his program did not pass. Moody was successful in some government reorganization. He also cleaned up the highway department, which had been criticized under the Fergusons, and abandoned the liberal clemency policy for prisoners. And Moody worked at changing Texas' image as an anti-business state. "The day of the political trust-buster is gone," he told one Eastern journalist.

Progressives and prohibitionists still had a major influence on the Democratic Party, and 1928 was a watershed year for them. Moody easily won re-nomination and re-election. But the state party was drifting away from the direction of national Democrats. Big-city politicians and political machines controlled by recent immigrants gained influence in the national party. Their political positions and apparent values were foreign to many Texans. When Al Smith, a wet and a Roman Catholic, won the presidential nomination at the national Democratic convention in Houston, Texans were hard-pressed to remain faithful to the "party of the fathers." Moody, who had been considered a potential national figure, ruined his political career trying to straddle the fence, angering both wets and drys, Catholics and Protestants. Former governor Colquitt led an exodus of so-called "Hoovercrats" from the state Democratic convention in 1928, and for the first time in its history, Texas gave its electoral votes to a Republican, Herbert Hoover, in the general election.

Through the 1920s, oil continued to increase in importance in Texas' economy. New discoveries were made at Mexia in 1920, Luling in 1922, Big Lake in Reagan County in 1923, in the Wortham Field in 1924 and in Borger in 1926. But oil still did not dominate the state's economic life.

As late as 1929, meat packing, cottonseed processing and various milling operations exceeded the added value of petroleum refining. And as the 1920s ended, lumbering and food processing shared major economic roles with the petroleum industry. During the decade, Texas grew between 35-42 percent of U.S. cotton and 20-30 percent of the world crop. Irrigation and mechanization opened new areas of Texas to cotton production. In 1918, the U.S. Department of Agriculture reported 50,588 bales of cotton grown on the Texas Plains. Eight years later, more than 1.1 million bales were grown in the region, mostly around Lubbock.

But Texas with the rest of the nation was on the threshhold of a major economic disaster that would have irreversible consequences. The Great Depression was at hand.

Depression and War 21

TEXAS suffered with the rest of the nation through the Great Depression of the 1930s. Historians have noted that the state's economic collapse was not as severe, however, as that which struck the industrialized states. Texas' economy had sputtered through the decade of the 1920s, primarily because of the fluctuation of the price of cotton and other agricultural products. But agricultural prices were improving toward the end of the decade.

The Fergusons attempted a political comeback in the gubernatorial election of 1930. But Texans elected Ross S. Sterling, the founder of Humble Oil Co. and a successful businessman. Early in the Depression, Texans remained optimistic that the economic problems were temporary, another of the cyclical downturns the nation experienced periodically. Indeed, some Texans even felt that the hardships would be beneficial, ridding the economy of speculators and poor businessmen. Those attitudes gave way to increasing concern as the poor business conditions dragged on.

A piece of good luck turned into a near economic disaster for the state in late 1930. C. M. "Dad" Joiner struck oil near Kilgore, and soon the East Texas oil boom was in full swing. Thousands of wells were drilled. Millions of barrels of new oil flooded the market, making producers and small landowners wealthy. The major oil companies had been caught by surprise by the large discovery. They owned only 20 percent of the producing leases in the region. Independent oil operators discovered the field and did most of the development. Soon the glut of new oil drove market prices down from $1.10 a barrel in 1930 to 10 cents in 1931. Around the state many wells had to be shut in because they could not produce oil profitably at the low prices. The major companies also saw their reserves in other parts of the state losing value because of the declining prices.

The railroad commission attempted to control production through proration, which assigned production quotas to each well. The first proration order limited each well to about 1,000 barrels a day of production. Proration had two goals: to protect reserves through conservation and to maintain prices by limiting production. In August 1931, the Legislature approved a statute prohibiting the commission from prorating production to market demand. For several months, the railroad commission was hard-pressed to control production, facing resistance from producers as well as adverse court rulings. In February 1931, Gov. Sterling sent state troops into the East Texas Field to maintain order and to force compliance with the proration orders. A federal court later ruled the governor's actions illegal. Gov. Sterling was roundly criticized for sending troops into East Texas. Opponents said the action was taken to aid the major oil companies to the disadvantage of independent producers. Finally, in April 1933, the railroad commission prorated production on the basis, in part, of bottom-hole pressure in each well, and the courts upheld this approach. In Washington, Texas Sen. Tom Connally authored the Hot Oil Act, which involved the federal government in regulation by prohibiting oil produced in violation of state law from being sold in interstate commerce. Thereafter, Texas' producers accepted the concept of proration. Since Texas was the nation's largest oil producer, the railroad commission could set the national price of oil through proration for several decades thereafter.

Despite the problems, the oil boom helped East Texas weather the Depression better than other sections of the state. Farmers were hit particularly hard by 1931. Bumper crops had produced the familiar reduction in prices. Cotton dropped from 18 cents per pound in 1928 to six cents in 1931. That year Louisiana Gov. Huey Long proposed a ban on growing cotton in 1932 to eliminate the surplus. The Louisiana legislature enacted the ban, but Texas was the key state to the plan since it led the nation in cotton production. Gov. Sterling was cool to the idea, but responded to public support of it by calling a special session of the Legislature. The lawmakers passed a cotton acreage limitation bill in 1931, but the law was declared unconstitutional the following year.

Government statistics on unemployment in the period are incomplete, but in February 1932, Gov. Sterling estimated that 300,000 Texans were out of work. Many of them were destitute. One feature of the Depression had become the number of transients drifting from city to city looking for work. Local governments and private agencies tried to provide relief for the unemployed, but the effort was soon overwhelmed by the number of persons needing help. In Houston, blacks and Mexican-Texans were warned not to apply for relief because there was not enough money to take care of whites, and many Hispanics returned to Mexico voluntarily and otherwise. To relieve the local governments, Gov. Sterling proposed a bond program to repay counties for highways they had built and to start a public works program. Texans' long-held faith in self-reliance and rugged individualism was put to a severe test. As optimism faded, attempts were made to find a scapegoat. President Hoover and the Republican Party were the likely choices. The party had taken credit for the economic prosperity that the nation had enjoyed in the 1920s, but it had to assume responsibility for the collapse as well. Many Texans felt guilty about abandoning the Democratic Party in 1928. By 1932, many were looking to the federal government to provide relief from the effects of the Depression.

Texas Congressman John Nance Garner was a presidential candidate when the Democrats held their national convention. To avoid a deadlocked convention, Garner maneuvered the Texans to change strategy. On the fourth ballot, the Texas delegation voted for the eventual nominee, New York Gov. Franklin D. Roosevelt. Garner got the second place on the ticket that swept into office in the general election.

In Texas, Miriam Ferguson was successful in unseating Gov. Sterling in the Democratic primary, winning by about 4,000 votes. Her second administration was less turbulent than the first. State government costs were reduced, and voters approved $20 million in so-called "bread bonds" to help provide relief. In 1933, horse-racing came to the state, authorized through a rider on an appropriations bill. The law was repealed in 1937. Prohibition also was repealed in 1933, although much of

Texas remained dry under the local-option laws and the prohibition against open saloons. State government faced a series of financial problems during Mrs. Ferguson's second term. The annual deficit climbed to $14 million, and the state had to default on the interest payments on some bonds. Voters aggravated the situation by approving a $3,000 homestead exemption. Many property owners were losing their homes because they could not pay taxes. And while the exemption saved their homesteads, it worsened the state's financial problems.

Many Texas banks failed during the Depression, as did banks nationally. One of Roosevelt's first actions was to declare a national bank holiday in 1933. Gov. Ferguson closed state banks at the same time, although she had to "assume" authority that was not in the law.

In Washington, Texans played an important role in shaping Roosevelt's New Deal. As vice president, Garner presided over the Senate and maneuvered legislation through the upper house. Texans also chaired six major committees in the House: Sam Rayburn, Interstate and Foreign Commerce; Hatton W. Sumners, Judiciary; Fritz G. Lanham, Public Buildings and Grounds; J.J. Mansfield, Rivers and Harbors; and James P. Buchanan, Appropriations. With this influence, the Texas delegation supported the president's early social programs. In addition, Jesse Jones of Houston served as director of the Reconstruction Finance Corporation, the Federal Loan Administration and as Secretary of Commerce. Jones was one of the most influential men in Washington and second only to Roosevelt in wielding financial power to effect recovery.

As the New Deal developed, Texas benefited. Almost $1.5 billion was pumped into the state's economy in the early years of President Roosevelt's program. Farmers benefited from higher incomes, though they had restrictions placed on production. Ironically, the Agricultural Adjustment Act fulfilled many of the Populists' demands of a half-century earlier by providing price protection, an expanded money supply and easy farm credit. The Federal Emergency Relief Administration, created in 1933, provided aid for up to 298,000 people a year between 1933 and 1935. And the lumber industry, which had deteriorated in the late 1920s, rebounded, as the Civilian Conservation Corps, created to provide jobs for young people, aided in replanting many acres of depleted forest lands. By 1939, the industry was producing one billion board feet of lumber again, after dropping to almost one-third that volume in 1932.

The aid to farmers and cattlemen was particularly timely because the state began to experience another cycle of drought. Poor conservation practices had left many of the state's farmlands open to erosion. During the Dust Bowl days of the early- and mid-1930s, for example, the weather bureau in Amarillo reported 192 dust storms within a three-year period. Cooperation between state and federal agencies helped improve farmers' conservation efforts and reduced the erosion problem by the end of the decade.

Although the New Deal provided economic relief for many Texans, the state became divided politically over the thrust of the program late in the 1930s. In 1937, the break became most apparent. Frustrated that the U.S. Supreme Court had declared many of the New Deal programs to be unconstitutional, President Roosevelt proposed that the membership of the court be enlarged to allow him to appoint a new majority. Vice President Garner adamantly opposed the so-called "court-packing" plan, as did many elected officials in Texas. Although public officials' criticism became vitriolic, Roosevelt remained popular with voters, carrying the state in 1940, after Garner left the vice presidency, and in 1944.

Mrs. Ferguson did not seek re-election in 1934, and Attorney General James V. Allred was elected. Under his administration, several social welfare programs were initiated, including old-age pensions, teachers' retirement and workmen's compensation. Allred also signed legislation that created the Texas Centennial celebration, marking a century of independence from Mexico. It was hoped that the Centennial would generate jobs and money. Allred was re-elected in 1936.

Some of the New Deal's luster also dimmed when the nation was struck by another recession in 1937. Although Texas' economic condition improved toward the end of the decade, a full recovery was not realized until the beginning of World War II — when the state went through another industrial revolution.

In 1938, voters elected one of the most colorful figures in the state's political history to the governor's office. W. Lee "Pappy" O'Daniel, a flour salesman and leader of a radio hillbilly band, came from nowhere to defeat a field of much better known candidates in the Democratic primary and to easily win the general election. When re-elected two years later, O'Daniel became the first candidate to poll more than one million votes in a Texas election.

But O'Daniel's skills of state did not equal his campaigning ability, and throughout his administration, the governor and the Legislature were in conflict. In early 1941, long-time U.S. Senator Morris Sheppard died, and O'Daniel wanted the office. He appointed Andrew Jackson Houston, Sam Houston's aged son, to fill the vacancy. Houston died after only 24 days in office. O'Daniel won the special election for the post and was elected to a full term in 1942 in a close race with a young congressman, Lyndon B. Johnson.

Lt. Gov. Coke R. Stevenson succeeded O'Daniel and brought a broad knowledge of government to the office. Stevenson was elected to two full terms as governor. Thanks to frugal management and greatly increasing revenues during the war years, he left the state treasury with a surplus in 1947. Voters also solved the continuing deficit problem by approving a pay-as-you-go amendment to the constitution in 1942. It requires the state comptroller to certify that tax revenues will be available to support appropriations. Otherwise the money cannot be spent.

After the Japanese bombed Pearl Harbor on Dec. 7, 1941, Texans were in the forefront of the World War II effort. Texas Sen. Tom Connally, chairman of the Foreign Relations Committee, introduced the resolution declaring war on Japan on Dec. 8.

As in every war fought by the United States after Texas entered the Union, young Texans flocked to military service. More than 750,000 served, including 12,000 women in the auxiliary services. In December 1942, U.S. Secretary of the Navy Frank Knox said Texas contributed the largest percentage of its male population to the armed forces of any state. Thirty Texans won Congressional Medals of Honor in the fighting, and Audie Murphy, a young farm boy from Farmersville, was the most decorated soldier in the war.

Important contributions also were made at home. Texas was the site of 15 training posts, at which more than one and a quarter million men were trained, and of several prisoner-of-war camps.

Texas industry also flourished. Between mid-1940 and the peak of wartime production activity in November 1943, the number of manufacturing workers in Texas rose from 185,000 to 443,000. New industries that started up during the period included aircraft construction, ordnance and primary metals. Shipbuilders on the Texas Gulf coast employed 96,000 workers, and the aircraft industries employed 82,000. The state's petrochemical industry also expanded.

Between 1919 and 1939, Texas' manufacturing grew at a rate of 4.06 percent a year; in the next 15 years, the growth rate would accelerate to 9.38 percent annually. World War II changed the face of the world, but probably no region was affected more than Texas. The state was on the threshhold of becoming one of the nation's industrial giants.

Post-War Texas 22

WORLD War II irrevocably changed the face of Texas. During the decade of the 1940s, the state's population switched from predominantly rural to 60 percent urban. The number of manufacturing workers almost doubled. And as had been the dream of Texas leaders for more than a century, the state began to attract outside investment and new industry.

The state's politics became increasingly controlled by conservative Democrats after Gov. Allred left office. In 1946, Beauford H. Jester, a member of the railroad commission, gained the governorship. Under Jester in 1947, the Legislature passed the state's right-to-work law, prohibiting mandatory union membership, and reorganized public education with passage of the Gilmer-Aikin Act.

In 1948, Sen. W. Lee O'Daniel did not seek re-election. Congressman Lyndon Johnson and former Gov. Coke Stevenson vied for the Democratic nomination. In the runoff, Johnson won by a mere 87 votes in the closest — and most hotly disputed — statewide election in Texas' history. Johnson quickly rose to a leadership position in the U.S. Senate, and, with House Speaker Sam Rayburn, gave Texas substantial influence in national political affairs.

During the Jester administration several major constitutional amendments were adopted. Also, one of Texas' greatest tragedies occurred on April 16, 1947, when the French SS Grandcamp exploded at Texas City. This caused 4,000 injuries, with 512 dead. Property damage exceeded $200 million.

Although re-elected in 1948, Jester died in July 1949, the only Texas governor to die in office, and Lt. Gov. Allan Shivers succeeded him. During Shivers' administration, state spending more than doubled, reaching $805.7 million in 1956, as the governor increased appropriations for eleemosynary institutions, school salaries, retirement benefits, highways and old-age pensions. The 51st Legislature met for a total of 177 days in regular and special sessions in 1947, a record at the time.

Shivers broke with tradition, successfully winning three full terms as governor after completing Jester's unexpired term. Shivers also led a revolt by Texas Democrats against the national party in 1952. The governor, who gained both the Democratic and Republican nominations for the office under the law that allowed cross-filing that year, supported Republican Dwight Eisenhower for the presidency.

Many Texas Democrats broke with the national party over the so-called "Tidelands issue." Texas claimed land 12 miles out into the Gulf as state lands. The issue was important because revenue from oil and natural gas production from the area supported public education in the state. Major oil companies also backed Texas' position because state royalties on minerals produced from the land were much lower than federal royalties. President Harry S. Truman vetoed legislation that would have given Texas title to the land. Democratic presidential nominee Adlai Stevenson was no more sympathetic to the issue, and Texas gave its electoral votes to Republican Dwight Eisenhower in an election that attracted a two million-vote turnout for the first time in Texas. President Eisenhower signed a measure into law guaranteeing Texas' tidelands.

Scandal struck state government in 1954 when irregularities were discovered in the handling of funds in the veterans' land program in the General Land Office. Land Commissioner Bascom Giles was convicted of several charges and sent to prison. Several insurance companies also went bankrupt in the mid-1950s, prompting a reorganization of the State Board of Insurance in 1957.

In 1954, the U.S. Supreme Court ruled unconstitutional the segregation of schools, and for the next quarter-century, school integration became a major political issue. By the late 1960s, most institutions were integrated, but the state's major cities continued to wage court battles against forced busing of students to attain racial balance. Blacks and Mexican-Texans also made gains in voting rights during the 1950s.

Shivers had easily defeated Ralph W. Yarborough in the Democratic primary in 1952, but the divisions between the party's loyalists and those who bolted ranks to join Republicans in presidential races were growing. Shivers barely led the first 1954 primary over Yarborough and won the nomination with 53 percent of the vote in the runoff. Yarborough ran an equally close race against Price Daniel, a U.S. Senator who sought the governorship in 1956. Upon election as governor, Daniel left the Senate, and Yarborough won a special election to fill the vacancy in 1957. William A. Blakley, whom Yarborough defeated, had been appointed to the Senate seat by Shivers. In 1961, Blakley also was appointed to fill the vacancy created by Sen. Lyndon B. Johnson's election to the vice presidency. Blakley has the distinction of serving in both the Rusk and Houston successions in the Senate. Yarborough beat Blakley for a full term in 1958 and won re-election in 1964 before losing to Lloyd Bentsen in 1970 in the Democratic primary. Although a liberal, Yarborough proved to be unusually durable in Texas' conservative political climate.

The state budget topped $1 billion for the first time in 1958. A year later, a financial crisis gripped state government. Three special sessions were needed for the lawmakers to agree on a record appropriations bill. In 1960, voters approved a constitutional amendment that limited regular sessions to 140 days. The Legislature met for 205 days in regular and special sessions in 1961-62 and levied, over Gov. Daniel's opposition, the state's first broad-based sales tax in 1962.

Through the 1950s and 1960s, Texas' industrial base had expanded and diversified. Petroleum exploration, production, transportation and refining remained the cornerstones, but other industries grew. Attracted by cheap electricity, the aluminum industry came to Texas after World War II. Starting from the base developed during World War II, defense industries and associated high-tech firms, specializing in electronics and computers, centered on the Dallas-Fort Worth area and Houston. One of the most important scientific breakthroughs of the century came in 1958 in Dallas. Jack Kilby, an engineer at Texas Instruments, developed and patented the microchip that became the central part of the computers of the 1980s.

Sen. Lyndon Johnson unsuccessfully sought the Democratic presidential nomination in 1960, and John F. Kennedy subsequently selected the Texan as his running mate. Johnson is credited with keeping several Southern states, including Texas, in the Democratic column in the close election. Kennedy was a Roman Catholic and a liberal, a combination normally rejected by the Southern states. When Johnson left the Senate to assume his new office in 1961, John Tower won a special election that attracted more than 70 candidates and became the first Republican since Reconstruction to serve as a Texas senator.

During the early 1960s, Harris County was chosen as the site for the National Aeronautics and Space Administration's manned spacecraft center, now the Lyndon B. Johnson Space Center. The acquisition of the facility further diversified Texas' industrial base.

In 1962, John B. Connally, a former aide to Vice President Johnson and Secretary of the Navy under Kennedy, returned to Texas to seek the governorship. Gov. Daniel sought an unprecedented fourth term and was defeated in the Democratic primary. Connally won a close Democratic runoff over Don Yarborough and was elected easily. As governor, Connally concentrated on improving public education and state services and water development. He was re-elected in 1964 and 1966.

One of the major tragedies in the nation's history occurred in Dallas on Nov. 22, 1963, when President Kennedy was assassinated while riding in a motorcade. Gov. Connally also was seriously wounded. Lyndon B. Johnson was administered the oath of the presidency by Federal Judge Sarah T. Hughes of Dallas aboard Air Force One at Love Field. Lee Harvey Oswald was arrested for the murder of the president on the afternoon of the assassination, but Oswald was killed by Dallas nightclub operator Jack Ruby two days later. An extensive investigation into the assassination of President Kennedy was conducted by the Warren Commission. The panel concluded that Oswald was the killer and that he acted alone. Ruby, who was convicted of killing Oswald, died of cancer in the Dallas County jail in 1967 while the case was being appealed.

The assassination damaged the Republican Party in Texas, however. Building strength in Texas' conservative political atmosphere in 1962, eight Republicans, the most in decades, had been elected to the Texas House. And two Republicans — Ed Foreman of Odessa and Bruce Alger of Dallas — served in Congress. All were defeated in the 1964 general election.

In the emotional aftermath of the tragedy, Johnson, who won the presidency outright in a landslide election in 1964, persuaded the Congress to pass a series of civil rights and social welfare programs that changed the face of the nation. Texas was particularly hard hit by the civil rights legislation and a series of lawsuits challenging election practices. During the 1960s, the state constitutional limitation of urban representation in the Legislature was overturned. The poll tax was declared unconstitutional, and the practice of electing officials from at-large districts fell to the so-called "one-man, one-vote" ruling. As a result, more Republican, minority and liberal officials were elected, particularly from urban areas. In 1966, Curtis Graves and Barbara Jordan of Houston and Joe Lockridge of Dallas became the first blacks to serve in the Texas Legislature since 1898.

Lyndon Johnson did not seek re-election in 1968. The nation had become involved in an unpopular war in South Vietnam, and Johnson bowed out of the race in the interest of national unity. Democrats, however, stayed firmly in control of state government. Preston Smith was elected governor, and Ben Barnes gained the lieutenant governorship. Both also were re-elected in 1970. Although state spending continued to increase, particularly on education, the Legislature otherwise was quiet. A minimum-wage law was approved, and public kindergartens were authorized in 1969. At a special session, one of the state's major scandals developed. Gov. Smith allowed the lawmakers to consider special banking legislation supported by Houston banker Frank Sharp. Several public officials were implicated in receiving favors from the banker for seeing that the legislation passed. Texas House Speaker Gus Mutscher and Rep. Tommy Shannon were convicted of conspiracy to accept bribes in a trial held in Abilene. Mutscher subsequently completed his probation, had his rights restored and was elected county judge of Washington County.

But voters in 1972 demanded a new leadership in the state capital. Smith and Barnes were defeated in the Democratic primary, and Dolph Briscoe was elected governor. William P. Hobby Jr., son of the former governor, was elected lieutenant governor. In the fall, Texans gave presidential candidate Richard Nixon the state's electoral votes. Nixon carried 246 counties over Democrat George McGovern and received more than 65 percent of the popular vote, the largest recorded by a Republican in Texas.

The Legislature in 1973 was dominated by a reform atmosphere in the wake of the Sharpstown scandal. Price Daniel Jr., son of the former governor, was selected speaker of the House, and several laws concerning ethics and disclosure of campaign donations and spending were passed. Open meetings and open records statutes also were approved.

By 1970, Texas had become an even more urban state. The census found almost 11.2 million people in the state, ranking it sixth nationally. Three Texas cities, Houston, Dallas and San Antonio, were among the 10 largest in the nation.

Through the first half of the 1970s, several major changes were made in state policy. Liquor-by-the-drink had become legal, the age of majority had been lowered from 20 to 18, giving young people the right to vote, and the state's first Public Utilities Commission was created, hearing its initial case in September 1976.

Texas entered a period of unparalleled prosperity in 1973 when the Organization of Petroleum Exporting Countries boycotted the American market. Severe energy shortages resulted, and the price of oil and natural gas skyrocketed. The federal government had allowed foreign oil to be imported through the 1960s, severely reducing the incentives to find and produce domestic oil. Consequently, domestic producers could not compensate for the loss in foreign oil as a result of the boycott. The Texas Railroad Commission had long complained about the importation of foreign oil, and in 1972, the panel had removed proration controls from wells in the state, allowing 100 percent production. For the rest of the decade, domestic producers mounted a major exploration effort, drilling thousands of wells. Nevertheless, Texas' oil and gas production peaked in 1970 and has been declining since. Newly discovered oil and gas have not replaced the declining reserves. While Texans suffered from the inflation that followed, the state prospered. Tax revenues at all levels of government increased, and state revenues, basically derived from oil and gas taxes, spiraled, as did the state budget.

With the new revenue from inflation and petroleum taxes, state spending rose from $2.95 billion in 1970 to $8.6 billion in 1979, and education led the advance, moving from 42 percent of the budget to 51.5 percent. But there was no increase in state tax rates.

It was no surprise that education was one of the major beneficiaries of increased state spending. After World War II, more emphasis was placed on education across the state. Community colleges sprang up in many cities, and a total of 109 colleges were established between the end of the war and 1980. Quantity did not assure quality, however, and Texas' public and higher education seldom were ranked among national leaders.

In 1972, voters approved an amendment authorizing the Legislature to sit as a Constitutional Convention to rewrite the 1876 charter. Judge Robert W. Calvert, former chief justice of the Texas Supreme Court, served as chairman of the Texas Constitutional Revision Commission that held hearings around the state and proposed a new constitution to the Legislature in 1974. But the lawmakers met for several months, spent $5 million and failed to propose anything to be considered by voters. The public was outraged, and in 1975, the Legislature presented the work of the convention to voters in the form of eight constitutional amendments. All were defeated in a special election in November 1975.

Texas voters participated in their first presidential primary in 1976. Jimmy Carter of Georgia won the Democratic primary, and eventually the presidency, and Ronald Reagan carried the state's Republicans, but lost the party's nomination to President Gerald Ford.

In 1977, Texas farmers joined a national farm protest movement against price levels for their products, which, they said, were being sold below the cost of production.

The state proved politically volatile in 1978. First, Attorney General John Hill defeated Gov. Dolph Briscoe in the Democratic primary. A political newcomer, William P. Clements, upset Hill in the general election, giving Texas its first Republican governor since Reconstruction. And also for the first time since Reconstruction, state officials were elected for four-year terms. And a major shakeup occurred in the state's congressional delegation when six members of the U.S. House retired and three more were defeated at the polls. Texas, which usually had strong, experienced representation in Washington, included nine freshmen congressmen in its 24-member delegation.

Bibliography

Books

Adams, Frank Carter, **Texas Democracy: A Centennial History of Politics and Personalities of the Democratic Party 1836-1936, Vol. I**; Democratic Historical Association, Austin, 1936.

Adams, Willena C., editor, **Texas Cities and the Great Depression**; Texas Memorial Museum, Austin, 1973.

Ashcraft, Allan C., **Texas in the Civil War**; Texas Civil War Centennial Commission, Austin, 1962.

Ashford, Gerald, **Spanish Texas: Yesterday and Today**; Jenkins Publishing Co., The Pemberton Press, Austin, 1971.

Barker, Eugene C., editor, **Readings in Texas History**; Southwest Press, Dallas, 1929.

Barker, Eugene C., **The Life of Stephen F. Austin, Founder of Texas, 1793-1836**; Cokesbury Press, Dallas, 1926.

Barksdale, E.C., **The Genesis of the Aviation Industry in North Texas**; Bureau of Business Research, University of Texas, Austin, 1958.

Barnhill, J. Herschel, **From Surplus to Substitution: Energy in Texas**; American Press, Boston, 1983.

Barr, Alwyn, **Black Texans: A History of Negroes in Texas 1528-1971**; Jenkins Publishing Co., The Pemberton Press, Austin, 1973.

Barr, Alwyn, **Reconstruction to Reform: Texas Politics, 1876-1906**; University of Texas Press, Austin, 1971.

Becerra, Francisco, **A Mexican Sergeant's Recollections of the Alamo and San Jacinto**; Jenkins Publishing Co., Austin, 1980.

Bertrand, Louis, and Sir Charles Petrie, **The History of Spain: From the Musulmans to Franco**; Collier Books, New York, 1971.

Binkley, William C., **The Expansionist Movement in Texas 1836-1850**; University of California Publications in History, Vol. 13, University of California Press, Berkeley, 1925.

Binkley, William C., **The Texas Revolution**; Louisiana State University Press, Baton Rouge, 1952 (rpt. Texas State Historical Association, Austin, 1979).

Brown, Norman D., **Hood, Bonnet, and Little Brown Jug**; Texas A&M University Press, College Station, 1984.

Buenger, Walter L., **Secession and the Union in Texas**; University of Texas Press, Austin, 1984.

Campbell, Randolph B., and Richard G. Lowe, **Wealth and Power in Antebellum Texas**; Texas A&M University Press, College Station, 1977.

Casdorph, Paul, **The Republican Party in Texas, 1865-1965**; Jenkins Publishing Co., The Pemberton Press, Austin, 1965.

Castaneda, Carlos E., editor, **The Mexican Side of the Texas Revolution**; P.L. Turner Co., Austin, 1928 (rpt. Graphic Ideas, Inc., Austin, 1970).

Castaneda, Carlos E., **Our Catholic Heritage in Texas, Vols. 1-3**; Von Boeckmann-Jones Co., Austin, 1933-38.

Clarke, Mary Whatley, **Thomas J. Rusk: Soldier, Statesman, Jurist**; Jenkins Publishing Co., The Pemberton Press, Austin, 1971.

Connor, Seymour V., **Adventure in Glory: The Saga of Texas, 1836-1849**; Steck-Vaughn Co., Austin, 1965.

Cotner, Robert C., **James Stephen Hogg: A Biography**; University of Texas Press, Austin, 1959.

Crocket, G.L., **Two Centuries in East Texas**; Southwest Press, Dallas, 1932.

Davis, Ronald L., **Twentieth Century Cultural Life in Texas**; American Press, Boston, 1981.

De la Pena, Jose Enrique, **With Santa Anna in Texas: A Personal Narrative of the Revolution**, Trans. Carmen Perry; Texas A&M University Press, College Station, 1975.

DeLeon, Arnoldo, **The Mexican Image in Nineteenth Century Texas**; American Press, Boston, 1982.

DeLeon, Arnoldo, **The Tejano Community, 1836-1900**; University of New Mexico Press, Albuquerque, 1982.

DeLeon, Arnoldo, **They Called Them Greasers: Anglo Attitudes Toward Mexicans in Texas, 1821-1900**; University of Texas Press, Austin, 1983.

DeVoto, Bernard, **The Year of Decision: 1846**; Little, Brown and Co., Boston, 1943.

Dixon, Sam Houston, and Louis Wiltz Kemp, **The Heroes of San Jacinto**; Anson Jones Press, Houston, 1932.

Dodge, Bertha S., **Cotton: The Plant That Would Be King**; University of Texas Press, Austin, 1984.

Drinnon, Richard, **Facing West: The Metaphysics of Indian-Hating and Empire-Building**; New American Library, New York, 1980.

Durham, George, **Taming the Nueces Strip**; University of Texas Press, Austin, 1982.

Easterlin, Richard A., David Ward, William Bernard, and Reed Ueda, **Immigration**; Belknap Press of Harvard University Press, Cambridge, 1982.

Farber, James, **Texas, C.S.A.: A Spotlight on Disaster**; The Jackson Co., New York, 1947.

Fehrenbach, T.R., **Comanches: The Destruction of a People**; Alfred A. Knopf Co., New York, 1976.

Fehrenbach, T.R., **Lone Star: A History of Texas and the Texans**; MacMillan Co., New York, 1968.

Foner, Eric, **Nothing But Freedom: Emancipation and Its Legacy**; Louisiana State University Press, Baton Rouge, 1983.

Fornell, Earl Wesley, **The Galveston Era: The Texas Crescent on the Eve of Secession**; University of Texas Press, Austin, 1961.

Frantz, Joe B., **Texas: A Bicentennial History**; W. W. Norton & Co., New York, 1976.

Friend, Llerena B., **Sam Houston: The Great Designer**; University of Texas Press, Austin, 1954.

Gambrell, Herbert, **Anson Jones: The Last President of Texas**; Doubleday and Co., Inc., Garden City, N.J., 1948.

Gard, Wayne, **The Chisholm Trail**; University of Oklahoma Press, Norman, 1954.

Goodwyn, Lawrence, **The Populist Moment: A Short History of the Agrarian Revolt in America**; Oxford University Press, New York, 1978.

Gouge, William M., **The Fiscal History of Texas**; Lippincott, Grambo, and Co., Philadelphia, 1852.

Gould, Lewis L., **Progressives and Prohibitionists: Texas Democrats in the Wilson Era**; University of Texas Press, Austin, 1973.

Graham, Philip, **The Life and Poems of Mirabeau Buonaparte Lamar**; University of North Carolina Press, Chapel Hill, 1938.

Grant, Joseph M., and Lawrence L. Crum, **The Development of State Chartered Banking in Texas**; Bureau of Business Research, University of Texas at Austin, 1978.

Green, George Norris, **A Liberal's View of Texas Politics, 1890s-1930s**; American Press, Boston, 1981.

Green, George Norris, **A Liberal View of Texas Politics Since the 1930s**; American Press, Boston, 1981.

Green, George Norris, The Establishment in Texas Politics: The Primitive Years, 1938-1957; Greenwood Press, Westport, Conn., 1979.

Gregory, Jack, and Rennard Strickland, Sam Houston with the Cherokees 1829-1833; University of Texas Press, Austin, 1967.

Haley, J. Evetts, The XIT Ranch of Texas and the Early Days of the Llano Estacado; University of Oklahoma Press, Norman, 1954.

Hanke, Lewis, Aristotle and the American Indian: A Study of Race Prejudice in the Modern World; University of Indiana Press, Bloomington, 1959.

Harper, William G., The Texas Blue Laws; Exposition Press, Hicksville, N.Y., 1974.

Hawkins, Wallace, El Sal Del Rey; Texas State Historical Association, Austin, 1947.

Henson, Margaret S., Anglo American Women in Texas, 1820-1850; American Press, Boston, 1982.

Hewitt, W. Phil, Land and Community: European Migration to Rural Texas in the 19th Century; American Press, Boston, 1981.

Hinkle, Stacy C., Wings Over the Border: The Army Air Service Armed Patrol of the United States-Mexico Border 1919-1921; Southwestern Studies, Texas Western Press, El Paso, 1970.

Hogan, William Ransom, The Texas Republic; University of Texas Press, Austin, 1969.

Horgan, Paul, The Great River, Vols. 1-2; Rinehart & Co., Inc., New York, 1954.

Horsman, Reginald, Race and Manifest Destiny: The Origins of American Racial Anglo-Saxonism; Harvard University Press, Cambridge, 1981.

Innes, Hammond, The Conquistadors; Alfred A. Knopf, New York, 1969.

Institute of Texan Cultures, The Indian Texans; University of Texas at San Antonio, 1970.

Institute of Texan Cultures, The Spanish Texans; University of Texas at San Antonio, 1972.

Irby, James A., Backdoor at Bagdad; Southwestern Series, Texas Western Press, El Paso, 1968.

James, Marquis, The Raven: A Biography of Sam Houston; Blue Ribbon Books, Inc., New York City, 1929.

John, Elizabeth A.H., Storms Brewed In Other Men's Worlds: The Confrontation of Indians, Spanish and French in the Southwest, 1540-1795; Texas A&M University Press, College Station, 1975.

Jones, Billy M., The Search for Maturity: Saga of Texas, 1875-1900; Steck-Vaughn Co., Austin, 1965.

Jordan, Terry G., Environment and Environmental Perceptions in Texas; American Press, Boston, 1980.

Jordan, Terry G., Immigration to Texas; American Press, Boston, 1980.

Jordan, Terry G., Trails to Texas: Southern Roots of Western Cattle Ranching; University of Nebraska Press, Lincoln, 1981.

Leckie, William H., The Buffalo Soldiers: A Narrative of the Negro Cavalry in the West; University of Oklahoma Press, Norman, 1967.

Lindheim, Milton, The Republic of the Rio Grande; W.M. Morrison, Bookseller, Waco, 1964.

Lockhart, James, and Stuart B. Schwartz, Early Latin America: A History of Colonial Spanish America and Brazil; Cambridge University Press, Cambridge, 1983.

Lord, Walter, A Time to Stand: The Epic of the Alamo; Harper & Row, New York, 1961 (rpt. University of Nebraska Press, Lincoln, 1978).

Lukes, Edward A., DeWitt Colony of Texas; Jenkins Publishing Co., The Pemberton Press, Austin, 1976.

Malone, Dumas, **Jefferson the President: First Term 1801-1805**; Little, Brown and Co., Boston, 1970.

Malone, Dumas, **Jefferson the President: Second Term 1805-1809**; Little, Brown and Co., New York, 1974.

Martin, Roscoe, **The People's Party in Texas: A Study in Third Party Politics**; University of Texas Press, Austin, 1970.

Maxwell, Robert S., and Robert D. Baker, **Sawdust Empire: The Texas Lumber Industry, 1830-1940**; Texas A&M University Press, College Station, 1983.

Maxwell, Robert S., **Texas Economic Growth, 1890 to World War II: From Frontier to Industrial Giant**; American Press, Boston, 1981.

McDonald, Archie P., **Texas: All Hail the Mighty State**; Eakin Press, Austin, 1983.

McDonald, Archie P., **The Trail to San Jacinto**; American Press, Boston, 1981.

McDonald, Archie P., **Travis**; Jenkins Publishing Co., The Pemberton Press, Austin, 1976.

McDonald, Archie P., **The Republic of Texas**; American Press, Boston, 1981.

McKay, Seth S., and Odie B. Faulk, **Texas After Spindletop: Saga of Texas, 1901-1965**; Steck-Vaughn Co., Austin, 1965.

Meinig, D.W., **Imperial Texas: An Interpretive Essay in Cultural Geography**; University of Texas Press, Austin, 1969.

Merk, Frederick, **The History of the Westward Movement**; Alfred E. Knopf, New York, 1978.

Meyer, Michael C., and William L. Sherman, **The Course of Mexican History**; Oxford University Press, New York, 1979.

Miller, Hurbert J., **Jose de Escandon, Colonizer of Nuevo Santander**; New Santander Press, Edinburg, 1980.

Miller, Thomas L., **The Public Lands of Texas, 1519-1970**; University of Oklahoma Press, Norman, 1972.

Moneyhon, Carl H., **Republicanism in Reconstruction Texas**; University of Texas Press, Austin, 1980.

Myres, John Myres, **The Alamo**; E.P. Dutton and Co., 1948 (rpt. University of Nebraska Press, Lincoln, 1973).

Myres, Sandra L., **Native Americans of Texas**; American Press, Boston, 1981.

Newcomb, W.W. Jr., **The Indians of Texas**; University of Texas Press, Austin, 1961.

Norman, Mary Anne, **The Texas Economy Since World War II**; American Press, Boston, 1983.

Nunn, W.C., **Texas Under the Carpetbaggers**; University of Texas Press, Austin, 1962.

Pettigrew, Thomas E., George M. Fredrickson, Dale T. Knobel, Nathan Glazer and Reed Ueda, **Prejudice**; Belknap Press of Harvard University Press, Cambridge, 1982.

Pilkington, William T., **Imaging Texas: The Literature of the Lone Star State**; American Press, Boston, 1981.

Price, Glenn W., **Origins of the War with Mexico: Polk-Stockton Intrigue**; University of Texas Press, Austin, 1967.

Prindle, David F., **Petroleum Politics and the Texas Railroad Commission**; University of Texas Press, Austin, 1981.

Procter, Ben H., **Not Without Honor: The Life of John H. Reagan**; University of Texas Press, Austin, 1962.

Puryear, Pamela A., and Nath Winfield Jr., **Sandbars and Sternwheelers: Navagation on the Brazos**; Texas A&M University Press, College Station, 1976.

Raat, W. Dirk, editor, **Mexico: From Independence to Revolution, 1810-1910**; University of Nebraska Press, Lincoln, 1982.

Raat, W. Dirk, **Revoltosos**; Texas A&M University Press, College Station, 1981.

Ramsdell, Charles William, **Reconstruction in Texas**; Columbia University Press, New York, 1910 (rpt. University of Texas Press, Austin, 1970).

Red, William Stuart, **The Texas Colonists and Religion 1821-1836**; E. L. Shettles, Publisher, Austin, 1924.

Reed, S.G., **A History of the Texas Railroads**; St. Clair Publishing Co., Houston, 1941.

Rice, Lawrence D., **The Negro in Texas 1874-1900**; Louisiana State University Press, Baton Rouge, 1971.

Richardson, Rupert N., **Colonel House: The Texas Years**; Hardin-Simmons University Publications in History, Abilene, 1964.

Richardson, Rupert N., Ernest Wallace and Adrian N. Anderson, **Texas: The Lone Star State**; Prentice-Hall, Inc., Englewood Cliffs, N.J., 1970.

Richardson, Rupert N., **The Frontier of Northwest Texas, 1846-1876**; The Arthur H. Clark Co., Glendale, Calif., 1963.

Rodriguez, Louis J., **Dynamics of Growth: An Economic Profile of Texas**; Madrona Press, Austin, 1978.

Rosenbaum, Robert J., **Mexican Resistance in the Southwest**; University of Texas Press, Austin, 1981.

Rosenbaum, Robert J., **The History of Mexican Americans in Texas**; American Press, Boston, 1980.

Rutherford, Bruce, **Ferguson: The Impeachment of Jim Ferguson**; Eakin Press, Austin, 1983.

Samora, Julian, Joe Bernal and Albert Pena, **Gunpowder Justice: A Reassessment of the Texas Rangers**; Notre Dame Press, South Bend, 1979.

Sibley, Marilyn McAdams, **The Port of Houston, A History**; University of Texas Press, Austin, 1968.

Sierra, Justo, **The Political Evolution of the Mexican People**, trans. Charles Ramsdell; University of Texas Press, Austin, 1969.

Silverthorne, Elizabeth, **Ashbel Smith of Texas: Pioneer, Patriot, Statesman, 1805-1886**; Texas A&M University Press, College Station, 1982.

Smallwood, James, **The Great Recovery: The New Deal in Texas**; American Press, Boston, 1983.

Smallwood, James, **The Struggle for Equality: Blacks in Texas**; American Press, Boston, 1983.

Smithwick, Noah, **The Evolution of a State or Recollections of Old Texas Days**; H.P.N. Gammell, Austin, 1900 (rpt. University of Texas Press, Austin, 1983).

Smyrl, Frank H., **Texas in Gray: The Civil War Years, 1861-1865**; American Press, Boston, 1983.

Smyrl, Frank H., **The Twenty-Eighth Star: Texas During the Period of Early Statehood, 1846-1861**; American Press, Boston, 1983.

Sonnichsen, C.L., **Pass of the North: Four Centuries on the Rio Grande, Vol. I -1529-1917**; Texas Western Press, UT-El Paso, 1968.

Spratt, John Stricklin, **The Road to Spindletop: Economic Change in Texas, 1875-1901**; SMU Press, Dallas, 1955 (rpt. University of Texas Press, Austin, 1983).

Stambaugh, J. Lee, and Lillian J., **The Lower Rio Grande Valley of Texas: Its Colonization and Industrialization, 1518-1953**; The Jenkins Co., San Felipe Press, Austin, 1974.

Syers, Ed, **Texas: The Beginning 1519-1834**; Texian Press, Waco, 1978.

Taylor, Virginia H., **The Franco-Texan Land Co.**; University of Texas Press, Austin, 1969.

Timmons, W.H., **The Anglo-American Advance Into Texas, 1810-1830**; American Press, Boston, 1981.

Tinkle, Lon, **The Alamo** (13 Days to Glory, McGraw-Hill Book Co., New York, 1958); New American Library, New York.

Tolbert, Frank, **The Day of San Jacinto**; McGraw-Hill Book Co., Inc., New York, 1959.

Utley, Robert M., **The Indian Frontier of the American West 1846-1890**; University of New Mexico Press, Albuquerque, 1984.

Vigness, David M., **The Revolutionary Decades: The Saga of Texas, 1810-1836**; Steck-Vaughn Co., Austin, 1965.

Vigness, David M., **Spanish Texas, 1519-1810**; American Press, Boston, 1983.

Wallace, Ernest, **Charles DeMorse: Pioneer Editor and Statesman**; Texas Tech Press, Lubbock, 1943.

Wallace, Ernest, and David M. Vigness, **Documents of Texas History**; The Steck Co., Austin, 1963.

Wallace, Ernest, and E. Adamson Hoebel, **The Comanches: Lords of the South Plains**; University of Oklahoma Press, Norman, 1952.

Wallace, Ernest, **The Howling of Coyotes: Reconstruction Efforts to Divide Texas**; Texas A&M University Press, College Station, 1979.

Wallace, Ernest, **Ranald S. Mackenzie on the Texas Frontier**; West Texas Museum Association, Lubbock, 1965.

Wallace, Ernest, **Texas in Turmoil: The Saga of Texas: 1849-1875**; Steck-Vaughn Co., Austin, 1965.

Webb, Walter Prescott, and H. Bailey Carroll, editors, **Handbook of Texas, Vols. 1-3**; Texas State Historical Association, Austin, 1952 and 1976.

Webb, Walter Prescott, **The Great Frontier**; University of Texas Press, Austin, 1964.

Webb, Walter Prescott, **The Great Plains**; University of Nebraska Press, Lincoln, 1981.

Webb, Walter Prescott, **The Texas Rangers: A Century of Frontier Defense**; Houghton Mifflin, Boston, 1935 (rpt.University of Texas Press, Austin, 1980).

Weber, David J., **The Mexican Frontier, 1821-1846: The American Southwest Under Mexico**; University of New Mexico Press, Albuquerque, 1982.

Weber, David J., editor, **New Spain's Far Northern Frontier**; University of New Mexico Press, Albuquerque, 1979.

Weddle, Robert S., **San Juan Bautista: Gateway to Spanish Texas**; University of Texas Press, Austin, 1968.

Weddle, Robert S., **Wilderness Manhunt: The Spanish Search for LaSalle**; University of Texas Press, Austin, 1973.

Whisenhunt, Donald W., editor, **Texas: A Sesquicentennial Celebration**; Eakin Press, Austin, 1984.

Whisenhunt, Donald W., editor, **The Depression in the Southwest**; Kennikat Press, Port Washington, N.Y., 1980.

Whisenhunt, Donald W., **The Depression in Texas**; American Press, Boston, 1982.

Whisenhunt, Donald W., **The Depression in Texas: The Hoover Years**; Garland Publishing, Inc., New York, 1983.

Whisenhunt, Donald W., **The Development of Higher Education in Texas**; American Press, Boston, 1983.

White, Dabney, editor, and T. C. Richardson, author, **East Texas: Its History and Its Makers, Vols. I-IV**; Lewis Historical Publishing Co., New York.

Wilkinson, J. B., **Laredo and the Rio Grande Frontier**; Jenkins Publishing Co., Austin, 1975.

Williams, Clayton W. (Ernest Wallace, editor), **Texas' Last Frontier: Fort Stockton and the Trans-Pecos, 1861-1895**; Texas A&M University Press, College Station, 1982.

Williams, Lyle W., **Ranches and Ranching in Spanish Texas**; American Press, Boston, 1982.

Williams, T. Harry, Richard N. Current and Frank Freidel, **A History of the United States (to 1876)**; Alfred A. Knopf, Inc., New York, 1959.

Wilson, James A., **Hide & Horn in Texas: The Spread of Cattle Ranching 1836-1900**; American Press, Boston, 1983.

Wintz, Cary D., **Reconstruction in Texas**; American Press, Boston, 1983.

Wintz, Cary D., **Texas Politics in the Gilded Age, 1873-1890**; American Press, Boston, 1983.

Wright, J. Leitch Jr., **The Only Land They Knew: The Tragic Story of the American Indian in the South**; The Free Press (Division of MacMillan Publishing Co.), New York, 1981.

Wyatt-Brown, Bertram, **Southern Honor: Ethics and Behavior in the Old South**; Oxford University Press, New York, 1982.

Articles

Barker, Eugene C., **"The Annexation of Texas"**; Southwestern Historical Quarterly(SWHQ), Vol. L, No. 1, July 1946.

Barker, Eugene C., **"Land Speculation as a Cause of the Texas Revolution"**; Texas State Historical Quarterly (SWHQ), Vol. X, No. 1, July 1906.

Barker, Eugene C., **"The San Jacinto Campaign"**; SWHQ, Vol. IV, No. 4, April 1901.

Barker, Eugene C., **"The Texan Revolutionary Army"**; SWHQ, Vol. IX, No. 4, April 1906.

Bender, A.B., **"Opening Routes Across West Texas, 1848-1850"**; SWHQ, Vol. XXXVII, No. 2, October 1933.

Bender, A.B., **"The Texas Frontier, 1848-1861, Part II"**; SWHQ Vol. XVI, No. 1, July 1912.

Binkley, William C., **"The Activities of the Texan Revolutionary Army after San Jacinto"**; Journal of Southern History, Vol. VI, August 1940.

Bolton, H.E., **"The Spanish Occupation of Texas, 1519-1690"**; SWHQ, Vol. XVI, No. 1, July 1912.

Caldwell, Edwin L., **"Highlights of the Development of Manufacturing in Texas,1900-1960"**; SWHQ, Vol. LXVIII, No. 4, April 1965.

Calvert, Robert A., **"Nineteenth-Century Farmers, Cotton, and Prosperity"**; SWHQ,Vol. LXXIII, No. 4, April 1970.

Casdorf, Paul D., **"Norris Wright Cuney and Texas Republican Politics, 1883-1896"**; SWHQ, Vol. LXVIII, No. 4, April 1965.

Cohen, Barry M., **"The Texas-Mexico Border, 1858-1867"**; Texana, Vol. VI, No. 2, Summer 1968.

Cox, Isaac Joslin, **"The Louisiana Texas Frontier"**; SWHQ, Vol. X, No. 1, July 1906.

Crane, M.M., **"Recollections of the Establishment of the Texas Railroad Commission"**; SWHQ, Vol. L, No. 4, April 1947.

Davenport, Harbert, **"Notes on Early Steamboating on the Rio Grande"**; SWHQ, Vol. XLIX, No. 2, October 1945.

Elliott, Claude, **"Union Sentiment in Texas, 1861-65"**; SWHQ, Vol. L, No. 4, April 1947.

Ellis, L. Tuffly, **"Maritime Commerce on the Far Western Gulf, 1861-1865"**; SWHQ, Vol. LXXVII, No. 2, October 1973.

Foner, Eric, "The New View of Reconstruction"; American Heritage Magazine, Oct./Nov. 1983, Vol. 34, No. 6.

Gard, Wayne, "The Fence-Cutters"; SWHQ, Vol. LI, No. 1, July 1947.

Havins, T.R., "Texas Fever"; SWHQ, Vol. LII, No. 2, October 1948.

Holt, R.D., "The Introduction of Barbed Wire Into Texas and the Fence Cutting War"; West Texas Historical Association Yearbook (WTHA Yearbook), Vol. VI, June 1930.

Houston, Sam, "Houston's Last Speech in the United States Senate"; Texas Almanac of 1860, Galveston News, Galveston, 1860.

Inglis, G. Douglas, "The Men of Cibola: New Investigations on the Francisco Vazquez de Coronado Expedition"; Panhandle-Plains Historical Review, Vol. LV, 1982.

Kilgore, Dan, "Texas Cattle Origins"; The Cattleman Magazine, January, 1983.

Kingston, Mike, "Archaeology: A Slow Start in Texas"; Texas Almanac, 1984-85, Dallas Morning News, Dallas, 1984.

Kingston, Mike, "A History of the Texas Borderlands"; Texas Almanac, 1984-85, Dallas Morning News, Dallas, 1984.

Koch, Lena Clara, "The Federal Indian Policy in Texas, 1845-60"; SWHQ, Vol. XXVIII, No. 2, April 1925.

Labadie, N.D., "San Jacinto Campaign"; Texas Almanac of 1859, Galveston News, Galveston, 1859.

Marshall, Ray, "Some Reflections on Labor History"; SWHQ, Vol. LXXV, No. 2, October 1971.

Marshall, Thomas Maitland, "The Southwestern Boundary of Texas, 1821-1840"; SWHQ, Vol. XIV, No. 4, April 1911.

Martin, Roscoe C., "The Grange as a Political Factor in Texas"; Southwestern Political and Social Science Quarterly, Vol. VI, June 1925-March 1926.

Martin, Roscoe C., "The Greenback Party in Texas"; SWHQ, Vol. XXX, No. 3, January 1927.

Myres, Sandra, "Spanish Cattle Kingdom"; Texana, Vol. IV, No. 3, Fall 1966.

Neighbours, Kenneth F., "The Expedition of Maj. Robert S. Neighbors to El Paso in 1849"; SWHQ, Vol. LVIII, No. 1, July 1954.

Neighbours, Kenneth F., "Indian Exodus out of Texas in 1859"; WTHA Yearbook, Vol. XXXVI, 1960.

Neighbours, Kenneth F., "The Struggle Over the Upper Rio Grande Region in 1850"; SWHQ, Vol. LXI, No. 4, April 1958.

Norvell, James R ., "The Railroad Commission of Texas, Its Origin and History"; SWHQ, Vol. LXVIII, No. 4, April 1965.

Parvin, Bob, "In Search of the First Texans"; Texas Parks and Wildlife Magazine, October 1983.

Peterson, Robert L., "Jay Gould and the Texas Railroad Commission"; SWHQ, Vol. LVIII, No. 3., January 1955.

Porter, Kenneth Wiggins, "The Seminole Negro-Indian Scouts, 1870-81"; SWHQ, Vol. LV, No. 3, January 1952.

Reese, James V., "The Early History of Labor Organizations in Texas, 1838-1876"; SWHQ, Vol. LXXII, No. 1, July 1968.

Reese, James V., "The Evolution of an Early Texas Union: The Screwmans' Benevolent Association of Galveston, 1866-1891"; SWHQ, Vol. LXXV, No. 2, October 1971.

Rippy, J. Fred, "British Investments in Texas Land and Livestock"; SWHQ, Vol. LVIII, No. 3, January 1955.

Smith, Ralph A., "The Farmers' Alliance in Texas"; SWHQ, Vol. XLVIII, No. 3, January 1945.

Smith, Ralph A., "The Grange Movement in Texas, 1873-1900"; SWHQ, Vol. XLII, No.4, April 1939.

Smyrl, Frank H., "Texans in the Union Army, 1861-65"; SWHQ, Vol. LXV, No. 2, October 1961.

Spillman, W.J., "Adjustment of the Texas Boundary in 1850"; SWHQ, Vol. VII, No. 3, January 1904.

Steiner, Stan, "Jewish Conquistadors: America's First Cowboys?"; American West Magazine, Sept./Oct. 1983.

Vigness, David M., "Indian Raids on the Lower Rio Grande, 1836-37"; SWHQ, Vol. LIX, No. 1, July 1955.

Walker, Ralph, "Long's Lone Star Republic: The death of James Long and the Texas filibustering era"; American History Illustrated, Vol XVIII, No. 10, February 1984.

Watford, W.H., "Confederate Western Ambitions"; SWHQ, Vol. XLIV, No. 2, October 1938.

Weddle, Robert S., "San Juan Bautista: Mother of Texas Missions"; SWHQ, Vol. LXXI, No. 4, April 1968.

Wilcox, Seb S., "Laredo During the Texas Republic"; SWHQ, Vol. XLII, No. 2, October 1938.

TEXAS HISTORY

Five Days of Destiny in Texas

This article was written by Mike Kingston, editor, and was published in the 1986-87 Texas Almanac.

More than 54,750 days have passed since Texas declared its independence from Mexico. Though there have been wars and Indian raids, political debates and elections, most of the days since March 2, 1836, have been uneventful. Texans went about the mundane business of transforming a wilderness into a modern society. But among those thousands of days, a handful harbored events that transformed Texas, in some cases, and, in other instances, had a great impact on United States and world history.

The following are brief accounts of these "five days of destiny" in Texas history and their impact.

April 21, 1836

In the late afternoon of this spring day on the plains of San Jacinto in present-day Houston, Gen. Sam Houston and a small band of Texans defeated a troop of Mexican soldiers in a short battle. The following day, Gen. Antonio Lopez de Santa Anna, dictator of Mexico and commander of the troops, was captured while trying to escape the field of battle.

With Santa Anna's capture, the Texans affirmed the independence that they had declared from Mexico on March 2, less than two months before. Although the two nations remained belligerent for the next nine years, Texas stood as a republic, a member of the family of the world's nations, until its annexation to the United States in 1845. Texas' claim to the entire watershed of the Rio Grande to its source in Colorado was accepted by the United States, which went to war with Mexico to back it up. As a result of the war with Mexico, the United States acquired the present-day Southwest and California and became a truly continental nation. Harbors acquired on the West Coast allowed American merchants to open trade with the Orient, and the U.S. role in world affairs was greatly expanded. The fact that Texas existed gave the United States the opportunity to contest Mexico for the large territory that Spain had claimed, but not developed, for more than two centuries.

Without Houston's victory over Santa Anna at San Jacinto, how different would the face of the United States be today? No one knows, of course. Most historians feel

128

that the power of Manifest Destiny would have pushed the United States westward into the Mexican territories regardless of the excuses necessary to justify the movement. Texas' existence allowed the United States to claim purity of motive in its war with Mexico and to demand the large territory as indemnity for the expense of the war and the loss of American life.

On the other hand, if Santa Anna had prevailed, Mexican history might have been much different. The nation was in constant turmoil from 1828 until 1855. Centralists and republicans battled for control of the government, and the Mexican presidency changed hands 36 times during these turbulent years. Two major problems included continuing recriminations over the loss of half the Mexican state to the United States in the War of 1846 and the lack of a single leader who by force of personality could unify the country.

A victory over the Anglo-Texans at San Jacinto would have allowed Santa Anna to return to Mexico City a national hero. With that prestige, the government could have been stabilized — albeit under the centralists. Serious attention could have been given to colonizing Texas with Europeans and Mexican citizens, as had been planned but never accomplished by both Spain and Mexico. A stable Mexican government might have attracted more serious support from England and France in case of hostilities with the United States. And the face of North America might be much different today.

But the victory of the Texas army, made up mostly of "Old Texans" who had established homes and families in the Mexican state, opened the door for Anglo-American colonization of the Southwest and California.

January 10, 1901

Anthony Lucas was not a fly-by-night wildcatter. An experienced oil man and engineer, he was convinced that there was oil around the salt domes near Beaumont in Southeast Texas. On Jan. 10, 1901, Lucas' faith was richly rewarded. Legendary Spindletop, which opened the world's largest oil boom at that time, blew in on the evening of that winter day. And with it, the oil age opened for the world.

Within days, Spindletop exceeded Texas' previous annual oil production of 836,000 barrels, and by the end of the first year, the well gushed forth 3.2 million barrels of oil.

Lucas was not the only person who felt that there was oil near the salt domes. Patillo Higgins drilled wells in the area around Spindletop for a decade before his money ran out, but no oil was discovered. Higgins leased to Lucas the land on which Spindletop was located.

Oil had been produced at Corsicana for many years before Spindletop blew in, but never in the quantities reached after Lucas' discovery. Indians had used oil from seeps for medicine, and Spanish explorers caulked boats with the tar-like substance. During the 19th century, oil discovered near Nacogdoches was used on roads to keep down the dust and occasionally as a lubricant.

The staggering volume of oil unleashed by Spindletop and subsequent discoveries gave U.S. industry a cheap and plentiful source of energy. Railroads soon converted from coal to oil, and steamship companies were not far behind. With such a cheap and ready supply of energy, personal automobiles were within the reach of many Americans. The increased use of automobiles and trucks for transportation required an improvement of the nation's highway systems.

Texas became the nation's undisputed leader in oil production in 1930 with the discovery of the East Texas oil field by C. M. "Dad" Joiner. The glut of oil caused by this find drove oil prices down to ruinous levels, and the state stepped in to control production as a conservation measure. The conservation also allowed the Texas Railroad Commission to set the world price of oil from the 1930s until the Arab oil crisis of the 1970s.

Texas, the nation and the world were never the same after Anthony Lucas' historic discovery opened the gates to the oil age, which has brought both great prosperity and problems.

March 2, 1910

No military establishment had a more inauspicious beginning than the United States Air Force. On March 2, 1910, Lt. Benjamin D. Foulois was catapulted into the air for a seven and one-half minute flight around a drill field at Fort Sam Houston in San Antonio. A second flight that day resulted in a crash that damaged the plane and delayed Lt. Foulois' "training" for 10 days.

These flights capped the entrance of the United States Army into the air age. Shortly after the Wright brothers' successful flight at Kitty Hawk, N.C., in 1903, the military application of the new airplanes was recognized. In 1908, the army and the Wright brothers, Orville and Wilbur, entered into a contract to provide the first military airplane. The contract called for the machine to pass a series of speed and cross-country tests and for two military pilots to be trained by the inventors. Lt. Foulois was a member of the Aeronautics Board that supervised the tests.

An accident that killed an officer and injured Orville Wright at the Fort Myers, Va., proving grounds delayed the tests until June 1909. A month later, the plane passed the required tests, and two officers were trained to fly it at College Park, Md. Lt. Foulois was scheduled for flight training but received only three hours of in-the-air instruction from Wilbur Wright and another pilot before being ordered to another assignment. The young lieutenant did not solo until he reached San Antonio.

In November 1909, Lt. Foulois was called to the office of Gen. James Allen, Chief Signal Officer of the Army, and was asked how long it would take to crate the army's only airplane for shipment to San Antonio. "Twenty-four hours," Foulois replied. Also present at the meeting was James L. Slayden, congressman from San Antonio and chairman of the U.S. House Committee on Military Affairs. Foulois was ordered to "take plenty of spare parts" and to "teach yourself to fly" in San Antonio.

Fort Sam Houston had two advantages: The weather was good enough for year-round operations, and there was room enough to keep the flight training from interfering with regular troop operations.

Lt. Foulois arrived in San Antonio with nine-man ground crew on Feb. 5, 1910. In less than a month, the bi-plane — called "Old No. 1" — was assembled. On March 2, 1910, the young army officer soloed. As Foulois trained himself to fly, the need for improvements in the plane became obvious. First, Foulois saw that he needed to stay with the plane, and a safety harness to keep him in his seat was developed. Because the catapult system used to launch the aircraft was so unwieldy, Foulois and his ground team designed a landing gear, which was successfully tested in August 1910.

With a civilian pilot, Foulois also flew on the first operational flight in March 1911. Covering the distance between Laredo and Eagle Pass in a record time of about two hours, Foulois called the flight the first military air reconnaissance made with U.S. Army troops on the ground.

The flight training operations moved to College Park, Md., for a brief time but returned to Texas during World War I. From then until 1938, all U.S. military pilots were trained in Texas, and today the state remains a center for military aviation and for military aviation contractors. Foulois rose to the rank of major general and was Chief of Air Corps upon his retirement in 1935.

September 12, 1958

Today hundreds of devices use integrated circuits, those tiny pieces of silicon on which minute electronic circuits are printed. The use of these chips has created a "second industrial revolution." Without them, homes would be without computers; man might still have never walked on the moon or sent probes to nearby planets; and hundreds of conveniences that are taken for granted today might not exist.

In the late 1950s, however, the electronic industry was frustrated. Bell Laboratories had introduced the transistor in 1948, a great advance at the time. No longer were vacuum tubes needed in electric circuits, and this allowed for miniaturization of electronic devices. But the industry faced a numbers barrier: Engineers could design intricate circuits with 1,000, 100,000 or more components. But the human hand could not wire the components together. Even if it could have, the labor costs would have been astronomical. The technology simply was not available to bring to life the grand designs that were on many drawing boards.

Jack S. Kilby of Texas Instruments in Dallas provided the breakthrough that revolutionized the world.

Kilby joined TI in April 1958 to work on the "tyranny of numbers," as the problem was called. The solution being considered was to devise a method to fit components together without wiring. Kilby did not think the idea would work.

At the time, all TI employees took their vacation time at once in July. Kilby had not been with the company long enough for a vacation, so he spent the time alone at the office. It was time well spent. TI engineers had designed a silicon transistor, and Kilby realized that the company was committed to using the material.

Kilby began to consider what could be made of silicon. It was already known that the parts of standard semiconductor devices, diodes and transistors, could be made from silicon. The material simply was doped with the proper impurities to make it conduct electric current. The silicon products were not as good as those made with other materials, but they would work. And what has been called the "Monolithic Idea" was born. If you could make any component from one material, the components of an entire circuit could be placed in a monolithic block of that material. With all the components in a single chip, no wiring would be necessary.

After TI's vacation period ended, Kilby got approval from his supervisor to build a prototype integrated circuit. On Sept. 12, 1958, the device was successfully tested at the TI laboratories, and the "tyranny of numbers" was overthrown.

In California, Robert Noyce reached the same conclusion from a different direction. Kilby and Noyce are credited jointly for the Monolithic Idea, and both received the National Medal of Science for the work. Kilby, who holds several other patents, also is a member of the National Inventors' Hall of Fame.

The "second industrial revolution" got its big push forward in a Texas laboratory.

November 22, 1963

John F. Kennedy, the 35th president of the United States, was assassinated while riding in a motorcade in Downtown Dallas on Nov. 22, 1963. He was the first president to be killed in office since William McKinley died at an assassin's hand in 1901. A Texan, Vice President Lyndon B. Johnson, took office shortly after Kennedy was pronounced dead at Parkland Hospital in Dallas.

Historians have yet to write a final evaluation of the administrations of either Kennedy or Johnson. But Kennedy's death introduced a dual age of accomplishment and turbulence into American history.

Johnson, considered a master politician by most contemporary observers, received a great deal of cooperation and support from a guilt-ridden nation during the early days of his administration. Opposition to controversial portions of Kennedy's legislative program in the U.S. Congress evaporated. Under Johnson's guidance, civil rights legislation and sweeping social programs, like Medicare, were passed. Contemporaries have credited Johnson's legislative skill and the contrite attitude of the Congress with the success of the program.

Johnson also easily won a full presidential term in the election of 1964, and shortly thereafter, his administration ran into serious problems in the conduct of the war in Vietnam.

The death of Kennedy, which reintroduced violence into the political dialogue of the period, has been called the end of America's "age of innocence." As Johnson committed more U.S. troops to the fighting in Vietnam, opposition became increasingly violent. Riots over Vietnam and civil rights issues became common. In 1968, violence became more intense and spread to all phases of politics. Civil rights leader Martin Luther King Jr. and Sen. Robert F. Kennedy, a presidential candidate, were assassinated.

Republican Richard M. Nixon won a narrow victory over Hubert H. Humphrey in 1968, when a bitterly divided Democratic Party could not unite. Nixon's election marked the end of the legacy of the Kennedy assassination. The Republican's resignation during the Watergate scandal was unrelated. But it continued the instability in national leadership and fostered a feeling of insecurity.

In Dallas, the assassination prompted a lengthy period of introspection. A great deal of criticism — much of it unwarranted — focused on the city. In the two decades after the death, Dallas evolved a more mature, cosmopolitan attitude, while retaining its basic political conservatism.

Kennedy's death ended a period of normalcy for the nation. The turbulence and controversy in the years that followed caused a great many Americans to revaluate their country.

The elapsed time from the assassination is still too short for a final historical assessment of the post-Kennedy years. For those Americans who lived through it, however, the world has not been the same — nor is it likely to be again.

Who First Explored Texas?

This article by Mike Kingston, editor, was published in the 1984-85 Texas Almanac.
1519 is usually the date textbooks give for the first European exploration of the land that is now Texas. Alonso Alvarez de Pineda, a Spanish sea captain under the command of Gov. Francisco Garay of Jamaica, was dispatched to reconnoiter the northern coast of the Gulf of Mexico. His voyage was to cover the coastline from Florida to the limits of Hernando Cortez' colony of Villa Rica, about 35 miles north of present-day Veracruz, Mexico. The goal was to find a sea passage to the Pacific Ocean, but Alvarez de Pineda also was ordered to find a suitable site for a colony.

In the autumn of 1519, according to these accounts, Alvarez de Pineda found the mouth of a large, fluent river, which he explored for a distance of 20 miles inland. He traded with friendly Indians and later returned to establish a colony. Until recent historical research raised questions, the river that the explorer surveyed was said to be the Rio Grande, also called the "Rio de las Palmas" by early Texas historians. Hence, Alvarez de Pineda was considered the first European explorer of Texas.

Subsequent visits were made by others after Alvarez de Pineda's discovery, according to these versions of the exploration. Diego de Camargo, also under the command of Gov. Garay, reportedly journeyed to the Rio de las Palmas — the Rio Grande in these versions — in the summer of 1520, and a third group came later in the same year.

Therefore the Rio Grande and the Rio de las Palmas are inexorably entwined in Texas history. But they should not be, according to recent historical research. They are two distinct rivers, about 160 miles apart. And Alvarez de Pineda, though the first to map the coast of Texas, may never have set foot on the State's soil. At least he did not explore the Rio Grande as the popular versions of history contend.

Alvarez de Pineda is an elusive figure in Spanish history. He is mentioned by name only by Bernal Diaz del Castillo, an aide to Cortez and an early Spanish historian of the conquest of Mexico. Diaz del Castillo reported that Alvarez de Pineda took his ships to Cortez' colony of Villa Rica. Cortez took four of the captain's men captive and learned that Alvarez de Pineda had established friendly relations with Indians on the Rio Panuco, which the prisoners said was about 70 leagues north of Villa Rica.

With the loss of his men to Cortez, Alvarez de Pineda beat a quick retreat, returning to the supposedly friendly environs of the large, fluent river. Up this river he traveled 20 miles, finding 40 Indian villages in the process. Here Alvarez de Pineda and his men spent 40 days careening their ships. Historian Diaz del Castillo said Alvarez de Pineda later lost his life in an Indian uprising at the colony the explorer had founded in 1520. Other historians have credited the founding to Diego de Camargo. Upon returning to the colony with supplies, Camargo found the Indians in revolt. Alvarez de Pineda, among others, was slain, and Camargo later died of wounds suffered in the uprising. But both men were mortally wounded on the Rio Panuco.

Then came Garay, who after reverses in Jamaica, was desperate to found a colony. He learned that Cortez had established a settlement at the Rio Panuco. Garay then briefly visited the Rio Soto la Marina in 1523, finding the land inhospitable, before marching south to Cortez' colony on the Rio Panuco. There Garay was taken into custody by Cortez. But this twist: The Rio Soto la Marina was called the "Rio de las Palmas" until the 18th century, when it was renamed in honor of colonizer Jose de Escandon's home village in Spain. A tributary is still known as the Rio de las Palmas.

Texas historians have often confused the various rivers, despite the fact the waterways are clearly located, if not named, on a map presumably drawn by Alvarez de Pineda. Recent research by Robert S. Weddle, an authority on Spanish exploration of Texas, has attempted to correct many misconceptions about Alvarez de Pineda's explorations and the confusion that has developed about the Rio Grande and the Rio de las Palmas. Indeed, later maps noted the location of both the Rio de las Palmas and the Rio Bravo, which was the Spanish and Mexican name for the Rio Grande.

Despite efforts by Weddle and Donald E. Chipman to correct the misidentification of the Rio Grande as the Rio de las Palmas, the problem persists.

Weddle attributes the confusion to early Texas historians' lack of knowledge of Mexican geography. They seemed unaware of a large river — the Soto la Marina — between the Rio Panuco and the Rio Grande. The assumption was that when Garay landed at the Soto la Marina, he had returned to the river where Alvarez de Pineda had settled his colony.

This is purely a construction of Texas historians, Weddle points out. Eastern historians have long contended that Alvarez de Pineda careened his ships and stayed 40 days on the Mississippi River. "In any event, there has never been any direct connection between Alvarez de Pineda and the Rio de las Palmas, and certainly none between the Rio de las Palmas and the Rio Grande," Weddle asserts, basing his argument on the Spanish records and accounts by historian Diaz del Castillo.

But another element was injected into the debate in 1974. Ray Penrod, an amateur archaeologist from San Benito, excavated a site at Boca Chica near the mouth of the Rio Grande. At a depth of five to six feet, below the strata in which Penrod said he usually found Civil War and historical Indian materials, several old bricks or plaques were found. At first, the damp masonry blocks did not seem unusual, and they were stacked next to the excavation, as the digging continued. When dried, however, one glazed block told a different story. It was inscribed with Alvarez de Pineda's name, the date 1519 and an apparent reference to 270 soldiers, the number the explorer was thought to have brought with him. Were the bricks a monument left by Alvarez de Pineda to commemorate his visit to the mouth of the Rio Grande?

The inscribed plaque, though broken, apparently was about one foot square when whole. It was taken to the Rio Grande Valley Museum in Harlingen and placed on display. Examinations have been conducted by several scientists. Robert Rogers, a geologist at Pan American University in Edinburg, determined that the object was man-made and appeared to be deeply weathered. The material used in construction of the fired plaque also did not appear to be from the immediate region. And the plaque appeared to have fingerprints and markings from some type of cloth wrapping imprinted on the damp clay before it was glazed.

Dr. Nancy Troike, a paleographologer at the Institute of Latin American Studies at the University of Texas at Austin, viewed a picture of the plaque and determined that the writing style was not of 16th century vintage. The use of a slash across the stem of the numeral 7, for example, did not come into vogue in Europe until the 19th century. A tilde, such as that over the "n" in "Pineda" on the plaque was not used in this period. In addition, the style of printing on the plaque was not in use until long after Alvarez de Pineda was thought to have made his voyage of exploration.

Although museum officials want to authenticate the plaque, arrangements have not been made for testing it either through thermoluminescence or chemical methods. The former technique could determine in which time period the plaque was fired.

That, however, might not settle the argument about whether Alvarez de Pineda explored the mouth of the Rio Grande. Historian Weddle argues that "Even if the plaque was made 500 years ago, there is no evidence that it was inscribed at the same time." And other authorities agree.

Even with the questions that have arisen, few people think the roughly engraved plaque is a futile attempt to perpetuate a hoax. Weddle, for example, believes that it might be the work of 19th century conservationists who wanted to denote the spot where some early historians held that Alvarez de Pineda had landed on the Rio Grande.

While the Spanish records seem clear that Alvarez de Pineda did not venture up the Rio Grande, legends die hard. And authentic or not, the plaque only deepens the mystery.

Texas' Capital in Louisiana

This article by Mike Kingston, editor, was published in the 1986-87 Texas Almanac.
Many archaeological sites are lost to vandals long before they can be preserved for future generations. Texas can thank the residents of Robeline, La., for the preservation of the site of one of the Lone Star State's colonial capitals: the Los Adaes presidio.

A local historian, J. Fair Hardin, researched the location of the presidio and, on his recommendation in 1931, the Colonial Dames of the XVII Century provided Natchitoches Parish with funds to buy the site. Although little was done to excavate the presidio, the site was protected. In 1972, Robeline residents organized the Los Adaes Foundation and, in 1978, got the mission and presidio placed on the National Register of Historic Places. A year later, the 12-acre tract of land on which the presidio is located was deeded to the state with the understanding that a commemorative site would be developed. In 1985, the site was designated a National Historic Landmark.

The mission, San Miguel, at Los Adaes was established by the Spanish in 1716 to serve the Adaes tribe of the Caddo Indians. Three years later, French troops from Fort St. Jean Baptiste in present-day Natchitoches ousted the Spanish. But the Marquis de Aguayo in 1721 re-established the mission and built a fort nearby to offset the French influence in what was then a border area. From 1721 to 1773, Los Adaes served as the provincial capital of Texas.

H. F. "Pete" Gregory, professor of anthropology at Northwestern Louisiana State University at Natchitoches, began small excavations of the presidio site in 1964 and, in the next 20 years, established the perimeter of the fort. Dr. Gregory says the presidio site is unique in that no city has grown up around it. Therefore the undisturbed location is a treasure chest of 18th-century history for both Texas and Louisiana.

Though through much of Los Adaes' history, trade between the Spanish and nearby French was prohibited, Gregory has uncovered evidence of a well-developed trade between the adversaries. French-made artifacts are almost as common as Spanish. Pieces of English and French tableware, Indian pottery, European trade beads, weapons and other artifacts turned up in the excavations reflect strong cultural contact between the many peoples who lived and traded in the area.

Although drawings with dimensions were available, archaeologists were surprised at the size of the fort because of a quirk of the Spanish engineers. A common unit of measurement for the colonial Spanish was the vara, which is usually defined as a length of about 33 and one-third inches. At the Los Adaes presidio, however, a 40-inch vara was used, a full 20 percent longer than usual. The longer unit of measurement apparently also was used at some Spanish facilities in present-day Texas.

The hexagonal fort had three bulwarks and was surrounded by moats. Two four-pounder cannons were located in each bulwark. The facility, complete with a governor's mansion, chapel, barracks, stables and other amenities, was large enough to house 300 soldiers. That was a large establishment for the day.

Untouched in the current excavations are the nearby mission site and cemetery, which are on private land. The state has been in negotiations to acquire the 25-acre tract that should prove to be another treasure trove of 18th-century Spanish-French colonial history.

Despite the amount of work that already has been done at the site, archaeologist Gregory indicates than another 20 years of excavation are needed to fully explore these historic sites. Work proceeds as funds are made available by the state government.

The State of Louisiana has built an archaeological laboratory on the site to house the hundreds of artifacts that already have been recovered from the presidio and homes sites surrounding it. A museum and interpretive center are planned to make the site an even more exciting tourist attraction.

Los Adaes is the only capital of Texas to be located outside the present-day boundaries of Texas or Mexico. And it may be the best preserved for archaeologists of all the previous capitals. If so, it is a tribute to the pride and foresight of the residents of Robeline and to the State of Louisiana.

The 'Yellow Stone'

This article by Mary G. Crawford, associate editor, was published in the 1988-89 Texas Almanac.

Not all the gallant veterans of Texas' fight for independence were humans. One was a steamboat — a sidewheeler named the *Yellow Stone.*

The *Yellow Stone* was built in Louisville, Ky., in 1831 for John Jacob Astor's American Fur Company. The vessel was 120 feet long, with a 20-foot beam and a deep (six-foot) draft, constructed to specifications furnished by Pierre Chouteau Jr., western agent for Astor's fur trading company, for service on the Missouri and Yellowstone rivers. The boat's crew usually numbered about 21.

In summer, the *Yellow Stone* plied the waters of the upper Missouri, proudly displaying an oversize 12-foot by 18-foot American flag as it hauled furs, deerskins, bison robes and bison tongues downstream to market and returned with trade goods for the Indians. In winter, the *Yellow Stone* transported cotton and sugar cane among ports on the lower Mississippi until the spring thaw.

On a normal daylight run, the steamboat would burn 10 cords of wood, which meant that fuel itself was a considerable amount of its cargo. Ten cords of oak wood weigh 40 tons, of cottonwood 25 tons. In its six-and-a-half-year life, the *Yellow Stone* probably consumed 40,000 trees.

The *Yellow Stone's* last voyage on the Missouri was in July 1833. On that ill-fated journey, the crew was stricken with cholera, and all of them died except the captain and a young, semi-trained pilot named Joe LaBarge.

The next year and a half saw the *Yellow Stone* churning up the waters of the Mississippi under a succession of owners. In fall 1835, it was sold to the firm Thomas Toby and Brother of New Orleans, who had connections in Mexican Texas and who intended to employ the steamboat in intracoastal trade in the Gulf of Mexico.

The last day of December 1835 saw the *Yellow Stone* clearing the port of New Orleans headed for Texas under the command of Capt. Thomas Wigg Grayson, carrying 47 men of the Mobile Grays, volunteers looking for action in the Texas Revolution. These adventurous young men found their action: They all died at Goliad.

At that time, the Brazos and Trinity rivers were the only Texas waterways

138

considered navigable by steamboats, but the *Yellow Stone*, intended for use in the deeper waters of the Missouri and the Mississippi, had trouble even with them. Sandbars, snags and droughts plagued the boat during its entire career on the Brazos.

On March 31, 1836, the *Yellow Stone* inadvertently stumbled into Texas history. Now under the command of Capt. John E. Ross, the vessel was taking on a load of cotton at Jared Groce's landing in present-day Waller County about 20 miles up the Brazos from San Felipe.

The Alamo had fallen on March 6. Even before that, settlers had begun leaving their homes to escape the advancing Mexican army, and after Sam Houston learned of the crushing defeat at the San Antonio mission, he left Gonzales and "advanced to the rear" toward the Colorado River with the Texas army, urging civilians along the way to flee. The trickle of refugees became a deluge; the mass exodus was called the Runaway Scrape.

Houston's retreat brought him to Groce's landing on March 31 facing a Brazos River swollen by spring rains. Desperate to cross, he commandeered the *Yellow Stone* to ferry men, horses and equipment to the opposite bank. Capt. Ross stacked his cargo of cotton bales in such a way as to protect the boat's boilers and pilothouse from snipers in case of hostilities. On April 12, Capt. Ross, finally satisfied with the cotton armor and the load of fuel, ferried Houston and his men across the river. Two days later, Ross guided the steamboat, under a full head of steam, on a wild, bumpy ride downriver past a Mexican army encampment at Fort Bend. One over-eager Mexican soldier even tried in vain to lasso the smokestacks, the only parts of the superstructure peeking out from the tops of the cotton bales.

Capt. Ross proceeded to Galveston, picking up refugees along the way. On the island he found President Burnet, many other government officials and a large number of refugees. After the Texans' victory, the *Yellow Stone* transported Burnet and other officials to the battleground at San Jacinto at the request of Secretary of War Thomas J. Rusk. At Buffalo Bayou, the steamboat played host not only to Sam Houston, who needed medical treatment for a wounded ankle, but also Gen. Santa Anna, 47 of his officers and other Mexican soldiers. About 80 prisoners were taken to Galveston for incarceration. It is said that Burnet, never a fan of Houston's, refused to let Houston board the boat. But Capt. Ross would not budge until Houston was allowed on board.

A Mexican officer, writing of the voyage later, found it curious that, as the *Yellow Stone* passed the San Jacinto battleground, the Texas troops on board lined the rail and presented arms, accompanied by a solemn military drumbeat. "What was their object?" he wondered.

In the months that followed, the steamboat ran more errands for the army and the government of the new nation. Capt. Thomas Wigg Grayson, once more in command, advertised in the *Telegraph and Texas Register* of Oct. 19, 1836, offering $3 a cord for wood along the route between Quintana and Washington-on-the-Brazos. It is not known whether the steamboat ever resumed regular Brazos runs.

It is also not known if the owners were ever able to collect the money owed by the government of the fledgling nation. Bills were sent to the Texas government several times. Sam Houston himself urged the Congress to authorize payment for the services of the *Yellow Stone*. But there is no firm evidence that the bills were ever paid.

The *Yellow Stone* was once again thrust into the Texas limelight when Stephen F. Austin died on Dec. 27, 1836, at the age of 43. The steamboat was summoned to Columbia to pick up the entourage and transport it a few miles downstream to Peach Point Plantation, home of Austin's sister and her husband, Emily and James F. Perry. Austin was interred in the plantation's burial ground, the Gulf Prairie Cemetery. Austin's body was later re-interred in the Texas State Cemetery in Austin.

Hauling freight and a few passengers around the Gulf occupied the steamboat's next several months. The vessel made two or three runs up Buffalo Bayou to the new village called Houston, but it was too long to turn around in Buffalo Bayou without first backing into White Oak Bayou — a tricky maneuver.

The spring of 1837 found the sturdy sidewheeler carrying to Houston a printing press meant for the *Telegraph and Texas Register*. Gail Borden Jr., the developer of condensed milk and part-owner of the paper, accompanied the press.

The *Yellow Stone* made a few more deliveries in the Galveston area; after that, there is no further evidence of its existence. Some historians think the steamboat literally dropped from sight: They believe that it hit a snag and sank in Buffalo Bayou. The last scrap of documentation is a bill to the Texas navy department dated June 2, 1837 — one last attempt to get paid for services rendered. What is generally accepted to be the bell of the *Yellow Stone* is on display at the Alamo.

One thing is certain, however: The *Yellow Stone* earned an important place in the history of Texas.

Frontier Racial Attitudes

This article by Mike Kingston, editor, was published in the 1986-87 Texas Almanac.
So much of the history of 19th-century Texas is written in blood that one would think that there was a special meanness and intolerance exhibited by Americans who colonized the vast territory. Mexicans and Indians were victims of random and often deadly violence, and blacks were first enslaved and after emancipation were victims of gross discrimination that often was expressed in mortal force.

To understand the atmosphere of this period, two European colonization policies must be examined. The Spanish approach to developing Mexico and the American Southwest relates directly to the expression of Anglo-Saxonism that marked the American experience in 19th-century Texas.

Spain's great adventure in the New World began as a religious, as well as an economic, crusade. When Isabel and Ferdinand commissioned Christopher Columbus to find a new route to the Far East, the idea was to develop trade and to enter into an alliance with the rulers of the region against the Muslims who ruled Africa and the Middle East. From the beginning, however, the westward thrust was a manifestation of an effort to spread Christianity — first to the Far East and eventually to the remainder of the pagan world. Spanish missionary efforts began with the first contact with natives of the New World. Pope Paul III legitimatized the effort by granting Spain the right to develop all new lands discovered west of a line 100 leagues west of the Canary Islands, providing the Spanish spread the Christian faith.

Violence characterized Spain's initial contact with New World natives, justified on the grounds that the Indians resisted Christianity. Compounding the problem was the desire of the conquistadors to obtain wealth. Gold was more attractive to many European settlers than spreading the faith of the Spanish kings. This gulf between the temporal and spiritual marked the Spanish policy in the New World. From the beginning, Spanish monarchs were concerned about the treatment of the natives. Throughout the reconquest of the Iberian peninsula, the Spanish required conquered territories to pay tribute. Spanish numbers were few, and the Spanish leaders understood that expulsion of the conquered peoples would destroy the economy. Similar strategy was pursued in the New World. Spanish settlers in some cases were given encomiendas, in which use of the land and the natives was authorized by the crown. In exchange, the settlers were to instruct the natives in the faith, provide for their upkeep and defend them. Too often, the system degenerated into a form of slavery.

The early abuses of the system and the general mistreatment of the aborigines prompted a great debate in Spain. What was the proper policy to protect the natives? The Church and its missionaries urged a humane policy. But others advocated the Aristotelian theory of natural slavery: that some segments of mankind were born to slavery and to serve those whose lives should be devoted to virtue and leisure. Spaniards felt that they had sacrificed too much while regaining the peninsula from the Moors to do manual labor in the New World. The more tolerant view prevailed in the debates of the 16th century. Both Spanish kings and the popes officially mandated humane treatment for the natives and prohibited their enslavement. The uncertainty about how to regard the natives slowed the development of the New World. The 40-year delay between Coronado's exploration of the upper Rio Grande valley and the first settlement by Juan de Onate in 1598, in part, was caused by the debate. In 1573, the king of Spain issued an ordinance changing the nation's goal in the New World from one of "conquest" to "pacification." However, policies conceived in Spain and in Rome often were radically altered on the voyage across the Atlantic. The king's policy shall be obeyed, it was said, but the policy will not be executed. Consequently, the New World natives continued to be abused throughout most of the Spanish dominance.

But the Indians also had a role in the Spanish scheme for developing the New World. Racial prejudice was not a factor. In the 16th century, the great division was between Christians and infidels, not races. From the first days of Spanish colonization, colonizers intermarried with native women. The Indians also were looked upon as potential Spanish citizens. Unlike England and France, which had an excess of populations to develop the New World, Spain was thinly populated. Consequently, Spain had to use the New World natives to "colonize" the new lands. The mission system was a response to this need. Basically, missionaries gathered willing Indians to a church. The natives were schooled in the faith, taught trades and were protected by the military during the training period. When indoctrination was complete, the missionaries moved on. The goals were simple: The Indians would be conquered, converted, exploited and assimilated. In short, they would become productive Spanish citizens. Courageous missionaries braved the hazards of Northern Mexico and the American Southwest to establish the mission strategy. The success varied, but the system left a mark on the Southwest. Texas historian Elizabeth A. H. John evaluated the Spanish experience with the Indians like this:

". . . Contrary to the Black Legend, and notwithstanding flagrant violations of Indian rights, it is on the Spanish frontier that one finds the earliest commitment to due process for Indians and the only consistent efforts to foster self-governance of Indian communities."

Historian Ronald Sanders commented:

". . . But Spaniards were never bothered by the physical manifestations of race differences as northern Europeans have tended to be; it was doctrinal divergence, and the possibility of the taint of heresy being carried into the bloodstream, that primarily worked to arouse racism in them."

And Sanders observed that the ethnic diversity of Spanish history made the Spaniards instinctual anthropologists:

". . . Spaniards were foremost among those in the 16th century who could find alien racial traditions to be interesting and significant as long as they were not dangerous."

When Anglo-Americans encountered the frontier culture of Spain, they found a mixed race — Spanish and Indian — with a strong Roman Catholic affiliation. Both conflicted with the social attitudes of the Americans, who were predominantly Southerners.

A racial philosophy had gained strength in the United States, especially the South, in the early 19th century. The culture American colonists found in Spanish-Mexican Texas was both foreign and unacceptable to their racial concepts.

When the English embarked on their colonization of the New World, their attitudes toward the natives and the goals of the effort were little different from the Spanish. The letters of patent setting up the Virginia companies in London and Plymouth in 1606 stressed the conversion and civilization of the natives as the prime motive of settlement. But economic considerations later predominated.

Initially the English considered the natives "brutes." But by the 18th century, the idea of the "noble savage," free of the corruption of civilization, took hold. Throughout the early colonial period, the English pursued an officially humane policy. The church, Anglican and Roman, had long held that mankind came from a single creation by a supreme being. Therefore, although some segments of the human family might have greater advantages or better developed talents, all peoples were capable of improvement — infinitely perfectible. Many efforts were made to convert the Indians. In the 17th century, Protestants started schools and pursued a range of missionary activities among the natives. After 1622, when Indians in Virginia revolted and killed several hundred English colonists, attitudes began to change.

The British government pursued a legalistic policy, however, insisting that the natives be reimbursed when they gave up the right to use the land. Perhaps the one major difference in the Spanish and English attitudes concerned the Indians' relation to the land — or at least the use of the lands. While the Spanish usurped the natives' land for the crown, the English felt that the Indians were using the soil under the concept of usufruct. This meant that the natives did not own the land, but they were entitled to its use. When Indians "sold" land, they were giving up only a secondary right. The English crown, like the Spanish monarch, owned the land.

German Romanticists, however, began a movement that would completely change the attitudes of the English and Americans toward other peoples. The Germans developed an interest in uniqueness in language and in national and racial origins. Not surprisingly, they proposed that Indo-Europeans had exhibited special talents that spread civilization to the West. These special people had migrated from Central Asia, established a society based on democratic principles in Northern Europe and had brought civilization to the western world.

The English embraced the racial concept. But they emphasized the development of their "Anglo-Saxon" nation, founded by a race that expanded the special talents for self-government originally practiced in the forests of ancient Germany. While the attitude was embraced in England, it often was manifested in a policy that asserted that as a special people the English had special responsibilities to primitive people, not special privileges.

Americans were influenced by the English attitudes, and the concept of special responsibilities toward native peoples directed early expansionist policy after the American Revolution. But as the westward movement across the North American continent gained momentum, attitudes changed. Success begot confidence and then arrogance. The attitude of special responsibility was replaced with a concept that Americans had special privileges. Until 1829, the federal government held that native peoples could be trained in democratic principles and led to civilization. Thereafter, the direction of the national policy was simply to get the Indians out of the way of the advance of the Anglo-Saxon civilization. In the 1830s, Georgia made it clear that no Indians were wanted in the state, either on reservations or on private land. Room had to be made in the state for the Anglo-Saxons who would properly develop the rich agricultural land. It was made clear that Indians who remained would not be candidates for assimilation and citizenship; they would be second-class citizens like the free blacks. And many Indians were enslaved, a practice that began not long after the first English settlements were established.

Frontier attitudes in America generally reflected a hatred for Indians and their desire to retain their native lands. Every effort, legal and otherwise, was made to remove the aborigines. By the 1830s, the attitude finally forced the federal government to remove thousands of natives from the Deep South to Indian Territory. Thousands died on the infamous Trail of Tears and others unsuccessfully resisted. Blood was spilled, as Americans prosecuted their ill-disguised policy of racial superiority.

Between 1820 and 1850, the concept of the racial superiority of Anglo-Saxons gained popularity, although some observers criticized it. One asserted, "The allegations of superiority of race and destiny neither require nor deserve any answer; they are but pretences under which to disguise ambition, cupidity, or silly vanity." Abolitionists' agitation in the North beginning in the 1830s also forced Southerners to defend slavery on the basis of racial superiority. Scientific and pseudoscientific arguments that allegedly found traits of racial inferiority in blacks and Indians also became popular. Basically, if the South was to defend slavery, the institution must be blamed on the blacks. Conventional wisdom in the South held that blacks deserved to be slaves because they were racially inferior. The argument was not unlike that used by 16th-century Spaniards who invoked Aristotle's concept of natural slavery to defend mistreatment of Mexican Indians.

Early Anglo colonists in Texas no doubt harbored many of these attitudes, although during the early days of the Austin Colony, little evidence suggests that the Americans planned to be anything but good Mexican citizens. In other parts of the state, Americans were not so docile. The Fredonian Rebellion in 1827 grew out of an attempt by Anglos to divest old Spanish settlers of their land in East Texas.

The Anglo experience in Texas between 1821 and 1836 also raised questions in the settlers' minds regarding the Mexican's ability to operate a democratic government. Mexico, of course, was experiencing many difficulties establishing an administration after gaining independence from Spain. Internal feuds and a state of almost constant revolution impeded efforts. Nevertheless, Anglo-Texans were disgruntled by several governmental shortcomings.

Whatever latent attitudes toward Mexicans early Texas colonists might have held were reinforced and charged with emotion during the war for Texas independence in 1836. Wartime passions are exaggerated when the conflict involves peoples of different religions and of different races. The Mexicans, faced by the predominantly Protestant Texans, were Catholics, were a mixed race and were still associated with the Spanish. English propagandists promoted the idea of leyenda negra — the Black Legend. This concept held that the Spanish abused their New World charges and committed abominable outrages. Therefore they were to be hated. And this long-held belief added a third strike to Anglo-Texans' attitudes toward the Mexicans.

After Texas gained independence from Mexico, migration from the Southern states increased greatly. And the new settlers brought their racial attitudes with them. Indians had been removed from the South, and that policy was often pursued by Texans. Ironically, most Texas Indians welcomed the coming of the Anglo-Americans. But the attitudes of the newcomers assured conflict. Anglo officials at Nacogdoches complained in 1832, for example, that the Mexican military commander, Col. Jose de las Piedras, "has insulted us while in the exercise of our functions by saying that Americans and Indians are by him held in the same estimation, and as colonists on the same footing . . ."

Official government policy swung to extremes after Texas gained independence from Mexico. President Sam Houston, a friend of Indians since his youth in Tennessee, tried to reconcile the Indians and the Anglos and succeeded in maintaining an uneasy peace between the groups. But his successor, Mirabeau B. Lamar, waged relentless war against Indians and expelled several tribes from Texas in 1839.

German settlers in Central Texas in 1847 made a treaty with the Comanches, and both sides abided by the agreement. It had the distinction of being the only treaty that was kept with Indians in the state. Anglo settlers were not anxious to cooperate with the Indians and, possibly blinded by their racial attitudes, seriously misunderstood and underestimated the Indians. In 1841 Texan-Indian relations deteriorated after the ill-fated Council House Fight in San Antonio. Texans had asked to meet with Comanche leaders to discuss an exchange of prisoners. The Texans were outraged when the Indians brought only one white prisoner to the meeting. The Indians were locked in the Council House and were to be kept until more prisoners were released. But Comanches would fight to the death before being taken prisoner, and several of the chiefs did in San Antonio on that day. Anglo credibility suffered, and the Indian troubles escalated.

The experience of blacks in Texas was little different from that suffered elsewhere in the South. Under the Spanish and Mexican governments, free blacks had full rights of citizenship. Some were landowners and leaders in their communities. But after independence, free blacks were encouraged — subtly or otherwise — to leave. Unlike Mexicans and Indians, however, blacks had economic value, both as chattel and through the work they performed. After emancipation, blacks were tolerated in the state because they were needed as field workers. But the attitude that blacks were an inferior race lasted well into the 20th century.

Some Anglo-Texans seemed to consider it manly to abuse a Mexican, Indian or black. Resistance by the minority groups was considered brutality and another characteristic of inferior peoples. And resistance also invited massive retaliation.

Early Texans reflected the Southern culture from which most of them emerged. They held the same social attitudes and embraced the same concept of the racial superiority of the so-called Anglo-Saxon race. The violence of the times and the brutal discrimination against peoples of color in Texas probably can be explained, in part, by the absence of mediating institutions on the frontier. Society put few reins on individual behavior, and such institutions as were available were manned by officials who held the same attitudes toward the victims of frontier violence as did the perpetrators of the acts.

Peer pressure also entered into the actions of some early settlers. Noah Smithwick recalled a pitched battle in which runaway slaves courageously fought off an attempt by settlers to recapture them:

"That was unquestionably the worst fight I ever got into. I think now, looking back over a life of ninety years, that that was about the meanest thing I ever did. Though having been all my life accustomed to such things I did not then take that view of it. The capture of fugitive slaves was a necessity of the institution (of slavery)."

This frontier conduct was not unique to Anglo-Americans in Texas. The conquistadors and early Spanish colonists in the New World also reacted violently to frontier conditions. Historian Louis Bertrand had this observation about these 16th-century forerunners to the Anglos:

". . . As always happens in colonial countries, the character of the colonist was strengthened by the contradiction, or the hostility, of his surroundings. When he was subjected to the influence of foreign customs and new environment, some of his racial feelings and prejudices, some of his ideas, acquired fresh vigour. It happened also that, as the colonist was no longer in contact with the motherland, where national characteristics were in course of evolution, his own remained stationary. . . . The feelings, the instincts, the prejudices which he had brought with him from his native environment became intensified or exaggerated without being transformed."

And so it was on the Texas frontier. While Anglo-Texans carved a dynamic state out of a wilderness, they wrote a sad and tragic chapter in race relations.

'Unredeemed Texas'

This article, by Mike Kingston, editor, was published in the 1986-87 Texas Almanac.

Until the admission of Alaska into the Union in 1958, Texas was in land area the largest of the United States. More than 267,000 square miles are within its boundaries. But early Texas was not nearly as large, and present-day Texas is only a shadow of the "empire" envisioned by the state's early leaders.

As a Spanish province in 1681, the original Texas was located between the Trinity and Sabine rivers. The East Texas mission, San Francisco de los Tejas, was an unofficial capital because it was so far removed from the Spanish colonies in Northern Mexico. In 1693, this mission was abandoned.

For many reasons, the Spanish provinces in Northern Mexico had ill-defined boundaries. The southern, eastern and western limits would be well located. But the northern boundaries were obscure because, as a practical matter, they were determined by where the Plains Indians would allow colonists to settle.

When missions were established in the San Antonio area in 1718, the Medina River was considered the boundary between Texas and Coahuila. Jose de Escandon's colony of Nuevo Santander (today's Tamaulipas) was bounded on the north by the Nueces River in the mid-18th century. A description of the course of the Rio Grande in 1744 never mentioned the river's touching Texas. Indeed, the Rio Grande had never been a boundary except between the provinces of Nuevo Vizcaya (Chihuahua) and Nuevo Mexico in the early 18th century.

In 1685 and again in 1712, the French tried to set the Rio Grande as the western limits of the Louisiana Territory. But these claims were based on LaSalle's explorations, and Spain had a better case by virtue of its limited occupation of the area. President Thomas Jefferson tried unsuccessfully to press the French argument when the United States purchased the Louisiana Territory in 1803.

When Anglo-American colonization began, Texas' southwestern boundary with Nuevo Santander and Coahuila was the Nueces River. After Mexico gained its independence from Spain, Coahuila and Texas were combined into a single state in the Constitution of 1824.

The United States had a long-standing interest in acquiring Texas. Efforts were

147

made to purchase the territory from Mexico, first by President John Quincy Adams and later by Andrew Jackson. Commercial interests in the United States also wanted a port on the Pacific coast, and in 1835, President Jackson broadened an offer to include purchase of Texas and a route to the area of San Francisco Bay in California.

When Texans won their independence in 1836, Mexico was stunned at the declaration that the entire Rio Grande valley to its headwaters in Colorado was claimed as the new republic's western boundary. In the Treaty of Velasco, Gen. Santa Anna agreed to withdraw Mexican troops to the south side of the Rio Grande. On this basis, the First Texas Congress claimed to the Rio Grande watershed as the Republic's south and west boundary.

There were probably several reasons for this precedent-setting claim. First, Sam Houston was a close friend and confidant of President Jackson, and he knew of the designs Jackson had on expansion. The Rio Grande also was a natural, defendable boundary. And one early dream of Moses and Stephen F. Austin was to divert the lucrative trade between Missouri and Santa Fe from the Santa Fe Trail to ports in Texas, which were much closer to Santa Fe than the Mississippi River.

Thus the boundaries of the Republic of Texas had a much different configuration than that of the present state. The Republic had a land area almost 105,000 square miles larger than today's Texas, and it included land that is in the present states of New Mexico, Colorado, Wyoming, Kansas and Oklahoma.

Leaders of the Republic soon learned that claiming land and possessing it were entirely different matters. Efforts to extend the Republic's jurisdiction beyond the boundaries of the old Spanish province of Texas were usually unsuccessful. Between the Nueces River and the Rio Grande, an area known as the Nueces Strip, there was nothing but desert. Some early Texans favored leaving it that way to maintain a buffer against Mexican attacks on the settled area of the Republic. Governors of the northern Mexican states asked President Mirabeau B. Lamar to allow trade in the region, and the Texas Congress in 1839 authorized the chief executive to do so. Trade relations soon cooled, however, when Mexican agents were discovered among the traders. These agents used the cover to incite Indians to violence against the Texans, and the trade was soon curtailed.

Texas was too thinly populated to send its own citizens to colonize the Nueces Strip. For a time, the Republic toyed with the idea of giving the Franco-Texienne Co. a grant of 3 million acres of land to establish a series of military colonies along the western frontier, including colonies in the infamous Strip. But the Texas Congress rejected the idea in 1840, fearing that the foreign company would bring in too many French colonists. France then would have too great a foothold in the fledgling Republic. In 1842, empresario grants were given to several individuals to colonize the region, but only Henri Castro settled a successful colony.

President Lamar then turned his attention to Santa Fe. During Lamar's administration, the Republic's finances were severely strained. The Panic of 1837 in the United States had dried up credit sources, and the money issued by the Republic had depreciated in value to only a few cents on the dollar. The dream of diverting the trade from Santa Fe to Texas' ports was a great attraction to Lamar. Not only would the Republic's economy be improved, but the trade would generate much-needed customs revenues. Not all Texans agreed, however. When the Congress failed to approve the scheme, Lamar launched an expedition based on the 1839 authorization to open trade along the Rio Grande. In 1841, the Santa Fe Expedition left with orders to open trade. Based on unofficial reports of discontent with Mexican officials in Santa Fe, Lamar was confident of the success of the enterprise. Almost 300 soldiers and traders made up the Texas contingent. Little was known about the route from near Austin to

Santa Fe, and the expedition exhausted its supplies and suffered many hardships before reaching its destination.

The Santa Fe Expedition ended in disaster. Mexican officials learned of its coming and stirred up the populace against the "invasion" by Texas. Members of the expedition were taken into custody and, after undergoing many hardships on a lengthy march, were imprisoned in Mexico City.

Houston had replaced Lamar as president when word of the disaster reached Austin in 1842. Texans were outraged at the stories of mistreatment of the prisoners. The Texas Congress reacted by passing a bill annexing the northern states of Mexico, which included California. Houston vetoed the bill because, he argued, it would hold the Republic up to ridicule in the eyes of the world's nations. The disaster of the Santa Fe Expedition hurt the Republic's financial standing with European nations because it indicated that the government could not control the territory it claimed. And the affair raised doubts about the Republic's maintaining its independence.

Passions remained strong, however, as the citizens of the Republic demanded revenge against Mexico for the mistreatment of the members of the expedition who were taken prisoner. In December of 1842, a military contingent of 750 men was authorized to mount raids along the Rio Grande in retaliation for Gen. Adrian Woll's brief capture of San Antonio in September. Under Thomas Somervell, the party raided Laredo. But when Somervell could find no objectives of military value to pursue, he tried to disband the unit. Five companies of men wanted to continue the raids, and they elected William S. Fisher commander. This group attacked Mier in Mexico, was defeated and taken prisoner. These prisoners also were marched to Mexico City under great hardship, giving Texans another disastrous military operation to digest.

Upon learning of the Mier operation, officials in the United States, who were trying to mediate a settlement between Texas and Mexico, warned Texans to restrict military operations to territory claimed by Texas and to forgo any further incursions into Mexico. Two attempts by Texans to disrupt trade on the Santa Fe Trail in 1842 and 1843 also were unsuccessful and drew criticism from the United States.

Thereafter, the leadership of the Republic of Texas concentrated on the numerous other problems afflicting the young nation and continued to pursue the annexation of Texas to the United States.

In Washington, efforts were made by President James Polk to negotiate purchase of Texas and what is now the Southwest and California. But Mexico rejected the proposals. The United States was concerned with English and French interest in the Pacific coast. Mexico was warned that while the United States would not take action against Mexican development of California, it would take steps to prohibit California from becoming a French or English colony.

Despite warnings from Mexico, the United States and Texas reached an agreement on annexation in 1845. In anticipation of the agreement, President Polk sent Gen. Zachary Taylor with a military force to Corpus Christi in August of 1845. When the annexation was approved, Taylor was ordered in early 1846 to move to the mouth of the Rio Grande. The Mexicans were outraged that U.S. forces were moving into the disputed Nueces Strip while negotiations over Texas' sovereignty over the area were still under way. But with the approval of annexation, the United States was bound to defend Texas' claim to the territory.

When hostilities between the United States and Mexico broke out in the Lower Rio Grande Valley, Brig. Gen. Stephen Kearny was dispatched to occupy Santa Fe, which he took without resistance. But the action was providential for Texas' future claims to the territory. Kearny set up a civil government backed by the military. When Texas Gov. J. Pinckney Henderson learned of the action, he protested to President Polk against any action that would affect Texas' claims to the territory. Polk assured the

Texan that the state's claims were secure, but he added that the matter should be considered by the U.S. Congress.

In March of 1848, Gov. George T. Wood informed the Legislature that the failure of the state to organize the Santa Fe territory could result in the loss of claims to it. So in 1848 Santa Fe County, Texas, was established by the Legislature. Worth County, which included southern New Mexico, and El Paso and Presidio counties in Texas were created in 1849.

New Mexicans resisted, however. In a convention in October of 1848, they declared their opposition to slavery, which was allowed in Texas, and to having their territory dismembered. New Mexico had been a Spanish province since Juan de Onate established a colony near Santa Fe in 1598, almost a century before the first development in Texas. For many years, it was a self-governing province with no connection whatsoever to the Spanish activities in Texas. And the 19th-century New Mexicans wanted to keep their independence from Austin.

Robert S. Neighbors, an Indian agent, was commissioned in January of 1850 by Gov. Peter H. Bell to organize the territories claimed by Texas in New Mexico. Neighbors was successful in setting up a Texas government in El Paso County, thereby saving that region for Texas. But he was unsuccessful elsewhere.

In Washington, the question of Texas' boundaries had become entwined in the debate over slavery, and the new state was in danger of losing a great deal of the territory it claimed. The New York legislature, for example, became so concerned that it instructed the state's congressmen to oppose even Texas' claim to the Nueces Strip because no civil jurisdiction had been set up there prior to the Mexican War.

Texans were infuriated by the failure of the U.S. government to back up Texas' claims to New Mexico. Many felt that President Polk had assured Texas its claims would be honored and that Texans had voted for annexation on that basis. If the claims were not to be honored, some Texans felt, the whole question of annexation should be reconsidered.

But Texas' poor financial condition led to a compromise. As a Republic, Texas had acquired substantial debt. Repayment was pledged on the basis of customs receipts and on land sales. When annexed to the United States, Texas retained its public lands, but lost its customs revenues to the United States, which also refused to assume the public debt. Since Texas would lose part of its ability to service the outstanding debt if its land claims were not honored, it was decided that the U.S. government should pay the state $10 million in lieu of the claims. Knowing the passions of his citizens, Gov. Bell called a referendum to determine if Texans thought the compromise was satisfactory. They did by a count of 4,473 "for" and 1,988 "against." And thereby, they accepted the present boundaries of the State of Texas.

But there was one more chapter in the story of "Unredeemed Texas." At the beginning of the Civil War in 1862, Confederate Gen. Henry H. Sibley launched a campaign from El Paso to take the upper Rio Grande valley to cut off a possible invasion of Texas from New Mexico. After early successes, Gen. Sibley's supply train was captured by Union forces at Glorieta Pass and the Texans were forced to retreat.

Certainly, Sibley did not think the effort was worth the money and lives expended. But other historians argue that if Sibley had been successful, the United States would have been cut off from California during the Civil War. With a Confederate California, the South would have had access to gold mines, timber for ships and ports that could not be blockaded by the United States, three elements that cost them the war.

So the loss of Unredeemed Texas may have been bad news for the Lone Star State — but a boon for the United States.

Texas Declaration of Independence

On March 2, 1836, Texas' Declaration of Independence from Mexico was adopted at Washington-on-the-Brazos. Richard Ellis served as president of this convention of delegates chosen by Texans. Ellis appointed five on a committee to write the document but George C. Childress wrote it with little help from the others. He is known as the author of the declaration.

The following text contains the exact wording and punctuation of the original Texas Declaration of Independence, and the names of signers are exactly as written on the original document.

When a government has ceased to protect the lives, liberty and property of the people from whom its legitimate powers are derived, and for the advancement of whose happiness it was instituted; and so far from being a guarantee for the enjoyment of those inestimable and inalienable rights, becomes an instrument in the hands of evil rulers for their oppression; when the Federal Republican Constitution of their country, which they have sworn to support, no longer has a substantial existence, and the whole nature of their government has been forcibly changed without their consent, from a restricted federative republic, composed of sovereign states, to a consolidated central military despotism, in which every interest is disregarded but that of the army and the priesthood — both the eternal enemies of civil liberty, and the ever-ready minions of power, and the usual instruments of tyrants; When, long after the spirit of the constitution has departed, moderation is at length, so far lost, by those in power that even the semblance of freedom is removed, and the forms, themselves, of the constitution discontinued; and so far from their petitions and remonstrances being regarded, the agents who bear them are thrown into dungeons; and mercenary armies sent forth to force a new government upon them at the point of the bayonet; When in consequence of such acts of malfeasance and abdication, on the part of the government, anarchy prevails, and civil society is dissolved into its original elements; In such a crisis, the first law of nature, the right of self-preservation — the inherent and inalienable right of the people to appeal to first principles and take their political affairs into their own hands in extreme cases — enjoins it as a right towards themselves and a sacred obligation to their posterity, to abolish such government and create another in its stead, calculated to rescue them from impending dangers, and to secure their future welfare and happiness.

Nations, as well as individuals, are amenable for their acts to the public opinion of mankind. A statement of a part of our grievances is, therefore, submitted to an impartial world, in justification of the hazardous but unavoidable step now taken of severing our political connection with the Mexican people, and assuming an independent attitude among the nations of the earth.

The Mexican government, by its colonization laws, invited and induced the Anglo-American population of Texas to colonize its wilderness under the pledged faith of a written constitution, that they should continue to enjoy that constitutional liberty and republican government to which they had been habituated in the land of their birth, the United States of America. In this expectation they have been cruelly disappointed, inasmuch as the Mexican nation has acquiesced in the late changes made in the government by General Antonio Lopez de Santa Anna, who, having overturned the constitution of his country, now offers us the cruel alternative either to abandon our homes, acquired by so many privations, or submit to the most intolerable of all tyranny, the combined despotism of the sword and the priesthood.

It has sacrificed our welfare to the state of Coahuila, by which our interests have been continually depressed, through a jealous and partial course of legislation carried on at a far distant seat of government, by a hostile majority, in an unknown tongue; and this too, notwithstanding we have petitioned in the humblest terms, for the establishment of a separate state government, and have, in accordance with the provisions of the national constitution, presented to the general Congress, a republican constitution which was without just cause contemptuously rejected.

It incarcerated in a dungeon, for a long time, one of our citizens, for no other cause but a zealous endeavor to procure the acceptance of our constitution and the establishment of a state government.

It has failed and refused to secure on a firm basis, the right of trial by jury; that palladium of civil liberty, and only safe guarantee for the life, liberty, and property of the citizen.

It has failed to establish any public system of education, although possessed of almost boundless resources (the public domain) and although, it is an axiom, in political science, that unless a people are educated and enlightened it is idle to expect the continuance of civil liberty, or the capacity for self-government.

It has suffered the military commandants stationed among us to exercise arbitrary acts of oppression and tyranny; thus trampling upon the most sacred rights of the citizen and rendering the military superior to the civil power.

It has dissolved by force of arms, the state Congress of Coahuila and Texas, and obliged our representatives to fly for their lives from the seat of government; thus depriving us of the fundamental political right of representation.

It has demanded the surrender of a number of our citizens, and ordered military detachments to seize and carry them into the interior for trial; in contempt of the civil authorities, and in defiance of the laws and the constitution.

It has made piratical attacks upon our commerce; by commissioning foreign desperadoes, and authorizing them to seize our vessels, and convey the property of our citizens to far distant ports of confiscation.

It denies us the right of worshiping the Almighty according to the dictates of our own consciences, by the support of a national religion calculated to promote the temporal interests of its human functionaries rather than the glory of the true and living God.

It has demanded us to deliver up our arms; which are essential to our defense, the rightful property of freemen, and formidable only to tyrannical governments.

It has invaded our country, both by sea and by land, with intent to lay waste our territory and drive us from our homes; and has now a large mercenary army advancing to carry on against us a war of extermination.

It has, through its emissaries, incited the merciless savage, with the tomahawk and scalping knife, to massacre the inhabitants of our defenseless frontiers.

It hath been, during the whole time of our connection with it, the contemptible sport and victim of successive military revolutions and hath continually exhibited every characteristic of a weak, corrupt, and tyrannical government.

These, and other grievances, were patiently borne by the people of Texas until they reached that point at which forbearance ceases to be a virtue. We then took up arms in defense of the national constitution. We appealed to our Mexican brethren for assistance. Our appeal has been made in vain. Though months have lapsed, no sympathetic response has yet been heard from the Interior. We are, therefore, forced to the melancholy conclusion that the Mexican people have acquiesced in the destruction of their liberty, and the substitution therefor of a military government — that they are unfit to be free and incapable of self-government.

The necessity of self-preservation, therefore, now decrees our eternal political separation.

We, therefore, the delegates, with plenary powers, of the people of Texas, in solemn convention assembled, appealing to a candid world for the necessities of our condition, do hereby resolve and declare that our political connection with the Mexican nation has forever ended; and that the people of Texas do now constitute a free, sovereign and independent republic, and are fully invested with all the rights and attributes which properly belong to the independent nations; and conscious of the rectitude of our intentions, we fearlessly and confidently commit the issue to the decision of the Supreme Arbiter of the destinies of nations.

RICHARD ELLIS, president of the convention and Delegate from Red River.

Charles B. Stewart
John S. D. Byrom
J. Antonio Navarro
Wm. D. Lacey
Jno. Fisher
William Mottley
Stephen H. Everitt
Elijah Stapp
Wm. B. Scales
A. B. Hardin
Thos. J. Gazley
Sterling C. Robertson
Edwin Waller
Geo. C. Childress
Rob. Potter
JB Woods
Chas. S. Taylor
Robert Hamilton
Albert H. Latimer
Sam Houston

Edwin Conrad
Edwin O. LeGrand
Jas. Gaines
Sydney O. Penington
Jno. Turner
G. M. Barett
Jesse Grimes
John W. Moore
Saml. A. Maverick
Sam P. Carson
Thos. Barnet
Franco Rutz
Jesse B. Badgett
William Menefee
Mathew Caldwell
Lorenzo de Zavala
Geo. W. Smyth
Claiborne West
M. B. Menard
J. W. Bunton

R. M. Coleman
Jas. Collinsworth
Asa Brigham
Bailey Hardeman
A. Briscoe
Thomas Jefferson Rusk
John S. Roberts
Collin McKinney
James Power
David Thomas
Martin Parmer
Stephen W. Blount
Wm. Clark, Jr.
Wm. Carrol Crawford
Benj. Briggs Goodrich
James G. Swisher
S. Rhoads Fisher
John W. Bower
(from Bejar)

Test H. S. Kemble Secretary

Index